Bridging Banas

for Guided Reading

Resourcing for Diversity into Key Stage 2

Includes a review of reading series designed for Key Stage 2 children working below age-related expectations

Shirley Bickler

Suzanne Baker

Angela Hobsbaum

Produced by the Reading Recovery National Network

INSTITUTE OF
EDUCATION
UNIVERSITY OF LONDON

reading recovery national network

First published 2003 by the
UK Reading Recovery National Network
Institute of Education, 20 Bedford Way
London WC1H 0AL

www.ioe.ac.uk

British Library cataloguing-in-publication data
A catalogue record for this publication is available from the British Library

ISBN 0 85473 690 5

Designed by Peter Dolton

Production services by Book Production Consultants plc
25–27 High Street, Chesterton, Cambridge CB4 1ND.
Printed in England by CPI Group (UK) Ltd, Croydon, CR0 4YY

CONTENTS

Why 'Bridging Bands'? iv

Introduction 1

Guided reading in context 2

Assessment for learning 5

Empowering children to take control 10

Reading strategies 12

Resourcing for diversity 17

Reviews of guided reading series offering diversity of reading challenge 22

Bridging Bands: Overview, lessons and texts 43

An overview of colour banding 44

Band 6 Orange: lessons and text list 48

Band 7 Turquoise: lessons and text list 60

Band 8 Purple: lessons and text list 72

Band 9 Gold: lessons and text list 84

Band 10 White: lessons and text list 99

Band 11 Lime: lessons and text list 115

Titles in alphabetical order 129

Acknowledgements 169

WHY 'BRIDGING BANDS'?

Book Bands for Guided Reading: Organising Key Stage 1 texts for the Literacy Hour, the precursor to this volume, was first produced in 1998 and is now in its third edition. It met a felt need by enabling Key Stage 1 teachers to organise their sets of reading materials from a variety of publishers in a common gradient of challenge suitable for children from Reception through to Year 2 (Primary 1 to Primary 3 in Scotland and Northern Ireland). The National Literacy Strategy included references to the gradient of ten colour bands in their guidance for Early Literacy Support in Year 1 and Additional Literacy Support for children in Year 3.

As schools have become more conversant with the bands, we have received many requests from teachers to extend the banding and **bridge the transition** in terms of text reading provision from Key Stage 1 into Key Stage 2. We hope that teachers will be able to use the banded lists to provide children with support and continuity as they encounter a more demanding range of fiction and topic-based books. Many of the titles in the upper five bands of *Book Bands* third edition have been incorporated into this book, and we have added a further LIME band of titles to cater for children already reading at NC Level 3.

In addition, we have undertaken a comprehensive review of the publishers' series currently on the market for the diversity of reading ability within the average Key Stage 2 classroom. Rather than offering reading ages, we have made an estimate of the National Curriculum levels catered for within each series and the extent to which the areas of the English Curriculum are represented. There are many beautiful fiction and non-fiction books on the market now, designed to appeal to children for whom the titles in the colour banded listings are not appropriate. Please look at them and ensure that you set up a special section in your guided reading library to offer the highest quality, most inviting texts to those readers whose progress causes you concern.

July 2003

FURTHER INFORMATION

To order coloured labels for banding books: Sato UK Limited, Valley Road, Harwich, Essex CO12 4RR. Telephone 01255 240 000. Fax 01255 240 111.
Email enquiries@satouk.com

Reading Recovery Network, Institute of Education, 20 Bedford Way, London WC1H 0AL. Telephone 020 7612 6586. Fax 020 7612 6828.
Email readrec@ioe.ac.uk. Website http:www.ioe.ac.uk/cdl/readrec.html

INTRODUCTION

Transitions between one phase of education and the next are often associated with a dip in achievement. The best known is at age 11 when children move into secondary school, but another can occur when children move into Key Stage 2.

In Key Stage 1, learning how to read is a primary goal of the curriculum, and everyone in the education system is well aware of the need for all children to make a strong start in basic literacy. Funding for book provision during the initial years of the National Literacy Strategy highlighted the importance of every school providing a large range of attractive books to support shared and guided reading, two new teaching techniques in the daily Literacy Hour.

Educational publishers have risen to the challenge by producing Big Books and posters that enable teachers to demonstrate to a class of children what is involved in reading a range of text types at various stages, and a large range of guided reading books so that children can put their learning into practice. So large, in fact, is the range now on the market that literacy co-ordinators in schools find it increasingly difficult and time-consuming to make wise selections.

A RESOURCING ISSUE

Nevertheless, in some schools, children moving into Year 3 may have grown dependent on the format and vocabulary of just one or two reading schemes, and may have had very little experience of adjusting to the language of non-fiction texts and a variety of layouts, text types and authors. They may have become accustomed to reading well within the comfort zone, under-challenged in terms of vocabulary and increasing complexity of sentence structure, and heavily reliant on adult help. Failure to cope adequately with higher expectations in their new class may result in loss of skill and confidence, and detract from their enjoyment of reading.

Even where there is a well-organised range of guided reading sets clearly colour-banded, regularly audited and replenished at Key Stage 1, there may be an abrupt discontinuity in book provision at Key Stage 2 in the same school. Most of the fiction available for guided reading may consist of chapter books, with smaller font, a greater number of pages and more sophisticated language than the children have hitherto met. As the range of non-fiction texts widens, children may be expected to work in various subject areas before they have gained sufficient experience with new formats and text types. While many children are ready for this challenge, results of SATs at the end of Key Stage 1 suggest that a large number of children may not be well equipped for the sudden shift in focus – from learning to read to reading to learn – that they will encounter in Year 3.

GUIDED READING IN CONTEXT

A comprehensive literacy curriculum provides different kinds of reading and writing experiences for children at school. In the structured Literacy Hour introduced by the National Literacy Strategy, three main types of reading experience are regularly provided for children:

SHARED READING

Existing working systems solve easy tasks; harder texts invite children to go beyond current operating power and extend their control over that harder text.[1]

Using an enlarged-print in the form of a Big Book, poster or overhead transparencies, the teacher's role in shared reading is to lead the class in a collaborative exploration of a text. The chosen text is usually at a somewhat higher level of challenge than the pupils could read on their own. Because they are reading in unison supported by the teacher, they are able to achieve access to richer language and more complexity, and reach out to the next stages of reading development.

Working within a meaningful context, the teacher introduces learning objectives at text, sentence and word levels. Children meet the technical terms associated with books generally and with different types of layout, and they experience at first hand the language styles associated with a range of text types. Formal elements of grammar, punctuation, sentence construction, vocabulary and spelling are introduced as part of an authentic reading experience, and links are formed and strengthened with what children already know about print and the ways books work.

GUIDED READING

The teacher's role in guided reading is to scaffold literacy learning, that is, to actively enhance each student's understanding. This is in marked contrast to the practice of merely checking or testing comprehension after a text has been read by the student.[2]

Guided reading offers small groups of children the opportunity, within a supportive teaching framework, to explore unfamiliar but accessible texts. The teacher usually works with a group of children who are able to read texts at a similar level of challenge, although group participation may at times be based on other criteria. In this situation, the teacher scaffolds the learning situation so that the children can take over responsibility for putting into practice what they learnt in shared reading and in other literacy activities.

After a planned book introduction, the lesson objectives are shared with the children. Each child then reads independently his/her own copy of the book. The teacher's role during this part of the session is to listen in on individual readers in turn, discussing and supporting their problem-solving. Discussion and some formal teaching takes place after the text reading, and this is frequently followed by further independent work on the text by the children either straight away or later.

[1] Marie M. Clay, Seminar held at the Institute of Education, London, on 16 October 2002.

[2] Jeanne Biddulph, *Guided Reading: Grounded in theoretical understandings*, 2002. Online. <http://www.learningmedia.com/DOWNLOAD/GuidedReading.pdf> (accessed 7 July 2003), p. 3.

INDEPENDENT READING

All learners need practice, so that what at first requires conscious attention becomes automatic and fluent. The teacher needs to ensure that children have access to a range of stimulating materials at appropriate levels so that reading is enjoyable and rewarding for its own sake.

Reading to children is also an invaluable form of shared enjoyment in and out of the classroom, and broadens the range of texts that children can access.

GUIDED READING PROCEDURES

The following sections offer general guidelines related to each aspect of a guided reading session. Not all of the elements need to occur in every session, especially where the same text is used across more than one lesson. Descriptions of guided reading sessions based on different types of text can be found in this book preceding each colour banding listing, and detailed suggestions for teaching prompts and acknowledgements can be found in the section on **Empowering children to take control** (p. 10).

PREPARING FOR A GUIDED READING SESSION

The teacher selects a text that is of interest to the group, manageable in terms of length, and at an appropriate level of challenge (see the section on **Assessment for learning**, p. 5). The teacher needs to have in mind the competencies and learning needs of individuals in the group. Planning includes notes on teaching objectives, the book introduction, teaching focus and follow-up activities. There should be sufficient copies of the text for each child, and preferably the teacher as well. It is of paramount importance that the teacher reads the whole text carefully prior to the lesson.

BOOK INTRODUCTION

Meaning is the most important source of information. It is a source which lies outside the text in the sense that it depends upon what the reader is able to bring to the text. Research and practice show that a good introduction of the text to the reader before he or she attempts to read it will make the task easier. The reader:

- brings prior knowledge to the text
- carries out reading work in order to make sense of what he is reading
- and uses meaning as his ultimate check that all is well.[3]

Almost all the reading we do in life is silent, but this silence belies the active mental process carried out by readers as they reconstruct their own understanding of the author's message. Discussions that precede the reading of a new text serve to activate each reader's personal experience, set up expectations that enhance the reader's predictive skill, and create links with other learning taking place inside and outside the classroom.

By the time they reach Key Stage 2, pupils are usually called upon to use their experience to familiarise themselves to some extent with a new book. They are encouraged to read through the blurb themselves, study the title, author and cover illustrations, and leaf through the book to note layout and illustrations, and ascertain the text type. After this overview, the teacher may give an outline of a story, summarise the contents of a non-fiction text or model a stanza of poetry. The teaching objectives for the session taken from the NLS framework for learning are shared with the group. These will usually relate to the termly objectives for the year

3 Marie M. Clay, *Becoming Literate: The construction of inner control* (Heinemann, 1991), p. 292.

group. However, if a group of children are reading at a level well above or below the class norm, the objectives will be selected to meet the needs of the group. In all cases, the teacher's role is to help children make links with other aspects of the English Curriculum and other curriculum areas.

STRATEGY CHECK

There needs to be a brief reminder or explanation to the group to pay conscious attention to certain general reading strategies, or to specialised strategies related to particular text types. The group may rehearse their response to punctuation, work through a few examples of word solving, or briefly revise a relevant whole-class session.

INDEPENDENT READING AND METACOGNITION

For comprehension to occur, readers must first construct a text (a meaningful message) inside their heads. The effectiveness of any act of reading thus becomes a function of the degree to which the meanings in the text constructed by the reader match the meanings which the author of the text intended.[4]

Beginner readers develop considerable cognitive control as they learn to keep in balance different types of information on-the-run in order to comprehend the author's meaning. As the act of reading becomes more rapid, automatic and internalised, attention can be directed towards an awareness of how a wide range of texts are constructed, and how writers achieve certain effects in their writing.

A teacher's expertise is revealed by the manner in which s/he poses questions for children to bear in mind as they read, praises and prompts the quality of their problem-solving as they work through the text, and thoughtfully acknowledges their views and ideas as they interact mentally with the author. In this way, children develop independent control and deepen their understanding of how texts work. This appreciation can then inform and enrich their own writing.

RETURNING/ RESPONDING TO THE TEXT

After reading independently, children in the group are often encouraged to make general comments, offer their own opinions supported by evidence from the text, and evaluate their performance in relation to the strategy check for the session. The teacher then develops the teaching objectives further and often organises **follow-up activities** including re-reading the text, carrying out word-level activities such as vocabulary and spelling investigations, and rehearsing poetry or dramatic performances.

4 Brian Cambourne, *The Whole Story: Natural learning and the acquisition of literacy in the classroom* (Ashton Scholastic, 1988), p. 158.

ASSESSMENT FOR LEARNING

This section of the book aims to explore the links between

- capturing and analysing a child's moment-by-moment processing, comments and decisions;
- establishing an individual's performance on a gradient of text challenge;
- using information from assessment and informal observation to scaffold further learning.

In the guided reading plans preceding each band listing, there are further examples of the ways in which learning objectives are shared with children, feedback is given to develop individual children's self-awareness and independent control, and opportunities are given for pupils to review, reflect on and extend their learning.

GUIDED READING AND ASSESSMENT

INFORMAL OBSERVATION

Guided reading provides rich opportunities for informal monitoring and feedback designed to develop pupils' insight, self-assessment and control. The teacher, concentrating on just a small group of children, is also able to gauge the effectiveness of the whole-class teaching as they work on text.

However, teachers need to distance themselves from their teaching role at times and use standardised procedures to measure progress and plan subsequent programmes. More formal assessment may also be required at the school management level.

GROUP READING TESTS

Results from standardised reading tests, whether they consist of isolated words or sentences, comprehension passages or cloze exercises, are reassuring to school managers and educational administrators. Tests come with precise instructions and conversion tables, and they provide straightforward results that can be compared year on year within and between schools. Above all, they can be administered to the whole class in a relatively short period of time under uniform conditions.

Their shortcomings, unfortunately, are considerable. Children making rapid or satisfactory progress will probably score well in any type of assessment, but many tests are less reliable at the extremes than in the middle range of the population. How accurate the norms are will depend on how recently the test was standardised and how appropriate the standardisation sample was. Standardised tests do not of themselves suggest the next stage in teaching, and 'more of the same' in terms of reading materials, activities and style of teaching might not be the most profitable conclusion to draw from satisfactory performance. Group reading tests offer little diagnostic insight into the difficulties individual children may be experiencing. Answers are either right or wrong, and the reasons for difficulties may not be apparent. Because standardised tests are not related to the way the curriculum is delivered, the results do not necessarily indicate how a teacher might best respond back in the classroom.

USING A GRADED READING SERIES

When teachers become very familiar with the progression in one particular reading series over a period of time, they may use their experience to match pupils with texts with reasonable accuracy: 'Red Group's up to Stage 6'. This system offers some kind of progression, but does not provide a broad basis of evidence upon which the teacher can plan or adjust the curriculum for all the children in a class. It does not easily translate into National Curriculum levels or specific curriculum targets that allow schools to track progress and development over time.

RUNNING RECORDS

RECORDING TEXT READING

Taking and analysing **running records** of text reading involves capturing what children know about reading in general, and how they apply their knowledge and experience on-the-run when faced with a new book or passage. It is an authentic snapshot of the complex reading process, particularly when followed by a discussion about the message, impact and implications of that passage.

A GRADIENT OF TEXT CHALLENGE

Detailed assessment of a child's processing is most valuable when the chosen texts are neither too difficult nor too easy for that child, i.e. at an **instructional level** (with 90–94 per cent accuracy). Where a school has set up a rich range of resources using a common gradient across different types of books and series, a teacher is able to establish the appropriate level of challenge both for assessment and for subsequent lessons. **A child or group's position on this gradient, then, becomes a short-hand description for their level of processing and a valid guide to their progress in text reading.**

VALUE OF RUNNING RECORDS

Finding a text on which a child performs at **instructional level** can be time-consuming, and recording the reading of 100–200 words accurately requires a certain amount of expertise and practice. The information that can be gleaned, though, is immensely valuable.

- The optimum band of text reading can be established for each child.
- Running records taken on different types of text, e.g. a non-chronological report, a short poem and an extract from a short novel, can indicate the reader's flexibility and experience.
- Errors and partially correct responses can be analysed in order to gain insight into a child's cognitive processing during text reading.
- Those insights can lead to sophisticated use of reading prompts that enable a child to improve their own reading.
- The children receive the benefit of the teacher's sole attention and can benefit from instant feedback of significant value and validity.
- Reporting to other professionals and to a child's parents is based on detailed and meaningful evidence that can easily be shared with others.
- Children working at a similar band can be grouped for effective guided reading.

GRADIENT OF CHALLENGE FOR YEAR 3 PUPILS

BAND	COLOUR	NC LEVEL	START OF Y3	END OF Y3
BEYOND BAND 11		Level 3+	Extended challenge desirable	
BAND 11	LIME	Level 3		
BAND 10	WHITE	Working Towards Level 3		
BAND 9	GOLD	Level 2	Average	
BAND 8	PURPLE	Level 2		
BAND 7	TURQUOISE	Working Towards Level 2	Additional group support desirable	
BAND 6	ORANGE	Working Towards Level 2		
BANDS 3–5	GREEN BLUE YELLOW	Level 1	Additional individualised literacy support required	
BANDS 1–2	RED PINK	Working Towards Level 1		

CAPTURING TEXT READING PERFORMANCE

A teacher needs to practise recording conventions with average readers before running records can be used as a reliable assessment technique. Once these are well rehearsed, the teacher is able to devote full attention to each child, chatting briefly about the procedure and enlisting co-operation in a relaxed way.

It is not necessary for the recorder to have a printed copy of the text, although it can be helpful when recording very rapid, able readers. It is essential, of course, to write down the name of the child, the title of the book and page numbers of the text on which the child's performance is to be recorded, and, crucially important, the recording date. A running record only has validity for a few weeks; children regularly engaging with a wide variety of new texts can make rapid progress.

GETTING GOING

Choose a relatively easy text to start with. If a child's previous records are available, they may indicate the current band at which the child was working. An alternative method of establishing a starting point is to ask the child to read a passage of about 100 words silently, and then ask for a paraphrase. If the child reads quite rapidly and is able to give many accurate details, repeat this procedure at a higher band. If it is apparent that the child cannot manage the text, repeat at a lower band until it is clear that the passage can be read and some facts recalled.

Supply the title of the book, and then make a detailed record without interrupting the reading or giving the child any clues or prompts. It may be necessary to urge him/her to 'have a go' at an unfamiliar word. Tell the child a word if the reading has come to a standstill, but count this as an error.

Procedures for taking running records and recording conventions can be found in the NLS document, *Guided Reading: Supporting transition from KS1 to KS2* (London: DfES 2003) and in Marie M. Clay's *An Observation Survey of Early Literacy Achievement* (Auckland, NZ: Heinemann Education, second edition 2002).

The *PM Benchmark Kit: An assessment resource for emergent–12 years R.A.* by E. Nelley and A. Smith (Cheltenham: Nelson Thornes 2000) provides a very useful gradient of assessment texts from Band 1 (working towards Level 1) to Band 13 at the upper end of Key Stage 2. There are running record forms and useful literal and inductive comprehension questions for each text, and helpful instructions on using the kit.

ESTABLISHING AN INSTRUCTIONAL LEVEL

Where a child makes only one error in every 10–20 words, i.e. reads with 90–94 per cent accuracy, we say that this book is at an **instructional level** for the child. This indicates that the challenge is not so great that s/he loses control, and not so easy that it provides very limited learning opportunity. Other texts listed within the same band should provide similar teaching and learning opportunities, although there is always individual variation in terms of prior experience and preference.

It is important to take a running record on a book from the next band up to establish the **highest possible instructional level**. More than 10 errors in 100 words indicates a **hard level** for the child, and that s/he needs to build experience at the band below.

Accuracy rate

Step 1	Count the number of words in a passage, excluding the title
Step 2	Count the uncorrected errors
Step 3	Express errors as a ratio of total number of words, e.g. 6 errors in a total of 120 words: 1:20
Step 4	Convert to accuracy rate, e.g. 95%

Conversion table

Error rate	Accuracy	
1:100	99%	
1:50	98%	Texts read at an instructional-to-easy level
1:35	97%	
1:25	96%	
1:20	95%	
1:17	94%	Observation of reading pace and control,
1:14	93%	together with an analysis of errors,
1:12.5	92%	provides teachers with the most valuable
1:11.75	91%	information at this accuracy rate
1:10	90%	
1:9	89%	
1:8	87.5%	The reader tends to lose control and
1:7	85.5%	is unable to use a balance of searchlights
1:6	83%	information
1:5	80%	

Self-corrections indicate that the reader is **monitoring** his/her own reading carefully, and using a balanced range of information from the print, from the sentence syntax and from the meaning of a passage. However, too much self-correction may indicate impulsive guessing using insufficient print information, and may break the flow of phrases and sentences. A child who has established this style of reading may need to work with guidance on easier texts until a better flow, i.e. more fluent reading, is established.

OBSERVING PHRASING AND FLEXIBILITY

The **pace and quality** of reading should be noted on every running record, along with the ability of a child to adjust to different text types. A fictional text usually needs to flow quite rapidly, with careful attention to punctuation to support longer phrasing, and direct speech. Non-fiction demands a slower, more deliberate pace with pauses to check information and refer to illustrations and diagrams. Poetry may require rehearsal while the reader explores the metre and rhyme elements, and decides on an appropriate manner to fit humour, melancholy or metaphorical language. The same exploratory approach may be necessary with plays and texts that use dialect, oral language and vocabulary unfamiliar to the reader.

There are more specific suggestions in the following chapter about using information from running records in guided reading.

EMPOWERING CHILDREN TO TAKE CONTROL

THE SEARCHLIGHTS MODEL

There is now a broad consensus of opinion among educators about what is meant by the 'act of reading':

A reader orchestrates information from print detail, word order arising from the syntax of spoken language, experience of written text and knowledge of the world, predicting and confirming the message on-the-run in order to match his/her thinking to that of an author.[1]

The teacher's role is to support this complex balancing act, where necessary

- sharing an appreciation of the message or the language of the text
- praising efforts to adjust phrasing and correct errors
- prompting the child to consider neglected information
- reminding him/her to monitor their own reading
- modelling language flow to make the meaning clearer
- discussing and predicting implications and inferences arising from the text
- clarifying terminology, meaning and pronunciation
- valuing the child's relevant experience in order to support his/her response to the text
- making links with curriculum areas covered in whole-class sessions.

ANALYSING THE EVIDENCE

Evidence from recent running records at an instructional level helps the teacher to establish the band at which the reader functions most actively, to identify a reader's strengths, and to plan for future progress.

At instructional level, a child makes one uncorrected error in every 10–20 words. However, a score of 93 per cent, say, does not take into account the quality of the reading. If the reader's pace is slow and expressionless, or rushed and full of self-correction, the teacher may decide to select books from a lower band for the child and work on phrasing. Encouraging a child to look ahead before reading a phrase, then pause and look ahead again may help him/her to develop a more relaxed reading style with a focus on the meaning.

It is easy to take for granted processing that is going well – reading that makes sense most of the time; reasonable language flow; a certain amount of checking and adjusting; a smile or comment in response to the content. If the text has been wisely selected by the teacher to provide valuable information, **errors will occur**. Resist the temptation to focus on these at the outset! Share the emotional response. Praise the pace and phrasing – getting these right is crucial for all reading. Pick up on the attempts to self-correct whether they are successful or not; **self-corrections indicate that the reader is self-monitoring.** Praise the reader for using, for example, meaning, syntax and some of the print information, and point out how a bit more attention to one aspect of information is all that is needed.

1 Paraphrased from Marie M. Clay, *Becoming Literate: The construction of inner control* (Heinemann, 1991), p. 6.

WORD-SOLVING

Children working on books within the 'Bridging Bands' listed in this book will meet an increasing proportion of words outside their spoken and receptive vocabulary. Those learning English as an additional language will need to adopt a particularly flexible, exploratory approach to pronunciation, given English spelling irregularities. All children benefit greatly from listening to text read aloud, sharing the reading of material that is somewhat above their current processing ability, and discussing unfamiliar vocabulary. Clocking up 'reading mileage' enables children to meet the same words and expressions in a variety of contexts, thereby enriching their knowledge of the language.

As children gain experience in word-solving, they learn to search for alternative pronunciations for unfamiliar words, e.g. 'vapour' could be 'va-**pour**' with an accent on the familiar-looking second syllable, but a check with the illustration may activate the memory of the correct pronunciation heard in conversation. 'Cr**y**-stal' modelled on 'cycle' is a logical pronunciation, but the reader needs to be prompted to search for other feasible alternatives. Letter order is crucial; for example a short word such as 'trial' looks very similar to 'trail' but is unlikely to fit the same context, and a closer look reveals the tell-tale difference in letter-order. It can be helpful for the child to re-read the phrase or sentence containing a correctly solved word to consolidate the meaning and pronunciation.

A common difficulty for those encountering longer words for the first time in print is reading through all the syllables. Some formal revision identifying the six vowels in English (including **y**, particularly in a final position) and the syllables that accompany them should help. Provide regular opportunities for children to return to texts encountered in guided and independent reading in order to locate specific spelling patterns or three-, four- and five-syllable words.

PACE, PHRASING AND EXPRESSION

Understanding written text requires the reader to recreate mentally the sounds and images of oral language. This is particularly true of direct speech, where the full meaning may be embedded within the speaker's tone, as reading the following passage aloud demonstrates:

> *Hugo's mother was going to have a baby. Very soon. She kept saying to Hugo, 'I'll only be gone for three days. I'm not asking you to choose a new mother. Just who you're going to stay with till I get back. So, come along, Hugo. Where's it going to be? Granny's house?'*
>
> (Opening paragraph from *Care of Henry* by Anne Fine, Walker Books, 1996)

Taking careful note of punctuation is the first step, together with the importance placed by the teacher on phrasing and expressiveness. Role-play, drama, play-reading and poetry-reading provide valuable opportunities to enhance enjoyment and appreciation of language. Choose books that offer scope for fun and word play for those children who are reluctant to read. They may need help to rehearse the first pages orally in order to establish a satisfactory tone for their inner reading voice.

Most non-fiction demands a more measured pace than narrative. Young readers whose experience has been mostly with reading fiction tend to race through the factual texts in the same band, since they may seem deceptively easy. To slow them down and ensure that they think about the information carefully as they read, set short-term comprehension questions in advance.

> As you read the next paragraph, find out how the rock was broken into pieces and moved to Hadrian's Wall.

> OR

> Study the pie-chart and then find out what information was collected.

More suggestions for working on specific texts can be found in the reading strategies chart and the lesson plans that accompany each band.

READING STRATEGIES

The chart opposite offers a summary of relevant reading strategies for teachers to work on before, during and after guided reading sessions. The suggested wording to be used by the teacher is intended to empower children to predict, collect evidence, reason, check for themselves, remember and problem-solve independently.

Specific praise and reinforcement for correct and partially correct responses is particularly empowering.

PRIOR TO READING

STRATEGY	SUGGESTED PROMPTS AND ACKNOWLEDGEMENTS
Book orientation	**Prompt**
	What type of book do you think this is? What makes you think that?
Locate title, author, illustrator, blurb, table of contents.	Where can we find out what kind of information this book deals with?
	Have you read any other books like this?
Use cover and look quickly through the book to check layout and predict text type.	**Acknowledge**
	I like the way you leafed through the book / read the blurb / checked the author's biography / scanned the table of contents or chapter headings / studied some of the illustrations/ worked out what type of text this is.
Anticipation	**Prompt**
	I wonder why this text is entitled ...? Let's write your suggestions down and check as we read.
Set up general expectation regarding contents, style.	Have you read anything else written by this author / poet / playwright / journalist? Did you enjoy it?
	Have **you** ever tried skate-boarding / seen a badger / visited a garden centre?
Involvement with the content.	**Acknowledge**
	Good – you're thinking hard about the front cover illustrations and title to get some clues.
Relate text type and content to the prior experience of the readers.	Good question – see if you can discover the reason as you read.
	Yes – it will be interesting to find out if it's similar to the other book you read.
Prediction and comprehension	**Prompt**
	Read the first verse / paragraph and think about what time of day / season this takes place.
Alert readers to the need to think actively while reading.	Are these two characters in the same family or are they just friends? How do you think they feel about each other? Check your ideas as you read on.
	Where can you look to find out that information?
Set up specific lines of thought to follow, connections to make, and implications to check.	**Acknowledge**
	I like the way you checked blurb again to find out who Mrs. Jenkins was.
	Good, you found a useful clue in the way the poet / author described the sky / the trees.
Scan contents page to discover the scope or find a specific section.	You located the key words in the first paragraph that helped you decide.
	Good – what made you look in that section / on that chart?

WORKING WITH CHILDREN AS THEY READ INDEPENDENTLY

Valuable information about a reader's processing of text can be gained from the running record, particularly if errors and self-corrections are analysed carefully to indicate which searchlight information is being used consistently, and which tends to be neglected.

Children working below the average class level may need to be reminded to listen to their own reading in order to check their syntax, or ask themselves if a passage makes sense, as well as being encouraged to attempt unfamiliar vocabulary.

It is quite common for otherwise fluent readers at this stage simply to stall when they meet an unfamiliar word, and wait for someone else to supply it. It is important to urge these children to 'have a go' and praise them for reading the first syllable or even sounding the first letter. Direct them to significant features within the word, and help them search for familiar elements.

Pace, expression and phrasing are highly important, and merit high praise and recognition. Finding the appropriate way to read an ever-increasing variety of text-type is a significant challenge for this age-group as their experience as readers increases.

STRATEGY	SUGGESTED PROMPTS AND ACKNOWLEDGEMENTS
Monitoring, word-solving and self-correcting	**Prompt**
Encourage readers to solve unknown words using print detail and checking that it fits meaning and syntax.	Start reading the word and think what would make sense. Now say it again slowly and check the spelling. You know another word like that, e.g. boat / throat; because / causes. Can you find two words you know in that compound word (e.g. sandstorm)? Now read the sentence again and see if it makes sense.
Foster a closer analysis of longer words using analogy, morphology, syllabification, etc.	Find the part of the word you know. Now read all the syllables (e.g. con**den**ses). Check the diagram. Can you figure out what it means? Could you hear the rhythm in that rap? Read it again so that it sounds like verse.
Adjust reading pace to master more complex phrasing, dialogue and different text types.	Try reading that again, pausing at the commas and emphasising the important part of the sentence.
	Acknowledge
Make full use of punctuation to extract full meaning from text.	Good – you stopped and checked the glossary. Well done – it didn't sound right so you re-read it. I like the way you sounded that word out, and then re-read the sentence to check the sense. Good. It could be 'grinned its teeth' but in fact it's pronounced 'grind' like 'kind'. Can you work out what that means?
Refer to the contents page, glossary or index to locate further information or check meaning.	It didn't sound right the first time you read it, so you changed the way you phrased it. Well done. Good – you used the parts of the word you knew to read through the whole word. It was a good decision to slow down and think carefully about the facts as you were reading.

AFTER READING

WORKING AT THE TEXT AND SENTENCE LEVELS

STRATEGY	SUGGESTED PROMPTS AND ACKNOWLEDGEMENTS
Return to text (text level)	**Prompt**
	Let's talk about the way the story opens / develops / reaches the climax (conflict).
Examine the formal text structure.	Why do you think giraffes spread their legs when they drink? How does the author describe their
Search for implicit meanings.	skin? Which go faster – lions or giraffes? Why do we need a narrator in this play?
Appreciate author's choice of language.	Why did you go to the page on 'habitats'?
Compare different types of presentation.	**Acknowledge**
	You found the part that tells why she was upset. Good, you scanned that page to find evidence.
Focus on elements of theme and character.	You read the verse to yourself again – well done. So that's why you think he was wrong.
Summarise sections of the text.	I like the way you thought carefully before you answered.
Return to text (sentence level)	**Prompt**
	Why does the author use commas on page 6? How should you read that sentence?
Deepen understanding of punctuation.	How do you think Dad would say that to show he is angry / pleased / impatient / tired / excited?
	Why does it say: you will need / are made up of / gets brushed with / put soil in the pot?
Extend understanding of verb agreement, function of adjectives, and role of pronouns.	Some of the words are in speech bubbles. Which ones will you read first? What about the words at the top of the page / in brackets / in italics?
Relate the use of verbs in 1st, 2nd and 3rd person with different text types.	**Acknowledge**
	Well done. You paused at the comma, and it made sense. Why did you speak softly there?
Investigate and explain a range of devices for presenting text.	How did you know 'this' (pollination) means 'bees carry pollen' / 'they' meant 'bridges'?
	I like the way you all read as though you really were the characters in the play.
	You keep re-reading that part slowly to work out what it means – well done.

WORD ANALYSIS

Training children to note and remember the spelling of words once they have read a passage helps to set up a lifetime repertoire of visual recall for word detail. Most of us, when we forget how to spell a word, will write down what it sounds like and then look at it critically in order to activate our visual lexicon.

Those children who read a great deal will reinforce their recall many times over. Less experienced readers lack the same opportunities to over-learn and therefore need to pay particular visual attention, and perhaps reinforce this by pronouncing the word several times to note how the sequence of sounds is represented.

STRATEGY	SUGGESTED PROMPTS AND ACKNOWLEDGEMENTS
Return to text (word level)	**Prompt**
	Look on page 14 and find three words with different spellings of the long 'e' phoneme.
Secure reading of Y1/2 high frequency words and words with long vowel phonemes.	Let's look at 'reply'. How could we spell 'replied' or 'replies'? Now try it with 'spy' and 'try'.
	Some of you had trouble reading this (should). You read a word like that in this book – see if you can find it. Now practise writing could /would / should.
Use analogy with known words to read unfamiliar words.	Find these words, say them and clap the syllables. Now write each syllable.
	If these words were listed alphabetically, would they be near the beginning, middle or end?
Extend control of multi-syllabic words and spelling patterns.	
	Acknowledge
	You noticed 'us' in 'thrust' / 'all' in 'stalled', and then you could read through the whole word. Can you find some other words like that on page 14?
Explore use of verbs, adjectives, root words, synonyms, antonyms.	I like the way you broke that word up into four syllables and then joined them up to read it. Here are some other words with several syllables: see if you can put them into columns depending on how many syllables they have.
Collect new words from reading and extend vocabulary.	Did the dictionary help you to understand it? Now try with these words from the story.
	Well done. You went straight to the middle of that encyclopaedia to find 'mongoose'.
Extend understand of alphabetic order.	You found three other compound words in that story. Good work.

Resourcing for diversity

RESOURCING FOR DIVERSITY

The term 'diversity' applies both to the range of reading ability found in the average primary classroom, and to the variety of texts all the children need to experience. This section lists and reviews the major published series at present on the market specifically designed to cater for those children whose literacy progress is a cause for concern to their parents, to their teachers and to themselves. Its purpose is to advance the case for a diversity of high quality text provision, informed text selection and highly skilled text-based teaching for all children.

TEXT-BASED TEACHING

When learners experience difficulties, it is very tempting for teachers to isolate the difficult elements and set up practice sessions or even whole programmes to deal with the problem areas. Curiously, it would not occur to them as parents to take the same steps if the child had difficulty learning to ride a bike – that is, set up prolonged steering practice or bouts of pedalling. The essence of reading, like bike riding, is keeping in balance different physical challenges and different types of attending in order to develop a new kind of **complex brain functioning**. A skilled teacher in both activities sets up a structured situation with enough support to make the learner feel safe, and enough challenge for him/her to experience the reward of successful effort. The motivation to try and to keep trying comes mainly from the thrill of carrying out the whole authentic activity independently, and without too much conscious effort.

A powerful underlying principle of the National Literacy Strategy, and of the Standard Assessment Tests, is that children should be working on texts. Teaching in a **meaningful context** enables the learner to stay in control of his/her own learning. With the main focus of attention on the text message, the learner sees how print detail, grammatical agreement, metaphorical language or specific text layout apply in one specific text and then another, so that over time the general principles become familiar and understood at a deep level. While there is a place for de-contextualised spelling, punctuation and grammatical exercises, these are most effective when they arise directly out of reading and writing text, and are remembered best when linked back to a variety of texts.

HIGH QUALITY TEXTS

It has often been the case in the past that materials designed for children reading below age-related expectations have been exclusively fiction, and easily distinguishable from books read by the rest of the class by inferior quality of content, illustration and layout. The simple fact that they were so easily distinguishable was already a disincentive. Happily, there is now an increasing range of engaging, high quality books on the market designed to offer older primary children access to the full class curriculum, and similar in quality to the materials that other children are reading.

In particular, there is an increasing range of **non-fiction** to choose from. Information texts share the appeal that magazines, newspapers, environmental print and technical texts have for adults:

- the purpose for reading is readily apparent
- the layout and illustrations provide specific support for the message
- the text tends to be relatively brief compared with novels and other sustained narrative
- non-fiction lends itself to discussion and shared communication.

A less confident reader can compensate for slow pace and some inaccuracy by paying close attention to the illustrations and maximising on personal experience and general knowledge. The incentive to find out specific information may boost his/her persistence in grappling with unfamiliar vocabulary and phrasing.

ADVANTAGES OF GUIDED READING

Children working below age-related expectations can gain a great deal from guided reading procedures, whether they are taught in small groups or individually. A **skilled, well planned book introduction** helps to activate prior knowledge, provides an overview of how that particular book is set out, and allows them to practise some vocabulary and unfamiliar sentence structures if necessary. In highlighting strategies that children will require, the teacher makes links with their previous experience and with relevant aspects of class teaching, and the children can feel they are in control before embarking on the actual reading of a new book.

Probably the biggest challenge for those working with weaker readers is to resist the temptation to give too much support, and to focus instead on **empowering the child** as they read. Warm acknowledgement of good phrasing, successful problem-solving and self-correction when the reading is going well helps develop self-awareness and strengthens the reader's independent control. Even more important is praise and encouragement for attempts to read unfamiliar words, *even* when these are unsuccessful, for re-running to change phrasing or to make a fresh attempt at a word, or for realising that something didn't make sense. Encourage the stalled reader to 'have a go', or in more specific terms: 'start saying the word and think what would make sense'. There are many more suggestions about prompts and acknowledgements during independent reading on pages 14 to 16.

Once the group has read the text, discussed and commented on the content and worked on appropriate text and sentence level objectives, they may like to take the book away and re-read it, if it is a narrative, and investigate further a non-fiction book. Children who have difficulty with spelling or with reading unfamiliar words, benefit greatly from **follow-up work** that takes them back to the print detail, for example to find six compound words; or find different spellings for the sound 'er'. This type of exercise helps to strengthen their visual memory and make links between formal spelling practice, reading and writing, and is more meaningful than many worksheet tasks.

The following chart reflects the authors' attempts to categorise the many types of reading series available that are designed to cater for diversity in Key Stage 2 primary classrooms.

1 DIFFERENTIATED SERIES OFFERING A RANGE OF READING CHALLENGE IN KS2

Three levels of text in each book	**Lightning** (fiction and non-fiction)	**Ginn** Harcourt Education
	Pelican Guided Reading & Writing (fiction and non-fiction)	**Longman** Pearson Education
Parallel texts at different levels of challenge	**Bookwise** 3 levels of challenge (fiction and non-fiction) For Y3 titles see main listings	**Nelson Thornes**
	Literacy Land Info Trail (non-fiction only) Standard and Access versions Y5/Y6 only For Y3 titles see main listings	**Longman** Pearson Education
	Literacy World Satellites (fiction and non-fiction) linked to Heinemann Literacy World	**Heinemann** Harcourt Education
	Literacy Web Spiders (fiction and non-fiction) linked to Oxford Literacy Web	**Oxford University Press**
Reduced challenge – fiction-only	**Longdale Park** linked to Collins Pathways	**Collins** HarperCollins
	Wolf Hill linked to Oxford Reading Tree	**Oxford University Press**
Extended challenge	**Fast Tracks** (fiction and non-fiction)	**Kingscourt** McGraw-Hill
	Literacy World Comets (fiction only) For Y3 titles see main listings	**Heinemann** Harcourt Education

2 SERIES DESIGNATED BY PUBLISHERS FOR KS2 'RELUCTANT READERS'

Fiction and non-fiction	**Pelican HiLo Readers**	**Longman** Pearson Education
	Wildcats	**Kingscourt** McGraw-Hill
Fiction-only	**4U2read.ok**	**Barrington Stoke**
	Comix	**A&C Black**
	Sam's Football Stories	**Brilliant Publications**
	Skyways	**Collins** HarperCollins
	Sparklers	**Nelson Thornes**
Suitable for upper KS2 readers (for individual titles see main listings)	**Famous People, Famous Lives** (non-fiction)	**Franklin Watts** Watts Publishing Group
	Crunchies (fiction)	**Orchard Books** Watts Publishing Group
	Rockets (fiction)	**A&C Black**

Detailed descriptions of each series listed above together with authors' reviews can be found on pp. 30–6

3 SERIES DESIGNED FOR KS2 PUPILS WORKING SIGNIFICANTLY BELOW AGE-RELATED EXPECTATIONS

Fiction and non-fiction	**fuzzbuzz**	**Oxford University Press**
	Jumpstart/Jumpstart Extra	**Collins**
		HarperCollins
	Wellington Square	**Nelson Thornes**
Fiction only	**Bangers and Mash**	**Longman**
		Pearson Education
	Zoom	**Ginn**
		Harcourt Education
Fiction at P-scale/Level 1	**Inclusive Readers**	**David Fulton**

Detailed descriptions of each series listed above together with authors' reviews can be found on pages 37–42

4 KS1 SERIES SUITABLE FOR OLDER READERS WORKING BELOW NC LEVEL 2 (BANDS 1–5)*

Fiction and non-fiction	**Alphakids; Alphakids Plus**	**Horwitz Gardner**
	Cambridge Reading: 'Range of Cultures'	**Cambridge**
	and non-fiction titles	**University Press**
	Literacy Land Genre Range: Traditional Tales	**Longman**
	Info Trail	Pearson Education
	Literacy Links Plus	**Kingscourt**
		McGraw-Hill
	PM Starters; PM Storybooks	**Nelson Thornes**
	Individual titles	Range of publishers
Fiction only	**Dr Seuss Beginner Books**	**Collins**
		HarperCollins
	Storyworld: Once Upon a Time & Fantasy strands	**Heinemann**
		Harcourt Education
Non-fiction only	**Alphaworld**	**Horwitz Gardner**
	Discovery World	**Heinemann**
		Harcourt Education
	PM Non-fiction	**Nelson Thornes**
	National Geographic Windows on Literacy	**Rigby**
		Harcourt Education
	Rigby Star Quest	**Rigby**
		Harcourt Education
	Storyteller	**Kingscourt**
		McGraw-Hill

*A general indication only as not all titles will be suitable. See *Book Bands for Guided Reading* 3rd edition (2003) for banding of individual titles

REVIEWS OF GUIDED READING SERIES OFFERING DIVERSITY OF READING CHALLENGE

INTRODUCTION

In this section, the main reading series currently on the market for 7–11-year-olds that extend the range of reading challenge beyond those listed in the main colour-banded listings are described and reviewed.

CATALOGUE DESCRIPTIONS

The first part of each review is a direct quotation from the publisher's catalogue. It includes the intended age groups and 'reading ages' (where provided) and a brief description of the contents of each series and the publisher's intentions. The term 'for reluctant readers' is used by different publishers to describe a range of series, but usually denotes what they consider to be high interest material accompanied by briefer, simpler texts with more illustrations than usual for KS2 pupils.

AUTHORS' REVIEWS

In the second section, the Book Bands authors have attempted to give an impression of appearance and general features of the books themselves compared with other series on the market. Some series are designed to offer a comprehensive range of texts that are not easily distinguishable from the mainstream series; some, mostly fiction, consist of just a handful of books intended to encourage children to read for enjoyment; and others are based on a particular approach to literacy learning.

GRADIENT OF DIFFICULTY

A small but extremely important section gives an indication of the range of text challenge for each series in terms of the National Curriculum Levels. Monitoring of text challenge is crucial for all children, especially those for whom these series at intended. Regular running records accompanied by comprehension questions enable teachers to measure progress in text reading in terms of a gradient of text difficulty This in turn can be translated into National Curriculum Levels, and the information used for monitoring purposes and for resourcing sensitively for individual needs. Where a group of children uses one particular series exclusively for a number of years, they may become unwittingly locked into a particular gradient of difficulty, be it too easy or too daunting.

STRENGTHS AND LIMITATIONS

All the series were reviewed, compared and re-reviewed over a period of months and the views of teachers working with experience of such materials were sought. Nevertheless judgements made in these sections inevitably reflect the personal tastes of the authors. No single series can offer the range to which every child is entitled, and the authors strongly recommend that a selection of different types of books from a range of publishers be made when setting up a rich resource for children working below age-related expectations.

1 DIFFERENTIATED SERIES OFFERING A RANGE OF READING CHALLENGE IN KS2

THREE LEVELS OF TEXT IN EACH BOOK

SERIES: LIGHTNING	PUBLISHER: GINN

Publisher's description

> *... Guiding Reading successfully at KS2...*
> *... provides the structure to help you get results'*

Target audience

Guided Reading Years 3–6
Listed below are the titles for Year 3

Description

8 books per year; series still in development
Individual whole texts with a range of genre coverage
Each book contains 3 levels of text intended to cater for a range of reading challenge

Support materials

Programme organiser
CD-Rom per year

YEAR 3 TITLES	SET	BAND RANGE	GENRE
Me, Miss!	Brown Level	8–9	Plays in familiar settings
Snake's Pyjamas, The	Brown Level	sophisticated	Poetry of the senses and shape poems
Tales from the Playground	Brown Level, T1	7–9	Narrative in familiar settings
You're It! Playground Games	Brown Level, T1	7–8	Non-chronological reports
Legends of the Lake	Brown Level, T2	9–11	Traditional tales in semi-graphic format
Magical Models	Brown Level, T2	9–10	Procedural texts
Ask the Experts	Brown Level, T3	8–10	Letters
M.C. Gang Investigates, The	Brown Level, T3	9–10	Detective stories by well-known author

1 DIFFERENTIATED SERIES OFFERING A RANGE OF READING CHALLENGE IN KS2

THREE LEVELS OF TEXT IN EACH BOOK

SERIES: PELICAN GUIDED READING & WRITING   PUBLISHER: LONGMAN

Publisher's description

'Differentiated content for 3 ability levels in every book...'

Target audience

Y1–Y6

Listed below are the titles for Year 3

Description

72 books in series; 4 books per term, 2 fiction, 2 non-fiction

Individual whole texts with a range of genre coverage

Each book contains 3 levels of text intended to cater for a range of reading challenge

Support materials

Teacher's Books including copymasters for each title

YEAR 3 TITLES	SET	BAND RANGE	GENRE
Settings and Cliffhangers	Y3T1	9–10	Narrative story starters
Pirate Plays	Y3T1	8–9	Humorous plays
Handful of Hobbies, A	Y3T1	9–10	Non-chronological information/procedural
Book of Teeth, A	Y3T1	9–11	Non-chronological report
Anansi and Brer Rabbit Stories	Y3T2	7–9	Traditional stories
Poems to Perform	Y3T2	9–11	Performance poetry
Make it with Paper	Y3T2	9	Procedural text
Recipes from Different Countries	Y3T2	7–9	Mainly procedural text with geographic links
Letters to Edward	Y3T3	7–11	Letters
Characters All at Sea!	Y3T3	8–11	Story extracts
Playing with Words	Y3T3	8–10	Sound effect poems
Children's Letters	Y3T3	6–11	Letters

1 DIFFERENTIATED SERIES OFFERING A RANGE OF READING CHALLENGE IN KS2

PARALLEL TEXTS AT DIFFERENT LEVELS OF CHALLENGE

SERIES: LITERACY WORLD SATELLITES	PUBLISHER: HEINEMANN

Publisher's description

'The Satellites strand of Literacy World provides a range of humorous, fast moving and thought provoking books, especially written to aspire and motivate less able readers'

Target audience

Age range: 7–11

Description

Guided reading in line with NLS KS2 curriculum guidelines year by year

36 books altogether, 4 stages, 9 books per year, each set colour-coded to match main series

Fiction: 2 novels, 2 short story collections, 1 play anthology per year

Non-fiction: 4 books per year (simplified versions of Literacy World)

Support materials

Reading and Language Skills book provides follow-up activities for fiction

Teacher's Guides includes differentiated worksheets

Guided Reading cards for every book

Literacy World software provides a range of differentiated activities

BRIDGING BANDS REVIEW

General comments

- Not easily distinguishable from main series, apart from different fiction titles
- Text presentation is uncluttered and illustrations are in full colour
- Sentence structures in both fiction and non-fiction remain straightforward throughout
- A comprehensive series of books varying in size, layout and text type
- Specifically designed for guided reading

Gradient of difficulty

- Working Towards NC Level 2 → NC Level 3 at Year 6

Strengths

- Mirrors the curriculum content of the rest of the class
- Non-fiction is a simplified version of the standard series and looks virtually indistinguishable from it apart from discreet logo
- High quality of text presentation
- Genuinely amusing and appealing
- Comprehensive range of text types including graphic novels, plays, biography, science experiments

Limitations

- Children start within striking distance of Level 2, but may not reach NC Level 4 by Year 6. Children may be locked into a lower gradient of learning.
- The font of the non-fiction is particularly small.

1 DIFFERENTIATED SERIES OFFERING A RANGE OF READING CHALLENGE IN KS2

PARALLEL TEXTS AT DIFFERENT LEVELS OF CHALLENGE

SERIES: WEB SPIDERS	PUBLISHER: OUP

Publisher's description

'A structured scheme for KS2 readers who are struggling to read but are still in mainstream classrooms'

Target audience

Age range: 7–11

Reading age: 5.5–9.5

Description

36 books altogether, 3 books per term focused on a single topic; 1 fiction and 2 non-fiction per topic.

Covers a full range of text types and objectives following the termly guidance of the NLS framework

Support materials

1 Teacher's Guide per year

BRIDGING BANDS REVIEW

General comments

- Full colour illustrations throughout; clear, colourful and lively layout
- Designed to appeal particularly to boys
- Non-fiction books could be integrated with the general school resources as 'brief reads' offering valuable and easily accessible links with a variety of topic areas
- Could be used in KS3 and beyond

Gradient of difficulty

- NC Level 1 → Working Towards NC Level 4

Strengths

- Designed to deliver the breadth of the NLS
- Attention-grabbing non-fiction texts and illustrations
- Texts begin at a simple level and rise to within striking distance of end of KS2 expectations
- Non-fiction appeals to a wide age range

Limitations

- Fiction gradient of challenge seems more gradual than the non-fiction
- Fiction lacks variety and compelling story lines

1 DIFFERENTIATED SERIES OFFERING A RANGE OF READING CHALLENGE IN KS2

REDUCED CHALLENGE – FICTION ONLY

SERIES: LONGDALE PARK	PUBLISHER: COLLINS

Publisher's description

'High interest low language level easy reads to motivate reluctant readers KS2'

Target audience

Age range: 7–11

Description

24 books altogether, 6 books per year

Support materials

None specific

Support included in yearly Pathways to Literacy Teachers Notes. Linked to vocabulary of main scheme

BRIDGING BANDS REVIEW

General comment

- All fiction, designed to provide differentiated guided reading
- Realistic stories revolving around a set of familiar characters
- All full colour
- Sustained reads
- Y3–Y5 books are certainly written at 'low language levels', however some of the language in the Y6 books does reach National Curriculum Level 4

Gradient of difficulty

- Working Towards NC Level 2 → NC Level 4

Strengths

- Outward appearance like other books in the scheme
- Stories deal with relevant age-appropriate social issues
- Characters reflect ethnic diversity

Limitations

- Restricted in text type, language and setting
- The group of children around whom these stories are based do not appear in the illustrations to 'grow up'* as the text complexity increases

* as claimed by the publisher

1 DIFFERENTIATED SERIES OFFERING A RANGE OF READING CHALLENGE IN KS2

REDUCED CHALLENGE – FICTION ONLY

SERIES: WOLF HILL	PUBLISHER: OXFORD UNIVERSITY PRESS

Publisher's description

'Motivating stories for reluctant readers, especially boys'

Target audience

Age range: 7–11
Reading age: 6–9

Description

36 books altogether arranged in 5 levels, in 6 month Reading Age bands, 6 books per pack with an extra pack at Level 1

Support materials

3 Teacher's Guides

BRIDGING BANDS REVIEW

General comment

- Colour-coded series with lively front covers and full colour illustrations that closely support the text
- All realistic stories in familiar settings; a lot of dialogue; narrative in the past tense
- Familiar characters and settings that recur throughout the series
- Intended to be read sequentially
- Humour designed to appeal to children

Gradient of difficulty

- NC Early Level 2 → Working Towards NC Level 4

Strengths

- Contemporary narratives that appropriately reflect intended age readership
- Equally appealing to boys and girls, in terms of content and illustrations
- Strong lively story lines dealing with real-life issues
- Short sentences, imaginative vocabulary, carefully introduced and revisited

Limitations

- Narrow range of text types
- Text challenge consists mostly of increasing text length (32–64 pp) and plot complexity
- Sentences mostly short and lack complexity (i.e. do not call for inference from the reader)

1 DIFFERENTIATED SERIES OFFERING A RANGE OF READING CHALLENGE IN KS2

EXTENDED CHALLENGE

SERIES: FAST TRACKS	PUBLISHER: KINGSCOURT

Publisher's description

'... an innovative series that shows middle and upper primary students how different genres are written'

Target audience

More able Y3–Y6

Description

36 books altogether in 2 series, each with 6 sets of different genres/text types, 3 books per set Each genre/text type comprises 3 components: a genre focus book, a long topic book and a short topic book

Support materials

Teacher's notes on CD-Rom

BRIDGING BANDS REVIEW

General comment

- A niche series designed to challenge talented independent readers
- Subject matter selected within the reach of younger KS2 children while presenting them with an enriched curriculum
- Broad range of text types and layout reflecting the range of the NLS
- Fiction has black and white illustrations; non-fiction has full colour spreads and photos

Gradient of difficulty

- NC Level 3 → NC Level 5

Strengths

- Imaginatively constructed series with unusually broad range of genres
- Rich content including contentious issues designed to develop critical thinking
- Mix of attractively presented fiction and non-fiction appealing to both girls and boys

Limitations

- ICT, science and technology strands would further extend the range

2 SERIES DESIGNATED BY PUBLISHERS FOR KS2 'RELUCTANT READERS'

FICTION AND NON-FICTION

SERIES: PELICAN HILO READERS	PUBLISHER: LONGMAN

Publisher's description

'Dynamic, visually arresting books designed to intrigue reluctant readers
High Interest/low readability books for reluctant and struggling 9–12 year olds'

Target audience

Age range: 9–12
Reading age: 7–9

Description

36 books altogether; 2 levels each containing 2 sets of 9 books, fiction and non-fiction

Support materials

Guided Reading cards for each title

BRIDGING BANDS REVIEW

General comment

- Very attractive presentation
- Fiction has black and white illustrations, non-fiction has full colour photos
- Contemporary age-appropriate content with explicit links to the NLS framework

Gradient of difficulty

- NC Level 2 → NC Level 3
- Non-fiction reaches Working Towards NC Level 4

Strengths

- Worthwhile content presented in a highly accessible manner
- Wide range of text types and non-fiction formats
- While very appealing to boys, there are plenty of titles to engage girls
- Exceptionally attractive to older children, including into KS3, in terms of content appearance and interest level

Limitations

- Restricted range of text challenge at lower and upper ends

2 SERIES DESIGNATED BY PUBLISHERS FOR KS2 'RELUCTANT READERS'

FICTION AND NON-FICTION

SERIES: WILDCATS	PUBLISHER: KINGSCOURT

Publisher's description

> *'...designed to provide high-interest books for lower-level readers*
> *Excellent for Guided Reading'*

Target audience

Age range: 6–12+ years

Description

72 books altogether arranged in 6 levels each with 12 titles
Each book is an anthology of different genres and text-types, both fiction and non-fiction

Support materials

Lesson plans
Copymasters for writing activities
Assessment Guidance
Teaching notes for KS3

BRIDGING BANDS REVIEW

General comment

- Standard size and format throughout
- Text presentation is uncluttered and illustrations are in full colour
- Series specifically designed for Guided Reading
- Each anthology contains 4 short reads in a variety of text types

Gradient of difficulty

- NC Level 1 → NC Level 4

Strengths

- Offers a range of fiction and non-fiction in every book and a wide variety of text type and layout throughout the series
- High quality of presentation
- The contents of each anthology are brief, attractive and distinctive
- Can be used flexibly to match the competency and development of individuals or groups
- Selections can be made to link with NLS framework in terms of text types and level of challenge from year to year

Limitations

- Standard size and format
- Essential to have familiarity with the books in order to match the NLS framework and cover a range of text type
- Quality of writing is higher in non-fiction than fiction

2 SERIES DESIGNATED BY PUBLISHERS FOR KS2 'RELUCTANT READERS'

FICTION ONLY

SERIES: 4U2READ.OK	PUBLISHER: BARRINGTON STOKE

Publisher's description

'Series for readers with a reading age of below 8 Differentiated versions of texts designed for reluctant, under-confident and disaffected readers'

Target audience

Interest age: 8–10; 10–12
Reading age: below 8

Description

14 titles altogether
Simplified versions of main catalogue paperback titles, both versions written by well-known authors
Same overall length as main title. Extra supporting illustrations and speech bubbles
6–8 chapters per book

Support materials

Audio cassettes available for some titles

BRIDGING BANDS REVIEW

General comment

- Small collection of novels by significant authors
- *4u2read.ok* logo is the only distinguishing feature on the cover
- Colour covers; greyscale illustrations; cream paper intended to be restful to the eye
- Strong appeal to boys, also for girls
- Clear font, short sentences and brief paragraphs, well spaced on the page
- Simplified vocabulary

Gradient of difficulty

- NC Level 2

Strengths

- Significant authors have written both the standard and simplified versions
- Easy reads with appeal to older children into KS3
- Interesting stories with engaging themes

Limitations

- Some loss of richness in story line compared with original
- Distraction of print showing through from next page

2 SERIES DESIGNATED BY PUBLISHERS FOR KS2 'RELUCTANT READERS'

FICTION ONLY

SERIES: COMIX	PUBLISHER: A&C BLACK

Publisher's description

'A fiction series to develop reading ability among 7–9-year-olds, especially boys…
Enough to get any reluctant reader totally engrossed'

Target audience

Age range: 7–9
Reading age: 6+

Description

18 titles available in both paperback and hardback editions
All fiction, integrated text and illustration, using comic strip conventions

Support materials

None

BRIDGING BANDS REVIEW

General comment

- Small fiction collection
- Enticing front covers in full colour; black and white illustrations
- Some have graphic novel/cartoon format; some simply have cartoon illustrations with narrative text
- Written by well-known authors

Gradient of difficulty

- NC Level 2 → NC Level 3

Strengths

- Contemporary and lively
- Imaginative language
- Some titles could be used for class teaching of graphic novels

Limitations

- Designed to engage boys rather than girls
- Narrative only and limited variety of text type

2 SERIES DESIGNATED BY PUBLISHERS FOR KS2 'RELUCTANT READERS'

FICTION ONLY

SERIES: SAM'S FOOTBALL STORIES	PUBLISHER: BRILLIANT PUBLICATIONS

Publisher's description

'...provides stimulation and motivation especially for boys ages 6–11, who are slower learners or reluctant readers'

Target audience

Age range: 6–11

Description

12 titles altogether: 2 sets of 6 books

Support materials

None

BRIDGING BANDS REVIEW

General comment

- Very small niche series, all narrative in a familiar setting
- Bright front covers, depicting boys (1 title about girls)
- Black and white illustrations, rather small font, with pronounced spacing between brief paragraphs

Gradient of difficulty

- Set 1 Working Towards NC Level 2
- Set 2 Working Within NC Level 2

Strengths

- Strong appeal to boys
- Wide age range appeal
- Strong social interaction portrayed

Limitations

- Quite long stories, but no chapters
- Limited variety of text types

2 SERIES DESIGNATED BY PUBLISHERS FOR KS2 'RELUCTANT READERS'

FICTION ONLY

SERIES: SKYWAYS	PUBLISHER: COLLINS

Publisher's description

'High-interest easy reads that your reluctant KS2 readers will love...'

Target audience

Age range: 7–11
Reading age: 6–9

Description

72 fiction books in 7 levels, 2–4 sets per level, each set contains 4 books on the same theme
Gradual introduction and repetition of vocabulary; controlled progression of reading levels

Support materials

Teacher's notes
Copymasters

BRIDGING BANDS REVIEW

General comment

- Full colour, age-appropriate illustrations throughout
- The illustrations dominate every page throughout the series
- Brief fiction reads with a broad range of characters and settings
- Stories have a strong narrative line, but plots vary in their credibility
- Caters for a very broad age range; could also be used in secondary and adult settings

Gradient of difficulty

- NC Level 1 → Working Towards NC Level 3

Strengths

- Wide variety of settings designed to provide strong motivation
- Brevity of text and illustrative style is particularly unthreatening to older readers working well below age-related expectations
- Strong narrative line throughout, even in the very easy books

Limitations

- Not specifically related to National Literacy Strategy requirements
- Uneven gradient of difficulty, e.g. 4a pack is easier than 1a
- Considering the number of books in the series, the gradient of difficulty is rather limited, and clustered around NC Level 2; not enough NC Level 1 reading experience for very inexperienced readers

2 SERIES DESIGNATED BY PUBLISHERS FOR KS2 'RELUCTANT READERS'

FICTION ONLY

SERIES: SPARKLERS	PUBLISHER: NELSON THORNES

Publisher's description

'High interest chapter books specifically written for Guided Reading in the Literacy Hour for reluctant readers...'

Target audience

Reading age 6–7.5

Description

4 levels, 7 books + 1 assessment book per level, in 6-month reading age levels

Support materials

4 teaching guides

BRIDGING BANDS REVIEW

General comment

- Attractive full colour covers similar to other age appropriate independent reading sets
- Chapter books with greyscale illustrations
- Each book contains picture-cued character summary, settings, chapter contents and glossary as well as author and illustrator blurb
- Carefully controlled amounts of text on the page; short simple sentences
- Age-related appeal

Strengths

- General presentation of the books is appealing
- Attractive text layout with particularly clear spaces between words and lines
- Strong support from illustrations
- Humorous, lively and realistic plots

Limitations

- Limited range of story and text types

Gradient of difficulty:

- NC Level 2 → NC Level 3

**3 SERIES DESIGNED FOR KS2 PUPILS WORKING SIGNIFICANTLY
BELOW AGE-RELATED EXPECTATIONS**

FICTION AND NON-FICTION

SERIES: fuzzbuzz	PUBLISHER: OXFORD UNIVERSITY PRESS

Publisher's description

> *'Tried and tested solution for special needs...'*

Target audience

Age range: KS2

Description

57 books in 3 levels; consisting of 8 sets of fiction, 1 set of non-fiction at Working Towards NC Level 2, and 3 plays

Support materials

Workbooks for sight vocabulary, phonic work
Teacher's Resource Books
Word cards
Language master cards
CD-Roms
Songs
Word book

BRIDGING BANDS REVIEW

General comment

- Very readily identifiable as a reading series, with bold colours and cartoon-style illustrations
- Highly structured series involving fantasy characters and plots
- Depends in initial stages on pre-learning of sight vocabulary prior to reading
- Punctuation and regular text features introduced one at a time in a planned sequence
- Story flow suspended at the end of each page while reader is directed to draw and write

Gradient of difficulty

- Working Towards NC Level 1 → NC Level 2

Strengths

- Highly predictable in terms of vocabulary and layout
- Zany 'characters' in fantasy settings are attractive to some children
- Appeals uniformly to boys and girls of any age
- Non-fiction is easily accessible and well-presented

Limitations

- Not designed for guided reading
- Early books contain very little print, later books are very text-heavy
- Strong emphasis on word learning and decoding print resulting in stilted language
- Restricted opportunities to use a balance of searchlight information
- Very limited variety of text type, plot and character

**3 SERIES DESIGNED FOR KS2 PUPILS WORKING SIGNIFICANTLY
BELOW AGE-RELATED EXPECTATIONS**

FICTION AND NON-FICTION

SERIES: JUMPSTART/JUMPSTART EXTRA	PUBLISHER: COLLINS

Publisher's description

'Easy Reads that ensure success for reluctant readers'

Target audience

Interest age: 6–9
Reading age: 5–8

Description

Jumpstart – 54 books in 3 stages: 3 sets of 6 books per stage; fiction, non-fiction and poetry

Jumpstart Extra – 30 books in 3 stages: 10 books per stage; non-fiction only

Simplified grammar structures; strictly controlled high-interest vocabulary; poetry with patterned text

Support materials

1 Teacher's Resource Book per level
2 Big Books
Workbooks
Flashcards

BRIDGING BANDS REVIEW

General comment

- Clearly identifiable as a series of readers
- Highly structured, full colour formatted covers and coloured illustrations with standardised layout
- Fiction readers revolve around a set of familiar characters
- Limited amount of text on a page

Gradient of difficulty

- Working Towards NC Level 1 → Working Within NC Level 2

Strengths

- Text is clear and straightforward
- Non-fiction and some of the fiction could be used for older pupils
- Some accessible poetry

Limitations

- Presentation and layout lacks variety
- No clear links with the NLS framework in terms of text types

3 SERIES DESIGNED FOR KS2 PUPILS WORKING SIGNIFICANTLY BELOW AGE-RELATED EXPECTATIONS

FICTION AND NON-FICTION

SERIES: WELLINGTON SQUARE	PUBLISHER: NELSON THORNES

Publisher's description

> '... for ... struggling readers, this scheme offers the broadest range of resources with a high interest level and low reading age'

Target audience

Age range: 7–13
Reading age: 6–8.5

Description

100 books in 5 levels including story books, non-fiction and plays

Support materials

Comprehensive range of support material including
Story tapes
CD-Roms
Activity books
Assessment Kit including books
Web site
Character cards
Big books and writing frames

BRIDGING BANDS REVIEW

General comment

- These books form part of a stand-alone multi-sensory literacy programme
- Colour-coded and formatted; readily recognisable as a reading scheme
- Long-standing series in schools, updated and expanded more recently to include ICT to support speaking, listening and writing

Gradient of difficulty

- Working Towards NC Level 1 → NC Level 2

Strengths

- Safe and predictable, with familiar characters and settings that recur throughout the series
- Repetition of a limited range of core vocabulary facilitates over-learning particularly at the early stages
- Non-fiction designed to cover a range of genres
- Comprehensive range of support materials including web-site

Limitations

- Sequential – intended to be read in order
- Fiction lacks vitality and visual appeal

3 SERIES DESIGNED FOR KS2 PUPILS WORKING SIGNIFICANTLY BELOW AGE-RELATED EXPECTATIONS

FICTION ONLY

SERIES: BANGERS AND MASH	PUBLISHER: LONGMAN

Publisher's description

'... a winning combination of phonics and fun'
Aimed at KS1/SEN

Target audience

Age range: 5–8

Description

36 books altogether in 3 levels: 6 core and 6 additional readers per level

Support materials

Workbooks
Big Books (1 per level)

BRIDGING BANDS REVIEW

General comment

- Small phonic-based fiction series
- Prominently numbered books, all written in the present tense
- Lively colour cartoon illustrations

Gradient of difficulty

- Core readers: NC Level 1 → Working Towards NC Level 2
- Extension readers: 13A–18A are better suited for reading to children

Strengths

- Appealing cartoon format
- Humorous, slapstick plots
- Brief, predictable reads

Limitations

- No variety of text types: all narrative written in the present tense
- Restricted opportunities to use a balance of searchlights information
- Conformity with phonic regularity tends to impede language flow

3 SERIES DESIGNED FOR KS2 PUPILS WORKING SIGNIFICANTLY BELOW AGE-RELATED EXPECTATIONS

FICTION ONLY

SERIES: ZOOM	PUBLISHER: GINN

Publisher's description

'... struggling readers, specifically designed to appeal to reluctant boy readers'

Target audience

Age range: 7–11
Reading age: 5–7

Description

48 books in 6 graded sets with 8 readers in each set

Support materials

Resource Book
Cassettes

BRIDGING BANDS REVIEW

General comment

- Colour-coded fiction scheme
- Coloured covers and illustrations throughout
- Different style of presentation used for each level in the series
- Sentences remain simple throughout the series

Gradient of difficulty

- Working Towards NC Level 1 → NC Level 2C

Strengths

- Motivating content and appearance for boys
- Brief, lively and unthreatening reads for older children working at KS1 levels
- Range of fiction genres

Limitations

- No sustained reading required
- Text types limited; mostly graphic style
- Little opportunity for word level development

3 SERIES DESIGNED FOR KS2 PUPILS WORKING SIGNIFICANTLY BELOW AGE-RELATED EXPECTATIONS

FICTION AT P-SCALE/LEVEL 1

SERIES: INCLUSIVE READERS	PUBLISHER: DAVID FULTON

Publisher's description

'Age-appropriate reading materials for children with moderate or severe learning difficulties'

Target audience

Age range: 7–11-year-olds with moderate or severe learning difficulties

Description

12 books: 3 x A3 books per year at KS2
Photocopiable differentiated versions of the text for use with individual children at 3 levels:
P-scales 5/6; P-scale 7/NC Level 1C; and NC Level 1B/2C.
The lower level texts are supported by Writing With Symbols

Support materials

Each title has an accompanying Teachers' Book, with weekly plans and activities for pupils at different levels linked to KS1 objectives in the NLS
There is also support for multi-sensory teaching approaches

BRIDGING BANDS REVIEW

General comment

- Shared books in full colour; pupils' photocopiable versions in black and white
- Illustrations reflect a range of disabilities and ethnic diversity
- Different genres and text types represented by each A3 book

Gradient of difficulty

- P-scale 5 → Working Towards NC Level 2

Strengths

- An imaginative way to provide access to the NLS for older pupils at very early stages of literacy learning
- Offers flexible access to each book
- Only series reviewed that begins at the pre-reading level

Limitations

- Text in shared books is often too small and dense for effective teaching by demonstration
- Pupils' reading materials lack the attraction of real books
- Very few books available at each year level

Bridging Bands: Overview, lessons and texts

AN OVERVIEW OF COLOUR BANDING

The assumption underpinning this chart is that individual children are able to read a certain band of text challenge with 90–94 per cent accuracy; that this is the highest band they are able to read at what is termed **instructional level** (see pp. 6–9); and that they are able to respond satisfactorily to comprehension questions on books banded at this level.

Describing children's current achievement in terms of a particular band of text reading links intimately with everyday classroom practice (see pp. 5–6 on assessment).

PROGRESSION OF SUCCESSFUL TEXT READING THROUGH KS1 INTO KS2

Band	National Curriculum Level	Colour	Year R	Year 1	Year 2	Year 3	Year 4
1	Working Towards Level 1	PINK	■				
2	Working Towards Level 1	RED	■	□			
3	Working Within Level 1	YELLOW	■	■			
4	Working Within Level 1	BLUE	□	■			
5	Working Within Level 1	GREEN		■	□		
6	Working Towards Level 2	ORANGE		■	■		
7	Working Towards Level 2	TURQUOISE		□	■	□	
8	Working Within Level 2	PURPLE			■	□	
9	Working Within Level 2	GOLD			■	■	□
10	Working Towards Level 3	WHITE			□	■	■
11	Working Within Level 3	LIME			□	■	■

■ Majority of pupils secure at this level

□ Normal range of achievement

A wider range of achievement in text reading may well occur within a class. The challenge for schools is to make provision for children falling above and below the ranges indicated, if necessary, on an individual basis.

AN OVERVIEW OF COLOUR BANDING

In order to place into context the six colour bands of texts included in this volume, it may be useful to examine briefly how the gradient supports and reflects the development of an independent reading process.

PINK AND RED BANDS
Working Towards NC Level 1

Text reading in the initial stages consists of mapping oral language onto print in a holistic fashion. Children bring to text reading their prior experience of books and how they work, their knowledge of terms such as 'front cover', 'page', 'word', and the relationships between illustrations and story. They bring their own spoken language skills and often a lively repertoire of literacy language and sense of story-telling.

As they work with simple storybooks, turning pages in order from front to back, and matching one-to-one their recitation of the text with clusters of letters on the page, they act as 'real readers'. The skilled teacher selects suitable high-frequency sight vocabulary from each book and provides additional opportunities for children in a group to learn and recognise these words in different contexts. They are encouraged to notice and remember significant features, for example double-**o** in *look*, **y** at the end of 'my', and extend their alphabet knowledge.

Teachers heighten children's awareness of correct and incorrect reading by prompting them to check initial and final letters, and teaching them to listen to their own reading and begin to understand how what they are saying is represented on the page. In praising children for noticing discrepancies between what they are pointing to and what the print actually represents, the seeds of self-monitoring and meta-cognitive control are sown.

This 'working towards', exploratory stage of text reading is similar to the exploratory stage of text writing. Keeping the excitement of communication and meaning-making intact, the teacher's role is to help each child establish one-to-one matching of spoken words and print, with accompanying spatial, manual and visual control. It is very easy for the burden of technical correctness to dampen a novice's enthusiasm and motivation. **Tolerating some errors while prompting children to construct their own knowledge of print detail is a major challenge for teachers.**

YELLOW, BLUE AND GREEN BANDS
Working Within Level 1

As children develop their literacy proficiency and make phonic links with their extending sight vocabulary, their concept of what a word is, and how words relate to one another deepens. Teachers draw attention to word endings, clusters of familiar letters and analogies, and support them to make connections with their growing ability to sound through words in order to write. Recognition of an expanding sight vocabulary becomes more rapid and requires less attention.

Re-reading texts serves to build up children's visual control so that they can dispense with pointing and make fuller use of basic punctuation, language flow and meaning. In the excitement of unravelling the mystery of decoding simple words, children sometimes slow down their reading and pay undue attention to print detail. The teacher's role is to keep the developing reading process on track so that children use a **balance of information** from different sources, and check their own understandings as they read.

Books in these bands gradually offer a greater range of somewhat longer sentences. Many published as part of a series re-cycle the same formats throughout a text in order to control vocabulary. While this is important in non-fiction texts throughout Level 1 in order to keep the information load at a reasonable level, children really enjoy and benefit from proper narrative. It takes considerable skill for authors to write strong narrative text while at the same time controlling vocabulary and incorporating links between words that allow opportunities for word study!

ORANGE AND TURQUOISE BANDS Working Towards Level 2

Children who are on track to achieve NC Level 2b and above will normally have reached Orange band and above by the beginning of Year 2. They should have a firm grasp of reading strategies in place by then and be able to

- read and write most of the 150 words listed in the YR and many of those on the Y1/2 NLS high frequency lists. This includes discriminating between words that are visually similar, such as they/there/then/these/three; our/out; come/came; etc.
- predict, monitor and cross-check syntax, meaning and print information, re-running and self-correcting where necessary
- adjust their reading in response to punctuation including speech marks to signify different characters talking
- recognise and begin to respond appropriately to a range of text types, e.g. take part in a play-reading, check a contents page and explore an alphabetically-organised text.

The teacher, sensitive to the importance of phrasing and fluency, broadens their attention to monitor meaning and establishes criteria for 'good reading'. Where 'word-barking' has become habituated, it will sometimes be necessary to return to texts at a lower band in order to broaden children's attention to include the monitoring of meaning.

PURPLE TO LIME BANDS Level 2 to Level 3

Further details relating to learning opportunities and text characteristics of books in Orange to Lime bands can be found at the start of each colour band listing.

Although the first nine colour bands represent the gradient that most 4–7-year-old children work through, this progression is still valid for older children learning English, and those working below age-related expectations.

Teaching objectives relate to the National Literacy Strategy Framework for Teaching. Y = Year group; T = Term 1, 2 or 3. In each term, objectives are numbered under the following categories: t = text level; s = sentence level; w = word level.

Band 6 ORANGE

NATIONAL CURRICULUM LEVEL 1

WORKING TOWARDS LEVEL 2: LEARNING OPPORTUNITIES

- Make good use of quite a brief introduction to a new book
- Refer to illustrations but work out vocabulary without heavy reliance on them
- Orchestrate information from meaning, syntax and print on the run
- Search for and use familiar elements within words to read longer words
- Use phonic knowledge together with context to solve unfamiliar words
- Rerun spontaneously to check meaning and self-correct
- Read somewhat longer phrases and more complex sentences than at earlier bands
- Attend to a range of punctuation and text layout to read dialogue, plays and simple non-fiction text appropriately
- Infer meaning from the text
- Check information in text with illustrations and personal experience and comment on the content
- Begin to use appropriate terminology when discussing different types of text

EXAMPLES OF TEXTS IN BAND 6

THE BIKE LESSON
Stan and John Berenstain

Dr Seuss Beginner Books, Collins
1964

ISBN 0 00 171327 2

Humorous extended rhyming narrative, sustained over 61 pages

Direct speech presented without conventional punctuation; speaker inferred

To be safe, Small Bear,
when you ride a bike,
you can not just take
any road you like.

Capital letters denote proper noun

Familiar vocabulary

Expressive reading requires attention to punctuation and poetic rhythm

Illustration suggests that Father Bear is disregarding his own advice, building anticipation of next event

THE SHOPPING LIST
Diana Foley
Illustrated by
Helen Humphries

Storyteller,
Kingscourt/McGraw-Hill
2003

ISBN 0 7901 2888 8

Narrative in a domestic
setting in which each family
member adds to the list

Reader must infer his
favourite item

He loved all the treats
on the list. But the thing
he liked best was not on it.

Mr. Jones poured
himself a glass of juice.
Then he picked up the pen
and added "juice" to
the shopping list.

12

Line break requires reader to
scan ahead to gather
meaning of whole sentence

Unfamiliar reading
vocabulary

Speech marks to indicate
emphasis rather than
spoken language

Illustration supports key
vocabulary

WALKING IN THE AUTUMN
Beverley Randell

PM Library,
Nelson Thornes
1998

ISBN 1 86961 239 6

Simple explanatory text
written in second person

Long sentence starting with
conditional clause. Line
breaks should help fluent
reading

Unfamiliar vocabulary,
supported by title and
illustrations

Writer addresses the
reader directly

In the autumn,
you can find acorns.

If you put one in a pot
and water it sometimes,
a baby oak tree will
come up in the spring.

You can find seeds with wings.
They fly like helicopters.
They turn around
and around in the wind.

Some of them will grow
to be trees, too,
in the spring.

seed

wing

Verb, more commonly
used as noun

Arrows must be interpreted
to indicate directionality

A SIMPLE RHYMING DICTIONARY
Pelican Big Books (small format)

BAND 6

ORANGE

NON-FICTION
Rhyming dictionary

Sue Palmer and Eugenia Low

Longman (1998)
ISBN 0582 339049

TEACHING
OBJECTIVES

- **Y3T1w15** To have a secure understanding of the purpose and organisation of the dictionary
- **Y2T2t16** To use dictionaries to locate words by using initial letter
- **Y3T2w22** To know the quartiles of a dictionary
- **Y3T2w19** To use dictionaries to learn or check the spellings and definitions of words
- **Y3T2w2** To blend phonemes for reading

TEXT SELECTION
NOTES

This 90-word dictionary has a useful introduction explaining how it works, and an index of rhymes.

The letters in red in the alphabet at the top of each page show which words are featured, and there are simple coloured illustrations to support the definitions. Each word is accompanied by rhyming words.

Most children will have had experience of dictionaries and their use in KS1. This book offers valuable practice to those Year 3 pupils who are still uncertain about the way dictionaries are organised, and to those who could benefit from further exploring rhyme.

LINKS TO WHOLE-
CLASS WORK

There is an accompanying Big Book version of this little book which could be used to revise and extend children's understanding of alphabetic ordering.

The rhyming sections provide a resource for children learning and revising different spelling patterns.

TEXT INTRODUCTION

Teacher reads the title of the book and asks the children to examine the front cover and discuss what they know about how dictionaries work.

Now turn to the title page and let's read the diagram explaining how this dictionary is set out.
Ask four children to read in turn the text boxes, and two other children to read the dictionary entries.

STRATEGY CHECK

Remind children about some common phonemes, e.g. **ur** (burst), **dge** (sledge), and split digraphs (huge).

Rehearse alphabetic order, e.g. would you look near the beginning, middle or end of the dictionary to find these words: wave, fry, mug, snail, crust?

INDEPENDENT READING

Write a selection of 8–10 words for all the children to locate, or give each one a different list. Ask them to read the definitions and the rhyming words.

Teacher works with individual children, reminding them of letters that go together to form phonemes and ensuring that they check the meanings that are supported by the illustrations.

RETURN TO THE TEXT

Let's have a competition to see who can find these words first: **boil, square, paw, team, ice, quack.**
Well done. I like the way you checked the alphabet at the top of the page.

Now ask the children to turn to the index of rhymes and discuss how it works. Then select four rhymes and ask them to locate them using the page reference and read the rhyming words.

LINK TO INDEPENDENT ACTIVITY

Ask the children to compose simple verses using rhyming words from the dictionary. Suggest that they work in pairs writing their own lists of words from some of the rhymes and then asking their partner to check them in the dictionary.

BAND 6

ORANGE

**PLAY VERSION
of traditional tale**

THE LITTLE RED HEN
Cambridge Plays

Gerald Rose

Cambridge University Press (2000)
ISBN 0 521 66455 1

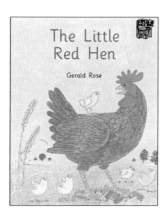

**TEACHING
OBJECTIVES**

- **Y3T1t5**   To recognise the key differences between prose and playscript, e.g. by looking at dialogue, stage directions and text layout
- **Y3T1t3**   To be aware of the different voices in stories using dramatised readings, showing differences between different characters
- **Y3T1s1**   To use awareness of grammar to decipher new or unfamiliar words, e.g. to predict from the text, read on, leave a gap and return; to use these strategies in conjunction with a knowledge of phonemes, word recognition, graphic knowledge and context when reading
- **Y3T2s6**   To note where commas occur in reading and discuss their functions in helping the reader
- **Y3T2w8**   To recognise how words change when -y is added

**TEXT SELECTION
NOTES**

Clear, attractive layout, full coloured illustrations and a somewhat extended script line for each character are featured in this folk tale adaptation by a well-known children's author.

The script is divided into five scenes. There are simple directions to indicate the setting of each scene and there is no narrator.

Sentences are brief and the vocabulary is carefully controlled. Speeches are depicted beside a coloured motif of the relevant character to support inexperienced readers.

**LINK TO WHOLE-
CLASS WORK**

Although the text difficulty is at Level 1, the teaching objectives for this book are appropriate for the age-group, and the subject matter will fit in well with the Y3 focus on traditional stories. The play also provides a model for composition.

TEXT INTRODUCTION

Pupils examine the front cover and discuss with the teacher what type of story this will be. As they look through the book, they are encouraged to comment on the layout and notice play-script elements.

Check the illustrations and describe what the setting of this story is. Now let's look at the title page. Each character has a picture next to it. It's really a key to help you read. How do you think it works?
Plays are often divided into scenes – parts of the story that happen at a different time and sometimes in different places. Let's check page 2 and read: 'Scene 1. In a field near the farmyard.' Can you find where the next scene begins?

Discuss what *wheat* is if necessary.

STRATEGY CHECK

Children select a role to read and the teacher explains that they need to follow closely so that they take their turn as soon as the previous character has finished.

Please let each person work out words on their own, and try to make your part sound like the animal talking. Have a practice of the voice you might use.
p. 2 What will you do where there are five pictures of characters next to a speech?

INDEPENDENT READING

Teacher directs children to read Scene 1, praising for prompt follow-on and appropriate expression.

p. 4 'Crusty': can you spot 'us'? Good, now start reading 'cr', then 'us' and carry on to the end.
p. 4 'busy': does 'bussy' make sense? What could it be?
p. 6 'sow': check the illustration to see what that means. This word is pronounced like 'grow'.

Scene 2: read the stage directions to yourselves. What do you think is going to happen? Let's see if you're right.

Scene 5: Ask children to anticipate how the play will end.

Were you right? Why did you think that?

RETURN TO THE TEXT

The teacher returns to the strategies for the lesson:
You followed on really well one after the other, and made your reading sound like talking. And you gave each animal a different kind of voice. How did you know that word was 'heavy'? Did you carry on and see if that made sense? Well done.

p. 22 In Little Red Hen's speech, there are four commas. Why? How should this be read? Would you like to try?
In her second speech, there are two more commas. Try that too.

Useful word level work on the text could involve identifying two-syllable words ending in **y**: busy, carry, crusty, hungry, ready.

FOLLOW-UP

The teacher links the play-script version with a narrative version, discusses the use of stage directions and speech marks and asks them to write out one page of the text in narrative form.

SERIES	PUBLISHER	SET (OR AUTHOR)	TITLE	BAND
All Aboard	Ginn	Stage 3: Non-fiction	Butterflies	6
			Workshop, The	6
		Stage 4: Non-fiction	Special Clothes	6
		Stage 5 Set A: Patt & Rhyme	Upside Down Harry Brown	6
		Stage 5 Set A: Sam & Rosie	Speedy's Day Out	6
		Stage 5 Set B: Sam & Rosie	Fun Run, The	6
			Have a Go, Sam	6
		Stage 5: Non-fiction	Biggest and Smallest	6
			Racing Pigeons	6
			Slugs	6
		Stage 6: Patt & Rhyme	Big Bad Bill	6
		Stage 6: Sam & Rosie	Great Lorenzo, The	6
			Lord Scarecrow	6
			Plum Magic	6
			Swan Rescue	6
		Stage 7: Sam & Rosie	Sonic Sid	6
Alphakids	Horwitz Gardner	Extending Level 18	Rosie Moon	6
		Transitional Level 13	Bakery, The	6
			Lost in the Park	6
			Snails	6
		Transitional Level 14	Big Dog, The	6
			Elves and the Shoemaker, The	6
			Insects	6
		Transitional Level 15	Butterfly, the Bird, the Beetle and Me, The	6
			Looking After Chickens	6
			We Need More Trees!	6
		Transitional Level 16	Animal Diggers	6
			Loudest Sneeze, The	6
			My Shells	6
			My Street	6
			School News, The	6
		Transitional Level 17	Sea Stars	6
Alphakids Plus	Horwitz Gardner	Early Level 11	Flying Machines	6
			Gorillas	6
			Your Amazing Body	6
		Early Level 9	Whales	6
		Transitional Level 12	Looking Like Plants	6
		Transitional Level 13	Getting Around	6
			Tigers	6
			Trail Riding	6
		Transitional Level 14	Making Pots with Dad	6
			Seahorses	6
		Transitional Level 15	Hunting in the Dark	6
			Last Word, The	6
			Shut in the Barn	6
			Silva the Seal	6
		Transitional Level 16	Three Wishes, The	6
		Transitional Level 17	Amazing Ants	6
			Dancing Dudley	6
			Princess Jo	6
AlphaWorld	Horwitz Gardner	Band 6: Orange	After the Storm	6

SERIES	PUBLISHER	SET (OR AUTHOR)	TITLE	BAND
AlphaWorld	Horwitz Gardner	Band 6: Orange	Present for Our Teacher, A	6
			Saving Up	6
			Storm is Coming, A	6
		Band 7: Turquoise	Seeds on the Move	6
Beginner Books	Collins	Berenstain, Stan & Jan	Bike Lesson, The	6
		Brown, Marc	Spooky Riddles	6
		Eastman, P D	Are You My Mother?	6
		Eastman, P D	Big Dog, Little Dog	6
		Heilbroner, Joan	Robert, the Rose Horse	6
		Sadler, Marilyn	It's Not Easy Being a Bunny	6
		Seuss, Dr	Great Day for Up!	6
		Seuss, Dr	Green Eggs and Ham	6
		Seuss, Dr	Hop on Pop	6
		Seuss, Dr	I Can Read with My Eyes Shut	6
		Stone, Rosetta	Because a Little Bug Went Ka-choo!	6
Blue Bananas	Mammoth	Mooney, Bel	I Don't Want to Say YES!	6
		Wilson, Jacqueline	Monster Eyeballs	6
Bright and Early Books	Collins	Tether, Graham	Hair Book, The	6
Cambridge Reading	CUP	Bridging Books	Flying Football, The	6
			Puppy Chase, The	6
			We're Going on a Picnic	6
			When Dad Went Fishing	6
		Y1: Non-fiction	Osprey	6
		Y1: Playscripts	Little Red Hen, The	6
Discovery World Links	Heinemann	Stage D	Animal Rescue	6
Genre Range	Longman	Emergent Letters	Ben's Get Well Cards	6
		Emergent Trad Tales	Blue Jackal, The	6
Individual Titles	Puffin	Allen, Pamela	Bear's Lunch, The	6
	Picture Puffin	Allen, Pamela	Bertie and the Bear	6
	HarperCollins	Berenstain, Stan	Old Hat New Hat	6
	Walker	Hughes, Shirley	Chatting	6
	Red Fox	Kumansky, K	You Can Swim Jim	6
	Walker	Larranaga, Ana Martin	Big Wide-Mouthed Frog, The	6
	Walker	Lloyd, D & Scruton, C	Cat and Dog	6
	Pan Ch P/backs	Rose, Gerald	Ahhh, Said The Stork	6
	Red Fox	Ross, Tony	Oscar Got the Blame	6
Info Trail	Longman	Beginner Geography	How to Read the Sky	6
		Emergent Geography	Come to My Party!	6
			Is Lightning Most Frightening?	6
		Emergent Science	How to Look After a Rat	6
			Is Simba Happy in the Zoo?	6
Lighthouse	Ginn	Orange: 1	Try Again, Emma	6
		Orange: 2	Animal Tails	6
		Orange: 3	Greedy King, The	6
		Orange: 4	Jolly Hungry Jack	6
		Orange: 5	Jo the Model Maker	6
		Orange: 6	Dog from Outer Space, The	6
		Orange: 7	Dream Team, The	6
		Orange: 8	Two Baby Elephants	6
Literacy Links Plus	Kingscourt	Early A	Water Falling	6
		Early B	Grandma's Memories	6

SERIES	PUBLISHER	SET (OR AUTHOR)	TITLE	BAND
Literacy Links Plus	Kingscourt	Early C	Boxes	6
			Brand-new Butterfly, A	6
			Gregor, The Grumblesome Giant	6
			Hippo's Hiccups	6
			Making Caterpillars and Butterflies	6
			Only an Octopus	6
			Philippa and the Dragon	6
			Pizza For Dinner	6
		Early D	Deer and the Crocodile, The	6
			Dinosaur's Cold, The	6
			Fastest Gazelle, The	6
			Frog Princess, The	6
			Half for You, Half for Me	6
			I Have a Question, Grandma	6
			Mice	6
			Queen's Parrot, The	6
			Rice Cakes	6
			Too Much Noise	6
			Why Elephants Have Long Noses	6
			Wind and Sun	6
		Fluent A	Knit, Knit, Knit, Knit	6
			Tommy's Treasure	6
		Fluent D	Ant and the Grasshopper, The	6
		Traditional Tales	Gingerbread Man, The	6
			Jack and the Beanstalk	6
Literacy Links Plus Topic	Kingscourt	Early C	Fascinating Faces	6
			King's Pudding, The	6
			Sally's Surprise Garden	6
		Early D	Little Half Chick	6
			Rice	6
		Fluent A	Big, Bad Cook, The	6
			Boy and His Donkey, A	6
		Fluent C	Hat Came Back, The	6
National Geographic	Rigby	Green Level	Mighty Machines	6
			People Live in the Desert	6
		Orange Level	Wind Power	6
Oxford Literacy Web	OUP	Non-fiction: Toys	How to Make Toys from the Past	6
			My Toys, Gran's Toys	6
		Poetry Stages: 1–5	Pit-a-Pat-a-Parrot	6
			This is the Mum	6
Oxford Reading Tree	OUP	Stage 6 & 7: More Owls B	Dad's Grand Plan	6
			Don't Be Silly	6
			Mirror Island	6
		Stage 6: More Owls	Christmas Adventure	6
			Fright in the Night, A	6
			Go-kart Race, The	6
			Laughing Princess, The	6
			Rotten Apples	6
			Shiny Key, The	6
		Stage 6: Owls	Kipper and the Giant	6
			Land of the Dinosaurs	6

SERIES	PUBLISHER	SET (OR AUTHOR)	TITLE	BAND
Oxford Reading Tree	OUP	Stage 6: Owls	Robin Hood	6
		Stage 8: Magpies	Kidnappers, The	6
		Stage 8: Playscripts	Kidnappers, The	6
			Viking Adventure	6
Oxford RT Branch Library	OUP	Traditional Tales	Donkey That Sneezed, The	6
			Jack and the Beanstalk	6
Pathways to Literacy	Collins	Year 2	Grabber	6
			Miss Blossom	6
			My Secret Pet	6
			One Puzzled Parrot	6
			Red Riding Hood	6
		Year 3	Bee In My Bonnet, A	6
Pelican Big Books	Longman	Dupasquier, Philippe	Dear Daddy…	6
		Palmer, Sue	Simple Rhyming Dictionary, A	6
		Waddell, Martin	Duck in The Hat, The	6
PM Non-fiction	Nelson Thornes	Green Level	In the Afternoon	6
			In the Morning	6
			Walking in the Autumn	6
			Walking in the Spring	6
			Walking in the Summer	6
			Walking in the Winter	6
		Orange Level	Budgies	6
			Cats	6
			Dogs	6
			Goldfish	6
			Guinea Pigs	6
			Mice	6
PM Storybooks	Nelson Thornes	Orange Set A	Biggest Tree, The	6
			Dinosaur Chase	6
			Jack and Chug	6
			Toby and BJ	6
			Toby and the Big Tree	6
			Toy Farm, The	6
		Orange Set B	Jessica in the Dark	6
			Just One Guinea Pig	6
			Mitch to the Rescue	6
			Pterosaur's Long Flight	6
			Sarah and the Barking Dog	6
			Toby and the Big Red Van	6
		Orange Set C	Busy Beavers, The	6
			Careful Crocodile, The	6
			Lost in the Forest	6
			Rebecca and the Concert	6
			Roller Blades for Luke	6
			Two Little Goldfish	6
PM Traditional Tales	Nelson Thornes	Orange Level	Chicken-Licken	6
			Gingerbread Man, The	6
			Little Red Hen, The	6
			Tale of the Turnip, The	6
			Three Billy Goats Gruff, The	6
			Three Little Pigs, The	6

SERIES	PUBLISHER	SET (OR AUTHOR)	TITLE	BAND
Rigby Star	Rigby	Orange Level	Chloe the Chameleon	6
			Fizzkid Liz	6
			Giant and the Frippit, The	6
			Hot Surprise, A	6
			How Turtle Got His Shell	6
Spotlight on Fact	Collins	Y1: Toys and Games	Toys of the Past 50 Years	6
Star Quest	Rigby	Orange Level	Clay Creatures	6
Storyteller	Kingscourt	Set 6	Dear Grandma	6
			Down in the Woods	6
			Families	6
			How Bat Learned to Fly	6
			How the Camel Got His Hump	6
			Lion Talk	6
			Meet Me at the Water Hole	6
			Off to the Shop	6
			Shoo, Fly!	6
			Shopping List, The	6
			Ski Lesson, The	6
			That's the Life!	6
			What am I Going to Be?	6
			Winter	6
			Year with Mother Bear, A	6
Storyworld Plays	Heinemann	Stage 8	Shark with No Teeth, The	6
			Tiger and the Jackal, The	6
Storyworlds	Heinemann	Stage 7: Once Upon a Time	Elves and the Shoemaker, The	6
			Frog Prince, The	6
			Pied Piper, The	6
			Tug of War, The	6

Band 7 TURQUOISE

NATIONAL CURRICULUM LEVEL 1

WORKING TOWARDS LEVEL 2: LEARNING OPPORTUNITIES

- Begin to take responsibility for reading title, blurbs, looking through new books, deciding the type of text, and predicting some of the content
- Extract meaning from the text while reading with less dependence on illustrations
- Use punctuation and text layout to read with a greater range of expression and control
- Sustain reading through somewhat longer sentence structures and paragraphs
- Tackle a higher ratio of more complex words, making use of phonic knowledge and syllables
- Approach different text types with increasing flexibility and note the key structural features
- Read simple directions and instructions and act on the information
- Discuss information, characters and reasons for events in the text and offer opinions on the effectiveness of the book

EXAMPLES OF TEXTS IN BAND 7

GROWN UPS MAKE YOU GRUMPY
Carrie Weston
Illustrated by Nick Schon

Lighthouse,
Ginn 2001

ISBN 0 602 30085 1

Storyline involves Jack's change of mood as he reflects on the literal meaning of idiomatic expressions

Synonyms to add variety

Jack thought about playing in Grandma's garden.
"Ooh, dear," says Grandma, "put your pullover on. You'll catch a chill."
She says it every time.
Jack wondered how fast a chill could run. Would he be able to catch it?
He grinned at the thought.

8

Different verb tenses indicate switch from narrative to internal monologue

Reader needs to understand that this is an idiomatic expression

Humour depends on word-play

Thought bubbles imply mental representation

DIARY OF A HONEY-BEE
Bill Keir

Literacy Links Plus, Kingscourt
1998

ISBN 0 7901 0250 1

Sequential report of part of a bee's lifecycle

Reader must infer that bees have different functions

DAY 42

At last, the bees are old enough to be field bees.
They fly around the fields and forests collecting nectar and pollen from flowers to bring back to the hive.
They make about a hundred trips a day.
When they bring nectar back to the hive, the hive bees make it into honey by chewing it and warming it.
If a field bee finds new flowers, she dances on the honeycomb to tell the other field bees where to go.

13

Despite relatively dense text at this band, line-breaks support reading for meaning

Technical vocabulary to be decoded and comprehended. Glossary includes all three terms

Complex sentence structure implying that dancing can communicate specific information

BIG BAD RAPS
Tony Mitten
Illustrated by
Martin Chatterton

Orchard Crunchies, Orchard Books
1996

ISBN 0 86039 365 9

Rap version of traditional tale challenges the reader to adapt to the special register

Whole verse is hyperbole for humorous effect

Poetic phrasing to fit metre

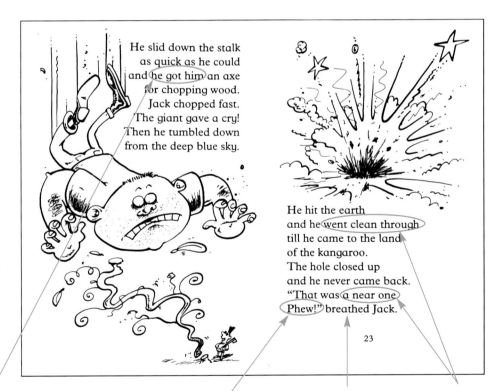

He slid down the stalk
as quick as he could
and he got him an axe
for chopping wood.
Jack chopped fast.
The giant gave a cry!
Then he tumbled down
from the deep blue sky.

He hit the earth
and he went clean through
till he came to the land
of the kangaroo.
The hole closed up
and he never came back.
"That was a near one
Phew!" breathed Jack.

23

Familiar expression – but hard to read

Character's relief implied

Colloquial expressions

BAND 7
TURQUOISE
FICTION Variation on traditional tale

THE LONELY TROLL
Alphakids

Shelley Jones

Illustrations by Meredith Thomas

Horwitz Gardner (1999)
ISBN 07253 1804 X

TEACHING OBJECTIVES

- **Y3T2t1**   To investigate the styles and voices of traditional story language
- **Y3T1s1**   To use phonological, contextual and graphic knowledge to work out, predict and check the meanings of unknown words and to make sense of reading
- **Y3T2t3**   To identify and discuss main characters, expressing own views and using words and phrases from texts
- **Y2T1w7**   To use word endings (-**ed**) to support reading and spelling

TEXT SELECTION

In this variation of the *Three Billy Goats Gruff*, Troll is a sympathetic character. In an attempt to win friends, he cleans himself up, prepares some sandwiches and waits on the bridge. One by one, each Billy Goat greets him with suspicion and spurns his overtures.

On their return, the goats find him reduced to tears. Misunderstandings are sorted and they happily join the picnic.

Words and pictures combine to create an engaging character whose appearance belies his affectionate personality.

LINK TO WHOLE-CLASS WORK

For children familiar with the well-known traditional tale on which his story is based, there are clear links with the class discussion on the features of this text type, e.g. the 'once upon a time' opening; repeated episodes, passages and phrases; a climax, and a happy ending. This text is at Level 1 but many of the Y3 teaching objectives can be exemplified and explored.

TEXT INTRODUCTION

Teacher reads the title and asks the children if they know what a troll is. Suggest that they look through the book at the illustrations, studying in particular the portrait on p. 3 with the picture of the children playing leap-frog over the troll.

p. 4 *Why do you think he's looking at himself in the pool? Check with the illustrations on page 5 to see if you're right.*

Do you think his plans work? Why not? He looks happy at the end though. I wonder why the goats decided to be friends with him.

STRATEGY CHECK

Remind the children how to work out unfamiliar words. Write on a whiteboard: 'He scrubbed his fingernails.'

Ask them to sound the phonemes in 'scrubbed':

Is 's-c-r-u-bb-e-d' a word? What could it be? Good, 'ed' just sounds like 'd'. Now find the two parts of this compound word: 'finger-nails'. Now read the sentence through. Does it make sense? Try this in your reading.

INDEPENDENT READING

The children read the story independently and the teacher works with individuals, praising their phrasing, self-correction and attempts at unfamiliar words.

p. 6 *You said, 'He starred hard at Troll.' It looks like 'starred' but does that make sense? Check the picture again.*

p. 8 (should): Write **could/would** and ask the child to read these and listen to the rhyme; then read **should**.

RETURN TO THE TEXT

I really like the way you made Troll speak so nicely to the Billy Goats. Now turn to p. 12. Let's read Troll's words on this page to make it sound like sobbing.

What sort of character was Troll? How do you know he was friendly? Good, you found the part that says, 'He smiled his lovely smile'. Any other ideas?

LINK TO INDEPENDENT ACTIVITIES

Write the following verbs on a whiteboard: **lived** (livd), **stopped** (stopt).

Ask the children to look through the story and find other -**ed** words and add them to one column or the other depending on sound of the final phoneme.

As a plenary activity, suggest that the children prepare a dramatised version of the story to present to the class.

BAND 7

TURQUOISE

EXPLANATORY TEXT
Non-fiction

TADPOLE AND FROG
Stopwatch books

Christine Back and Barrie Watts

A&C Black (1992)
ISBN 0 7136 3612 1

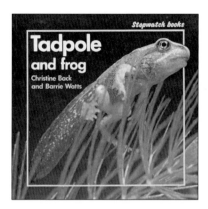

TEACHING OBJECTIVES

- **Y2T3t14**   To pose questions and record these prior to reading non-fiction to find answers
- **Y2T3t16**   To scan text to find specific sections, e.g. sub-headings
- **Y2T2t18**   To use alphabetically ordered texts, e.g. index
- **Y2T2t19**   To read flow charts that explain a process
- **Y2T3t18**   To evaluate the usefulness of a text for its purpose
- **Y3T1s1**   To use awareness of grammar to decipher new or unfamiliar words in conjunction with a knowledge of phonemes, word recognition, graphic knowledge and context when reading

TEXT SELECTION

To quote from an entirely accurate blurb: 'remarkable colour photos show how a tadpole forms inside a ball of jelly and then changes into a young frog'.

The text is clearly written and asks the reader to attend closely to the photographs. Headings are written as particularly simple sentences that could be read independently by NC Level 1 readers.

This title is also available in Big Book format.

LINK TO WHOLE-CLASS WORK

The size and general appearance of this book makes it an excellent link to non-fiction that is common in libraries, i.e. it looks like the type of book accessible by the more able readers in the class. It contains all the features of non-fiction that are discussed in whole-class sessions, contains much detail, yet remains accessible. It fits in with the KS2 science curriculum: *Living things in their environment*.

TEXT INTRODUCTION

Tell the children to look through *Tadpole and Frog* quickly and then discuss what type of book it is, giving reasons for their response, e.g. photographic and diagrammatic illustrations, headings and index.

Ask the children what they would like to find out about tadpoles and frogs, and record their questions. Model the question if necessary:

I'd like to know how long it takes for a tadpole to turn into a frog.

Now we'll take a close look at all the illustrations and talk about what we can see in them. Read the headings as we look.
p. 3 It does look like jelly. Can you see the little eggs inside it? That's called 'frog-spawn'. You try saying it.
p. 12 The tadpole breathes through these gills. The authors call them 'feathery' gills – can you see why?

STRATEGY CHECK

Think about our questions as you read this book and we'll talk about what you discovered when you've finished.

INDEPENDENT READING

Work with individual readers:

Start reading the word (liquid) and think what would make sense. Good, you spotted the 'q' and pronounced it correctly. Did that make sense? (photograph) **ph** at both ends of this word say 'f'. Try sounding it out. Now read from the beginning of the sentence. Yes, you need to change the way you said it. Well done.

I like the way you are checking the illustrations carefully.

RETURN TO THE TEXT

Return to the written questions and discuss with reference to the index. Ask children to locate the answers in the text and read out the relevant sentence.

Develop informed judgement about texts by asking for oral evaluations in terms of
* general appearance of the book
* the way it is written
* whether it supplies interesting information
* whether it inspires the reader to find out more.

INDEPENDENT WORK

Using the photographic flow-chart on pp. 24–25, the children could write and illustrate a simple account of the development of a frog. Suggest that they use the sub-headings throughout the text and the index to check information.

SERIES	PUBLISHER	SET (OR AUTHOR)	TITLE	BAND
All Aboard	Ginn	Stage 4: Non-fiction	Road Signs	7
		Stage 5: Non-fiction	Roller Coaster	7
			Wearing Glasses	7
		Stage 6: Patt & Rhyme	Kangaroos	7
			Lion's Roar, The	7
Alphakids	Horwitz Gardner	Extending Level 18	Betty Boots	7
			If I Were InvisibleÉ	7
			Sebastian Tidies Up	7
		Extending Level 19	Great Sebastian, The	7
		Extending Level 20	Bird Hide, The	7
		Transitional Level 15	Sebastian's Special Present	7
			Space Travel	7
		Transitional Level 16	Predators	7
		Transitional Level 17	Animal Builders	7
			Dress-up Parade, The	7
			Enjoy! Enjoy!	7
			Lonely Troll, The	7
Alphakids Plus	Horwitz Gardner	Transitional Level 15	Crocodile Watching	7
		Transitional Level 16	Crabs	7
			Seashore Crabs	7
			Skate Rider	7
		Transitional Level 17	My Grandpa Plants the Rainforest	7
			Sharks	7
AlphaWorld	Horwitz Gardner	Band 7: Turquoise	Classroom Animals	7
			Eyes	7
Beginner Books	Collins	Eastman, P D	Best Nest, The	7
		Eastman, P D	Sam and the Firefly	7
		Le Seig, Theo	Ten Apples Up On Top	7
		Palmer, Helen	Fish Out of Water, A	7
		Seuss, Dr	Cat in the Hat, The	7
Blue Bananas	Mammoth	Koralek, Jenny	Keeping Secrets	7
		Morse, Brian	Horse in the House	7
		Ritchie, Alison	Riff-Raff Rabbit	7
Book Project	Longman	Fiction Band 5	Blue Moo	7
			Day Poppy Said "Yes!", The	7
			Gregorie Peck	7
		Fiction Band 6	Day Poppy Went Out, The	7
			Jilly's Days	7
		Fiction Band 7	Nyamia and the Bag of Gold	7
Book Project Non-fiction A	Longman	Children Around the World	Growing Up in Australia	7
			Growing Up in Canada	7
			Growing Up in Denmark	7
			Growing Up in Japan	7
			Growing Up in South Africa	7
			Growing Up in Sri Lanka	7
		Food	Has it Gone Off?	7
Bright and Early Books	Collins	Berenstain, Stan & Jan	He Bear, She Bear	7
		Frith, Michael	I'll Teach My Dog 100 Words	7
	Collins	Le Seig, Theo	Tooth Book, The	7
		Perkins, Al	Hand, Hand, Fingers, Thumb	7
Cambridge Reading	CUP	Bridging Books	Apples!	7

SERIES	PUBLISHER	SET (OR AUTHOR)	TITLE	BAND
Cambridge Reading	CUP	Bridging Books	Drat that Cat!	7
			Sam's Snacks	7
			Who Stole the Fish?	7
		Y1 B: Narrative Recount	All By Myself	7
			Going to School	7
			Moonlit Owl, The	7
		Y1 C: Narrative Recount	Atul's Christmas Hamster	7
			Gracie's Cat	7
		Y1 C: Range of Cultures	Animal Wrestlers, The	7
			Chinese New Year, The	7
			Story of Running Water, The	7
		Y1: Non-fiction	Animal Senses	7
			Bridge, The	7
			Forest, The	7
			Scots Pine, The	7
		Y1: Playscripts	Story of Running Water, The	7
Crunchies	Orchard	Seriously Silly Rhymes	Old King Cole Played in Goal	7
		The One And Only	Bruno the Bravest Man	7
			Micky the Muckiest Boy	7
			Ruby the Rudest Girl	7
		Twice Upon a Time	Runaway Cakes and Skipalong Pots	7
Discovery World	Heinemann	Stage E	Everyday Forces	7
			Maps	7
Discovery World Links	Heinemann	Stage D	Road Safety	7
Genre Range	Longman	Emergent Trad Tales	Sleeping Beauty	7
Individual Titles	Little Mammoth	Ahlberg, Allan	Funnybones	7
	Puffin	Ahlberg, Allan	Miss Jump the Jockey	7
	Picture Puffin	Allen, Pamela	Who Sank the Boat?	7
	Walker	Baron, Alan	Red Fox Dances	7
	OUP	Beck, Ian	Goldilocks and the Three Bears	7
	Orchard	Beck, Ian	Ugly Duckling, The	7
	Red Fox	Burningham, John	Oi! Get Off Our Train	7
	Red Fox	Burningham, John	Would You Rather?	7
	Egmont	Cole, Babette	Trouble with Gran, The	7
	Random House	Gunson, Christopher	Over on the Farm	7
	Red Fox	Hutchins, Pat	Shrinking Mouse	7
	Random House	Hutchins, Pat	Silly Billy	7
	Collins Pict Lions	Kerr, Judith	Mog and the Baby	7
	Red Fox	Kitamura, S	When Sheep Cannot Sleep	7
	Walker	Lloyd, David	Duck	7
	Egmont	Lobel, Arnold	Frog and Toad Are Friends	7
	Red Fox	Marshall, James	Three by the Sea	7
	Red Fox	McKee, David	Tusk Tusk	7
	Orchard	Mitchell, R P	Gotcha Smile, The	7
	Walker	Prater, John	Greatest Show on Earth, The	7
	Picture Puffin	Rose, Gerald	Trouble in the Ark	7
	Red Fox	Selway, Martina	What Can I Write?	7
	Picture Puffin	Sutton, Eve	My Cat Likes to Hide in Boxes	7
	Walker	Waddell, Martin	Once There Were Giants	7
	Walker	Waddell, Martin	Pig in the Pond, The	7
Info Trail	Longman	Beginner Geography	Do All Rivers Go to the Sea?	7

SERIES	PUBLISHER	SET (OR AUTHOR)	TITLE	BAND
Info Trail	Longman	Beginner History	Did a Hamster Go into Space?	7
			Knucklebones	7
		Beginner Science	Feet	7
			Would You Be a Bee?	7
		Emergent Science	Don't Be a Beetroot!	7
Lighthouse	Ginn	Turquoise: 1	Grown-ups Make You Grumpy	7
		Turquoise: 2	Boring Old Bed	7
		Turquoise: 3	From a Bean to a Bar	7
		Turquoise: 4	Cat and Rat Fall Out	7
		Turquoise: 5	Clay Dog, The	7
		Turquoise: 6	How Big is it?	7
		Turquoise: 7	Monster in the Cave, The	7
		Turquoise: 8	What a Load of Rubbish	7
Literacy Links Plus	Kingscourt	Early B	What Tommy Did	7
		Early C	Emma's Problem	7
			Goodness Gracious!	7
			Just My Luck	7
		Early D	How Fire Came to Earth	7
			How Turtle Raced Beaver	7
			Monkey and Fire	7
			Trees	7
			Vagabond Crabs	7
		Fluent A	Cat Concert	7
			Diary of a Honey Bee	7
			Don't Worry	7
			Dragon Who Had the Measles, The	7
			Friends Are Forever	7
			Grandpa's Birthday	7
			Something Soft for Danny Bear	7
			Souvenirs	7
			Two Foolish Cats, The	7
		Fluent B	Dogstar	7
			Little Girl and Her Beetle, The	7
			Lonely Giant, The	7
			Oogly Gum Chasing Game, The	7
			Pumpkin House, The	7
			Skeleton on the Bus, The	7
			T-Shirt Triplets, The	7
		Fluent C	Rosie's House	7
		Fluent D	Boy Who Went to the North Wind, The	7
			Smallest Tree, The	7
		Traditional Tales	Chicken Little	7
			Rumpelstiltskin	7
			Three Billy Goats Gruff, The	7
Literacy Links Plus Topic	Kingscourt	Fluent B	Sidetracked Sam	7
		Fluent C	Fabulous Freckles	7
		Fluent D	Pookie and Joe	7
			Stranger's Gift, The	7
National Geographic	Rigby	Green Level	What Do You Know About Dolphins?	7
		Orange Level	Animal Armour	7
		Purple Level	Tunnels	7

SERIES	PUBLISHER	SET (OR AUTHOR)	TITLE	BAND
Oxford Literacy Web	OUP	Non-fiction: Animals	Dinosaur Alphabet	7
			Elephant Diary	7
			Keep Your Hamster Happy	7
		Non-fiction: Toys	All Kinds of Dolls	7
			How My Bike Was Made	7
			Kites	7
		Poetry Stages: 1–5	Beep Goes My Belly Button	7
			Teacher, Teacher	7
			Teeny Tiny Teddy, A	7
		Stage 7: Duck Green	Bird in the Bush, A	7
			Wolf Whistle, The	7
		Stage 7: Variety	Boy Who Talked to the Birds, The	7
			King's Ears, The	7
			Strange Dream, The	7
		Stage 8: Duck Green	Dinosaur Danger!	7
			Summer Fair, The	7
			Watch the Birdie!	7
		Stage 9: Duck Green	Daylight Robbery	7
			Dormouse Pot, The	7
			Miss Ross is Cross	7
Oxford Reading Tree	OUP	Stage 6 & 7: More Owls B	Joke Machine, The	7
			Submarine Adventure	7
			Willow Pattern Plot, The	7
		Stage 6: Owls	Outing, The	7
			Treasure Chest	7
		Stage 6: Robins	Dump, The	7
		Stage 7: More Owls	Bully, The	7
			Chinese Adventure	7
			Hunt for Gold, The	7
			Jigsaw Puzzle, The	7
			Motorway, The	7
			Roman Adventure	7
		Stage 7: Owls	Broken Roof, The	7
			Lost in the Jungle	7
			Lost Key, The	7
			Red Planet	7
		Stage 8: Magpies	Viking Adventure	7
		Stage 8: More Magpies	Flood!	7
		Stage 8: Playscripts	Day in London, A	7
			Flying Carpet, The	7
			Rainbow Machine, The	7
			Victorian Adventure	7
		Stage 8: True Stories	Travels with Magellan	7
		Stage 8: Woodpeckers	Kate and the Crocodile	7
		Stage 9: Magpies	Litter Queen, The	7
			Storm Castle	7
			Superdog	7
		Stage 9: More Magpies	Dutch Adventure	7
			Flying Machine, The	7
			Key Trouble	7
Oxford RT Rhyme & Analogy	OUP	Story Rhymes: Pack A	Mungle Flap, The	7

SERIES	PUBLISHER	SET (OR AUTHOR)	TITLE	BAND
Oxford RT Rhyme & Analogy	OUP	Story Rhymes: Pack A	Supersonic Engine Juice	7
			Who Wants to Play with a Troll?	7
Pathways to Literacy	Collins	Year 2	Hattie Hates Hats	7
			Make a Book Book, The	7
			Owl	7
			Rain Arrow, The	7
			Shoes	7
Pelican Big Books	Longman	Body, Wendy	Absolutely Brilliant Crazy Party, The	7
		Cullimore, Stan	Turtle Who Danced with the Crane, The	7
		Purkis, Sallie	Looking at Teddy Bears	7
PM Storybooks	Nelson Thornes	Turquoise Set A	Cabin in the Hills, The	7
			Jonathan Buys a Present	7
			Monkey Tricks	7
			Nelson the Baby Elephant	7
			Toby and the Accident	7
			When the Volcano Erupted	7
		Turquoise Set B	Bird's Eye View	7
			Hailstorm, The	7
			Little Dinosaur Escapes	7
			Number Plates	7
			Rescuing Nelson	7
			Seat Belt Song, The	7
		Turquoise Set C	Ant City	7
			Grandad's Mask	7
			Jordan's Lucky Day	7
			Nesting Place, The	7
			Race to Green End, The	7
			Riding to Craggy Rock	7
PM Traditional Tales	Nelson Thornes	Turquoise Level	Brave Little Tailor, The	7
			Elves and the Shoemaker, The	7
			Goldilocks and the Three Bears	7
			Little Red Riding Hood	7
			Stone Soup	7
			Ugly Duckling, The	7
Rigby Star	Rigby	Turquoise Level	Flyers	7
			Giant Jumperee, The	7
			Is the Wise Owl Wise?	7
			Korka the Mighty Elf	7
			Perfect Pizza, The	7
			That's Not My Hobby!	7
Rockets	A&C Black	Morgan, Michaela	Sausage and the Little Visitor	7
			Sausage and the Spooks	7
			Sausage in Trouble	7
			School for Sausage	7
		Rodgers, Frank	What Mr Croc Forgot	7
Spotlight on Fact	Collins	Y2: The Seaside	Along the Seashore	7
			Packing for A Holiday	7
Star Quest	Rigby	Purple Level	Peanuts	7
		Turquoise Level	Home for Bonnie, A	7
Stopwatch	A&C Black		Broad Bean	7
			Chicken and Egg	7

SERIES	PUBLISHER	SET (OR AUTHOR)	TITLE	BAND
Stopwatch	A&C Black		Tadpole and Frog	7
Storyteller	Kingscourt	Set 6	Please Don't Sneeze!	7
		Set 7	Amazing Tricks	7
			Bun, The	7
			Crocodile's Bag	7
			Fast Food for Butterflies	7
			Fowler's Family Tree	7
			Granny Garcia's Gifts	7
			Hat Chat	7
			It's About Time	7
			Lizzie's Lizard	7
			Parachutes	7
			Please Do Not Drop Your Jelly Beans	7
			Sarah's Pet	7
			Turtle Talk	7
Storyworlds	Heinemann	Stage 8: Once Upon a Time	Ali Hassan and the Donkey	7
			Little Red Riding Hood	7
			Three Wishes, The	7
			Tiger and the Jackal, The	7

Band 8 PURPLE

NATIONAL CURRICULUM LEVEL 2

WORKING WITHIN LEVEL 2: LEARNING OPPORTUNITIES

- Look through a variety of texts with growing independence to predict content, layout and story development
- Read silently or quietly at a more rapid pace, taking note of punctuation and using it to keep track of longer sentences
- Solve most unfamiliar words on the run
- Use knowledge of high-frequency vocabulary and syllables to read compound words and longer unfamiliar vocabulary
- Adapt to fiction, non-fiction or poetic language with growing flexibility, adjusting reading pace to the text type
- Take more conscious account of literary effects used by writers
- Discuss story themes, characters and settings with reference to words and phrases in the text
- Use a range of alphabetically-ordered text, e.g. indexes, glossaries
- Begin to make more conscious use of reading to extend speaking and writing vocabulary and syntax

EXAMPLES OF TEXTS IN BAND 8

ANIMAL LIFE CYCLES
Clare Llewellyn

Discovery World Links, Heinemann
2002

ISBN 0 435 33977 X

Each double-page spread is a self-contained account of one animal

Cyclic flowchart to illustrate process

Illustration needs to be interpreted in terms of caption

Technical vocabulary

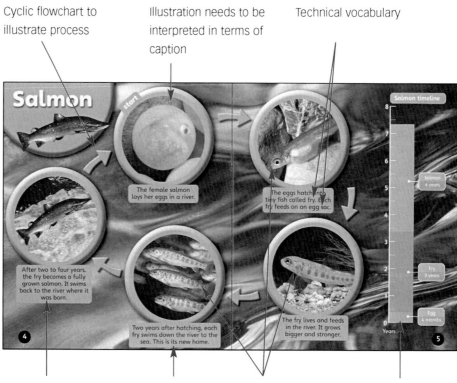

Present perfect verb tense indicates non-chronological report

Compound sentence structure

Relative size of objects requires explanation

Diagrammatic representation of same material in different format

THE MUNGLE FLAP
Roderick Hunt
Illustrated by
Nigel McMullen

Oxford Reading Tree,
Oxford University Press
1996

ISBN 0 19 916817 2

Apparently simple text
whose appeal lies in the
rhythm and sounds of the
words. The challenge for
the reader is to locate
the metre

Illustration does not support
text directly

Reader needs to locate internal rhymes
as well as those at the end of the line

We've got a (trap) for the Mungle (Flap) –
a great big Mungle net.
With (ropes) that (wrap)
(round) a (stretchy) (strap).
It's a very clever sort of trap.

6

Alliteration

PEANUTS
Claire Llewellyn

What's for lunch?
Franklin Watts
2003

ISBN 0 7496 4940 2

Expository text dealing with
different aspects of
production and processing

Passive verbs indicate
report register

Peanuts (can be made) into peanut butter.
To do this the peanuts are (ground), and
sugar and salt are added to the (paste).
This is (mixed) until it is very runny and
can be poured into jars.
It (sets) into peanut butter.

Verb, past tense of grind,
not the more familiar noun

Emboldened words are
defined in glossary

Relatively simple words
with technical meanings

25

PIPE DOWN, PRUDLE!
Colour Crackers

Rose Impey and Shoo Rayner

Orchard Books (1995/2002)
ISBN 1 84121 880 4 (hardback)
ISBN 1 84121 250 4 (paperback)

BAND 8
PURPLE
HUMOROUS NARRATIVE

TEACHING OBJECTIVES

- **Y2T3t6** To read and respond imaginatively to humorous stories
- **Y2T3t8** To discuss the meanings of words and phrases that create humour
- **Y3T3w16** To investigate common expressions from reading
- **Y2T2s7** To investigate and recognise a range of other ways of presenting texts, e.g. speech bubbles, enlarged print
- **Y2T3t2** To use phonological, contextual, grammatical and graphic knowledge to work out, predict and check the meanings of unfamiliar words and to make sense of reading

TEXT SELECTION

All 16 Colour Crackers are highly entertaining. The language is imaginative, the illustrations in full colour are excellent, the print is well set out on the page and there's a collection of really corny jokes at the end.

In this particular book, most of the direct speech is presented in speech bubbles throughout, so the layout somewhat resembles a short graphic novel.

LINK TO WHOLE-CLASS WORK

Although this is an easier text to read than those that most children in Year 3 would be working on in guided reading, some of the language is quite sophisticated and the jokes will appeal to the rest of the class.

A short dramatic presentation to the class based on the story or posters illustrating some of the expressions in the stories and the jokes could be very enjoyable.

TEXT INTRODUCTION

Read the title and sub-title to the children and ask them about parrots and what they think 'pipe down' means. Read the first three pages, imitating the parrot's voice and discuss the expressions: talk the 'legs off a donkey', 'the tail off a tomcat' and 'the ears off an elephant'.

Encourage the children to predict what might happen in the story.

STRATEGY CHECK

This story has lots of speaking in speech bubbles, so you need to think about who is doing the speaking. Watch out for the punctuation – especially the question marks and exclamation marks – and read it to yourself as if you were that character.

It is probably easier to read all the narrative first on each page and then the speech bubbles.

INDEPENDENT READING

Work with individual children, prompting and praising their phrasing and expression as well as their strategies for working out unfamiliar words.

I really like the way you went back and read that again as though you were Prudle.
Start sounding out those words. Keep going right to the end.
Now say it all again to hear if it sounds right. Well done! (sticky-backed plastic; Coronation Street; nosey parker; definitely; popular)

That's a compound word. Find the two words it's made of: (grandson; EastEnders; boyfriend; fingerprints)

RETURN TO THE TEXT

What did you think about that story? Do you think a parrot could be as clever as that? Which part did you like best? Read it out to us. That's great! You sounded just like the burglars.

Discuss the following expressions:
p. 14 'in her will'
p. 21 'who's a nosey parker?'
p. 34 'This place gives me the creeps.'
p. 39 'They took down the details.'
p. 45 'I'm the chief witness.'

LINK TO INDEPENDENT WORK

Ask the children to turn to the Crack-A-Joke page. Suggest that they take turns to ask their partner a joke.

Apart from a dramatic presentation or posters as already suggested, the children could write a book review. In it they would need to justify their opinions with reference to the plot, the main character and the language. If they were enthusiastic, they could locate and read other books in the series.

BAND 8

PURPLE

HISTORICAL REPORT

TRAINS NOW AND FIFTY YEARS AGO
The Longman Book Project

Robin Jones

Longman (1999)
ISBN 0 582 35804 3

TEACHING OBJECTIVES

- **Y3T1t17** To notice differences in style and structure of fiction and non-fiction writing
- **Y3T1t18** To locate information using contents, index, headings and sub-headings, and page numbers
- **Y2T3t14** To pose questions and record these in writing, prior to reading non-fiction to find answers
- **Y3T1t20** To read information passages and identify main points by noting key words or phrases
- **Y3T2w23** To organise words alphabetically, using the first two letters

TEXT SELECTION

Relatively simple historical texts are hard to find. This text is one in a useful series of six about the history of transport covering ships, planes, bicycles, buses and cars. The text is brief and straightforward. The photos on every page, both coloured and black-and-white, have informative captions and create a sense of the changes that have taken place both in technology and in society. The glossary is particularly carefully written, and there is a table of contents and an index.

LINK TO WHOLE-CLASS WORK

The content of this series has obvious links with the history curriculum: *Britain since 1930*, and can help children develop a sense of chronology and continuity.

The non-fiction elements are particularly clear and offer opportunities for children to use those terms such as 'index', 'glossary' and 'caption' that form part of whole-class discussions.

TEXT INTRODUCTION

The front cover invites a discussion based on the title of this book, particularly the similarity in design of the two trains.

Read through the contents page and think about the different sections. I'd like you to come up with some questions you'd like answered by this book.

Teacher records these questions.

STRATEGY CHECK

Ask the children to read the first section, 'Why we have trains' and then choose another chapter from the table of contents. As they read, they should note anything they don't understand, and information they would like to share with the rest of the group.

It's important to study the illustrations and captions carefully and check out what you are reading about.

INDEPENDENT READING

Pupils read independently to themselves within the group. By this stage, they will be reading very quietly or silently. The teacher works with one child and then another, encouraging individuals to read through unfamiliar words, self-correct where necessary and to check their own understanding.

RETURN TO THE TEXT

Well done, Sammy. You finished your section quickly and then read another section while you were waiting for the others.

Let's look at our written questions. Did you find out how steam engines work? Where did you find that information? I wonder where we look to find out more. Yes, the library would be a good place.

Teacher discusses other questions with the group and then gives them some practice in using the index:
- Where can we find information about the Mallard?
- What are 'express trains'?
- What kind of engines do trains have nowadays?
- What are 'branch lines'?

FURTHER READING AND INDEPENDENT WORK

Pupils compare the changes in trains with those in other vehicles using other books in this series; or find other books on transport to locate specific information on trains.

Put in alphabetical order these words from the text:
Coaches, canals, charge, carriages, cities, cab, coal

SERIES	PUBLISHER	SET (OR AUTHOR)	TITLE	BAND
All Aboard	Ginn	Stage 5: Non-fiction	Newts	8
		Stage 8: Non-fiction	Frogs and Toads	8
			Painting with Poster Paint	8
All Aboard	Ginn	Stage 8: Sam & Rosie	Bobby Glow-Worm	8
			Detective Tilak	8
			Toad Crossing	8
		Stage 9: Short Stories	Nognapped	8
Alphakids	Horwitz Gardner	Extending Level 18	Hot-air Balloons	8
			Looking After Their Young	8
		Extending Level 19	Cat and Dog	8
			Natural Disasters	8
			Real Princess, The	8
			Under the Sea	8
		Extending Level 20	Annie and the Pirates	8
			My Diary by Fairy Godmother	8
			Ugly Duckling	8
			Vote for Me!	8
		Extending Level 21	Sir Andrew the Brave	8
		Extending Level 22	Johann and the Birds	8
		Transitional Level 17	Staying Alive	8
Alphakids Plus	Horwitz Gardner	Transitional Level 15	Coastlines	8
		Transitional Level 16	Animals That Sting	8
		Transitional Level 17	Super Sea Birds	8
AlphaWorld	Horwitz Gardner	Band 7: Turquoise	Food for Animals	8
		Band 8: Purple	Amazing Plants	8
			Animal Close-ups	8
			Kites	8
Beginner Books	Collins	Berenstain, Stan & Jan	Bears' Christmas, The	8
		Berenstain, Stan & Jan	Bears' Picnic, The	8
		Berenstain, Stan & Jan	Berenstain Bears & Missing Dinosaur Bone	8
		Gurney, Nancy	King, the Mice and the Cheese, The	8
		Holland, Marion	Big Ball of String, A	8
Blue Bananas	Mammoth	Stewart, Paul	Millie's Party	8
		Young, Selina	Big Dog and Little Dog Visit the Moon	8
Book Project	Longman	Fiction Band 5	King Grumpyguts	8
		Fiction Band 6	Good Dog	8
Book Project Non-fiction A	Longman	Animals	Dragonflies and Their Young	8
			Rabbits and Their Young	8
			Three-spined Sticklebacks & Their Young	8
		Babies	How Babies Grow	8
			Ways of Carrying Babies	8
		Food	Hen's Eggs	8
			Sweets	8
		Homes	Beds	8
			Housework	8
			Water in the House	8
		Toys	Construction Toys	8
			Making Puppets	8
		Toys	Miniature Toys	8
Cambridge Reading	CUP	Bridging Books	Nibbles	8
		Y1 C: Narrative Recount	Tiger Dreams	8

SERIES	PUBLISHER	SET (OR AUTHOR)	TITLE	BAND
Cambridge Reading	CUP	Y1: Non-fiction	Bubbles	8
			Dinosaur (whole text)	8
			Harbour, The (whole text)	8
		Y2 A: Familiar Settings	Parrot Talk	8
			Strawberry Picking	8
		Y2 A: Fantasy Worlds	Grabbing Bird, The	8
		Y2 A: Narrative Recount	Ben's Amazing Birthday	8
			Dad's Promise	8
		Y2 A: Poetry	In the Mirror	8
		Y2 A: Range of Cultures	Dancing to the River	8
		Y2 B: Narrative Recount	Welsh Lamb, A	8
		Y2: Playscripts	Pyjama Party, The	8
Crunchies	Orchard	Colour Crackers	Hot Dog Harris	8
			Pipe Down, Prudle!	8
			Precious Potter	8
			Sleepy Sammy	8
			Stella's Staying Put	8
			Too Many Babies	8
			Welcome Home, Barney	8
		Little Horrors	Spider Man, The	8
		Raps	Big Bad Raps	8
		Seriously Silly Rhymes	Ding Dong Bell, Whats That Funny Smell?	8
		Seriously Silly Stories	Ghostyshocks and the Three Scares	8
		The One And Only	Boris the Brainiest Baby	8
			Harold the Hairiest Man	8
			Polly the Most Poetic Person	8
			Tina the Tiniest Girl	8
		Twice Upon a Time	Bad Bears and Good Bears	8
			Greedy Guts and Belly Busters	8
			Knock, Knock! Who's There?	8
			Over the Stile and Into the Sack	8
			Sneaky Deals and Tricky Tricks	8
Discovery World	Heinemann	Stage C	Day in the Life of a Victorian Child, A	8
			Minibeast Encyclopaedia	8
Discovery World Links	Heinemann	Stage C	How to Grow a Nasturtium	8
		Stage F	Animal Life Cycles	8
Find Out About	Franklin Watts		Wool and Fibre	8
First Explorers	Kingscourt	Level 1	Food for All	8
			Look Up	8
			Nests and Shelters	8
			On the Move	8
			Plants All Round	8
			Ponds and Rivers	8
			Sense This	8
		Level 2	Handle with Care	8
			People and Places	8
Individual Titles	Picture Puffin	Allen, Pamela	Mr Archimedes' Bath	8
	Frances Lincoln	Anholt, Lawrence	Camille and the Sunflowers	8
	Red Fox	Blake, Quentin	All Join in	8
	Harper Collins	Blake, Quentin	Patrick	8
	Red Fox	Brown, R	World That Jack Built, The	8

SERIES	PUBLISHER	SET (OR AUTHOR)	TITLE	BAND
Individual Titles	Heinemann	Bryant-Mole, Karen	Materials	8
	Transworld	Counsel, June	But Martin!	8
	Picture Puffin	Dodd, Lynley	Hairy Maclary from Donaldson's Dairy	8
	Picture Puffin	Dodd, Lynley	Slinky Malinki	8
	Hodder Wayland	Godwin, Sam	Rise and Shine	8
	Frances Lincoln	Hoffman, M & Binch, C	Grace and Family	8
	Egmont	Lobel, Arnold	Frog and Toad Together	8
	Red Fox	McKee, David	Two Can Toucan	8
	OUP	Paul, Korky	Winnie the Witch	8
	Macdonald	Rayner, Shoo	SuperDad the Super Hero	8
	Viking	Riddell, Chris	Platypus	8
	Colour Young Puffin	Rodgers, Frank	Robodog and the Big Dig, The	8
	Arrow Red Fox	Sendak, Maurice	Where the Wild Things Are	8
	Walker	Smee, Nicola	Finish the Story, Dad	8
	Roberts Rineherts	Ungerer, Toni	Three Robbers, The	8
	Walker	Waddell, Martin	Owl Babies	8
	Pan Ch P/backs	Zacharias, Thomas	But Where is the Green Parrot?	8
	Red Fox	Zion, G	Harry, the Dirty Dog	8
Info Trail	Longman	Beginner Science	Does Cheese Come From Cows?	8
		Emergent Geography	Alien Landing	8
			Birthday Treasure Hunt, The	8
		Emergent History	History of Football, The	8
		Emergent Science	Tongues	8
			Training with Ali and Emma	8
Lighthouse	Ginn	Purple: 1	Ozlo's Beard	8
		Purple: 2	Make a Bottle Garden	8
		Purple: 3	Best Pet, The	8
		Purple: 4	Jade Emperor and the Four Dragons, The	8
		Purple: 5	Mouse Stone, The	8
		Purple: 6	Rescue!	8
		Purple: 7	Stop Thief!	8
		Purple: 8	Wild Cat Guide, The	8
Literacy and Science	Neate Publishing	4–7-yr-olds	Animal Sets	8
			Body Parts	8
			Colours Around Us	8
Literacy Land	Longmans	Genre Range – Competent	Zoomababy & the Search for the Lost Dummy	8
			Zoomababy and the Great Dog Chase	8
		Story Street: Step 7	Jojo Makes the Team	8
			Rat for Mouse, A	8
Literacy Links Plus	Kingscourt	Early D	Gallo and Zorro	8
		Fluent A	Awumpalema	8
			Morning Star	8
			Turtle Flies South	8
		Fluent B	Alison Wendlebury	8
			Camping with Claudine	8
			Hare and the Tortoise, The	8
			Mrs Pepperpot's Pet	8
			Oh, Columbus!	8
		Fluent C	Best Birthday Present, The	8
			Look Out for Your Tail	8
			Monster of Mirror Mountain, The	8

SERIES	PUBLISHER	SET (OR AUTHOR)	TITLE	BAND
Literacy Links Plus	Kingscourt	Fluent C	Trojan Horse, The	8
			Why the Sea is Salty	8
			Yellow Overalls	8
		Fluent D	Crosby Crocodile's Disguise	8
			Misha Disappears	8
			Tony and the Butterfly	8
			White Horse, The	8
		Traditional Tales	Fisherman and His Wife, The	8
			Puss-in-Boots	8
			Why Flies Buzz	8
			Why Frog and Snake Can't Be Friends	8
Literacy Links Plus Topic	Kingscourt	Fluent A	Chano	8
			Froggy Tale, A	8
		Fluent A	Simple Solution!	8
		Fluent B	Beanbag	8
			Flying Fingers	8
		Fluent C	Big Catch, The	8
			Moon and the Mirror, The	8
		Fluent D	Forgotten Princess, The	8
National Geographic	Rigby	Turquoise Level	Corn	8
Oxford Literacy Web	OUP	Non-fiction: Animals	Salmon's Journey, The	8
			Spiders Are Amazing	8
			Tigers	8
		Stage 8: Variety	Moneypenny and the Pond	8
			Moneypenny Goes Camping	8
			Moneypenny's Big Walk	8
		Stage 9: Duck Green	Josh and the Beanstalk	8
			Magic Number, The	8
Oxford Reading Tree	OUP	Stage 7: Robins	Old Vase, The	8
		Stage 8: Magpies	Day in London, A	8
			Flying Carpet, The	8
			Rainbow Adventure, The	8
			Victorian Adventure	8
		Stage 8: More Magpies	Egyptian Adventure	8
			Evil Genie, The	8
			Pocket Money	8
			Save Floppy!	8
			What Was it Like?	8
		Stage 8: Robins	Kate and the Sheep	8
		Stage 8: True Stories	Alex Brychta	8
		Stage 9: Magpies	Green Island	8
			Survival Adventure	8
		Stage 9: More Magpies	Blue Eye, The	8
			Finest in the Land, The	8
			Rescue!	8
		Stage 9: Robins	Proper Bike, A	8
		Stage 10: Robins	Holiday, The	8
			Secret Plans, The	8
		TreeTops All Stars: Pack 1	Cosmo for Captain	8
			Farmer Skiboo	8
			Magic Porridge Pot, The	8

SERIES	PUBLISHER	SET (OR AUTHOR)	TITLE	BAND
Oxford Reading Tree	OUP	TreeTops All Stars: Pack 1	Two Brown Bears	8
		TreeTops Stage 10: Pack A	Jungle Shorts	8
			Squink, The	8
Oxford RT Branch Library	OUP	Traditional Tales	Magic Doctor, The	8
			Pied Piper of Hamelin, The	8
Oxford RT Rhyme & Analogy	OUP	Story Rhymes: Pack A	Bad Day, Good Day	8
			Scat, Cat!	8
		Story Rhymes: Pack B	King's Socks, The	8
Pathways to Literacy	Collins	Year 2	All Aboard	8
			Bronwen The Brave	8
			Ginger, Where Are You?	8
			Letters From Lucy	8
			You Can't Park an Elephant	8
Pelican Big Books	Longman	Cullimore, Stan	Cinderella	8
		Witherington, Anne	Food for Festivals	8
		Witherington, Anne	What Babies Used To Wear	8
PM Non-fiction	Nelson Thornes	Turquoise Level	Brown Bears	8
			Elephants	8
			Hippos	8
			Kangaroos	8
			Lions and Tigers	8
			Monkeys and Apes	8
PM Storybooks	Nelson Thornes	Purple Set A	Dog Called Bear, A	8
			Moppet on the Run	8
			Nelson Gets a Fright	8
			Pedlar's Caps, The	8
			Roller Blade Run, The	8
			Zala Runs for Her Life	8
		Purple Set B	Bike for Brad, A	8
			Green Dragons, The	8
			Muffin is Trapped	8
			New School for Megan, A	8
			Surf Carnival, The	8
			Troop of Little Dinosaurs, A	8
		Purple Set C	Gorgo Meets Her Match	8
			Jordan's Catch	8
			Marble Patch, The	8
			Riding High	8
			Toby at Sandy Bay	8
			Two Red Tugs	8
PM Traditional Tales	Nelson Thornes	Purple Level	Animal Band, The	8
			Boy Who Cried Wolf, The	8
			Hare and the Tortoise, The	8
			Puss-in-Boots	8
			Sly Fox and Little Red Hen	8
			Town Mouse and Country Mouse	8
Rigby Star	Rigby	Purple Level	Cherokee Little People, The	8
			Elves and the Shoemakers, The	8
			Jumping Jack	8
			King of the Birds, The	8
			Poles Apart	8

SERIES	PUBLISHER	SET (OR AUTHOR)	TITLE	BAND
Rigby Star	Rigby	Purple Level	Rabbit's Surprise Birthday	8
		Star Plus	Woodcutter and the Bear, The	8
Rockets	A&C Black	Anderson, Scoular	Muddled Monsters, The	8
		Anderson, Scoular	Perfect Pizza, The	8
		Rodgers, Frank	Mr Croc's Clock	8
		Rodgers, Frank	Mr Croc's Silly Sock	8
Star Quest	Rigby	Gold Level	Magnets	8
		Purple Level	Pedal Power	8
Starters	Walker	Crebbin, June	Dragon Test, The	8
		Crebbin, June	Hal the Highwayman	8
		West, Colin	Percy the Pink	8
Stopwatch	A&C Black		Ladybird	8
Storyteller	Kingscourt	Set 7	Knitting for Penguins	8
		Set 8	Adventures of the Robber Pig	8
			Camels and their Cousins	8
			Coyote, Fox, and Wolf Tales	8
			Dream Catchers	8
			Elephant Walk	8
			Feathers	8
			Fire! Fire!	8
			Frog Day	8
			Happily Ever After	8
			Look Inside	8
			Pandora's Box	8
			Rhyming Princess, The	8
			School Days, Cool Days	8
			Solve This!	8
			Wild Easts and the Wild West, The	8
			Winter Woollies	8
Storyworld Plays	Heinemann	Stage 9	Big Barry Baker on the Stage	8
			Jack and the Beanstalk	8
What's for Lunch?	Franklin Watts	Claire Llewellyn	Peanuts	8
			Rice	8

Band 9 GOLD

NATIONAL CURRICULUM LEVEL 2

WORKING WITHIN LEVEL 2: LEARNING OPPORTUNITIES

- Look through a variety of texts with growing independence to predict content, layout and story development
- Read silently or quietly at a more rapid pace
- Read aloud with intonation and expression, taking note of punctuation and using it to keep track of longer sentences
- Solve and self-correct most unfamiliar words on the run, re-reading at times to pull information together or alter phrasing
- Adapt to fiction, non-fiction and poetic language with growing flexibility
- Take more conscious account of literary effects used by writers
- Investigate and recognise a range of ways of presenting text, e.g. captions, headings, sub-headings, chapters, textboxes, etc
- Begin to make more conscious use of reading to extend speaking and writing vocabulary and syntax

EXAMPLES OF TEXTS IN BAND 9

THE BAD DAD LIST
Anna Kenna
Illustrated by David Elliot

Skyracer,
Collins
2003

ISBN 0 007 16739 3

Personal narrative in a familiar setting explores relationship between father and daughter

Direct speech carries emotional tone of relationship and must be read expressively

Paragraphs used to separate actions/ideas

I ran into the living room. Dad was supposed to be getting my cereal, but instead he was watching TV. "Dad!" I yelled. "Quick!"

He jumped up and followed me into the hall. The soapsuds were coming out the door. "What did you put in the machine?" I asked, fighting my way through the bubbles.

"The stuff in the blue plastic bottle."

I shook my head. "You're supposed to use the powder in the red and white box."

By the time we'd cleaned up, it was really late. I was trying not to cry as we sped to school. Dad was very quiet.

We passed the soccer ground. We were just about to turn into the main street when … "Whooo, Whooo".

An officer on a motorbike pulled Dad over.

12

13

Speeding is implied, indicating further problems

Incomplete sentence sets up anticipation

CHOCOLATE!
Mary Ellen Ray

Tristars,
Horwitz Gardner
2000

ISBN 0 72531 895 3

Historical information conveyed through narrative excerpts, as part of chapter on the history of chocolate

Readers must handle condensed text which introduces different kinds of information

Background knowledge of anthropology and geography assumed

Reader needs to understand ways of expressing duration and date

Tricky foreign name to pronounce

The Aztec Indians of Mexico grew cacao trees for many purposes. They ate the beans, and ground them to make a chocolate drink. The Aztec Indians also used cacao beans as money. They bought goods with the beans.

It was only about 300 years ago that chocolate was made into blocks. Before this, people drank chocolate, rather than ate it.

Many other ingredients were added, such as flower petals and black pepper!

In 1528 a Spanish person named Hernando Cortes went to Mexico. He enjoyed the chocolate so much, he took some cacao beans home to Spain.

People in other countries soon found out about chocolate and were very excited about it. Chocolate became very popular.

REPTILES
Paul McEvoy

Go Facts,
A&C Black
2002

ISBN 0 7136 6603 X

Non-fiction text using a flow-chart to accompany sequential description

Little technical vocabulary; focus is on significance of temperature regulation

Emboldened type indicates definition in glossary

Report uses present tense

Illustrated sequence numbered and coloured to match text

A Lizard's Day

How does a lizard spend the day?

1. **Early Morning** At sunrise a lizard moves slowly. It warms itself in the sun before going hunting.
2. **Late Morning** The warm lizard can move quickly. Lizards hunt and catch insects and small animals.
3. **Afternoon** After feeding, the lizard rests in the sun to **digest** its food.
4. **Night** At night the lizard finds a safe place to sleep. During the night the lizard's body cools down. In the morning the lizard can only move slowly.

BAND 9

GOLD

POETRY

MARVEL PAWS
Cambridge Reading

Poems chosen by Richard Brown and Kate Ruttle

Illustrated by David Parkins

Cambridge University Press (1996)
ISBN 0 521 49996 8

TEACHING OBJECTIVES

- **Y2T2t9** To identify and discuss patterns of rhythm, rhyme and other features of sound in different poems
- **Y2T2t11** To identify and discuss favourite poems and poets, using appropriate terms (poet, verse, rhyme, etc) and referring to the language of poems
- **Y3T1t6** To read aloud poems, comparing different views of the same subject
- **Y3T1t8** To express their views about a poem, identifying specific words and phrases that support their viewpoint
- **Y3T2t4** To choose and prepare poems for performance, identifying appropriate expression, tone, volume and use of voice

TEXT SELECTION

Collections by well-known poets that have a consistent and accessible level of challenge are rare. 'Pets' is the theme of this selection of ten short, modern poems that are ideal for guided reading.

Imaginative use of language is matched by lively, uncluttered colour illustrations.

LINK TO WHOLE-CLASS WORK

The more shared poetry reading experience that children have had, the greater will be their ability to search for the rhythm in a new poem, and appreciate the language. These poems should fit well into the Year 3, Term 2 recommended range, and opportunities that children have to rehearse and perform their favourites for classmates, parents and others should enhance their enjoyment.

TEXT INTRODUCTION

Talk with the children about the title, and the illustrated verse on the back cover. Ask them to speculate about the contents.

Now turn to the special index of first lines at the back of this book. Read them to yourself and decide which one you'd like to try first.

STRATEGY CHECK

Poems should be read quite slowly to begin with because each word is important and has been chosen carefully by the poet for a special reason. Treat the punctuation like traffic lights, pausing and stopping when they tell you.
Then read the poem through again and think about the words and ideas that the poet has chosen and why.

INDEPENDENT READING

The teacher works with individual readers.

I do like the way you sound as though you're enjoying every single word.
Well done. You were pausing at the commas and dropping your voice at the full stops.
Start sounding out that word and think what would make sense there (whiskers).

The teacher pauses after each child has read a poem, asks for their comments and whether they would recommend that poem, and then the children choose and read two or three more.

RETURN TO THE TEXT

Ask the children to find 'My Parakeet' by referring to the contents page. After they have read or re-read it, discuss the reason for the recurring **ee/ea** sounds and spellings. Ask for their ideas on the phrase 'the green-pearl of my eye'. Then re-read it in unison, making the first verse sound like the parakeet pick-picking.

Now choose 'Marvel Paws', 'My Dog Spot', 'Jemima Jane' or 'Mice'. Read through the poem and write down all the rhyming words, and see if there's a pattern to the poem.

Good. You can see that they come on every second line.
And you noticed that although the words rhyme, the spellings are very different.

There are two poems about cats in this book. Read them and then we'll discuss the differences in the way that Eleanor Fargeon and Tony Mitton portray cats.
Why do you think Marvel Paws is 'an empty dish, an upset jug and a missing fish'? What does the poet mean by this?

FOLLOW-UP AND INDEPENDENT WORK

The children may like to read the remaining poems, select a favourite and learn it by heart to recite to the class or assembly, individually or in a group.

BAND 9

GOLD

EXPLANATORY TEXT
Technology

FIND OUT ABOUT PAPER

Henry Pluckrose

Franklin Watts (2002)
ISBN 0 7496 4777 9

TEACHING OBJECTIVES

- **Y2T3t14** To pose questions and record these in writing prior to reading non-fiction to find answers
- **Y3T1t17** To notice differences in style and structure of fiction and non-fiction writing
- **Y3T1t20** To read information passages, and identify main points or gist of text
- **T3T3s2** To identify pronouns and understand their functions
- **Y3T1w1** To collect new words from reading
- **Y3T3w14** To explore homonyms, e.g. *beat, light, shape*

TEXT SELECTION

The eight books in the 'Find Out About' series explore various aspects of everyday materials. They consist of full-page photographs of superb quality with clearly worded text-boxes designed to engage readers of all ages. This title charts the process of paper-making from forest to library and newspaper stand, and shows some of the many uses of paper and cardboard.

LINK TO WHOLE-CLASS WORK

Reading a non-fiction text of this type and discussing how the language differs from narrative helps children to compose their own reports in various areas of the curriculum. This particular book has clear links with the Design and Technology Curriculum topic 4: *Knowledge and understanding of materials and components.*

TEXT INTRODUCTION

In order to set up expectations prior to reading, ask children in the group what they would like to find out about paper.

List these on a whiteboard, e.g. how paper is made; different types of paper; who invented paper, etc.

STRATEGY CHECK

This book does not have headings or chapters to separate the different parts. As you are reading, think about the headings you would have put if you had been the author.

INDEPENDENT READING

As each child reads the text silently, work with individuals, asking them to read aloud quietly. In particular, check that they understand how the words 'it', 'they', 'their' and 'these' refer to nouns in the previous sentence, e.g.

p. 5 *Chemicals are added to the pulp.* **They** *make the paper smooth to write on.*

p. 16 *Postage stamps are printed on large sheets of paper too. Tiny holes along* **their** *edges make is easy to tear each stamp …*

RETURN TO THE TEXT

I liked the way some of you were re-reading sentences and checking the photographs to make sure you understood exactly what the author was describing.

Ask the children to identify the different sections of the book, briefly stating the content of each.

Ask the children to define the terms **beat** (p. 5), **light** (p. 12), **to shape** (p. 17) in context, and discuss other meanings for these terms. This work could be extended using dictionaries.

Let's check our own predictions about what this book would tell us about. Yes, some aspects were covered and some were not. Perhaps you could do some research in the library to find out more.

FOLLOW-UP AND INDEPENDENT WORK

There are some very interesting words in this book (e.g. **doilies, silhouette, origami, saliva, delicate**). Choose three of them, and construct a quiz for your partner. Look up the words in your dictionary and write the meanings, and then see if your partner can guess them.

Ask the group to construct a collage from a wide range of different types of paper.

SERIES	PUBLISHER	SET (OR AUTHOR)	TITLE	BAND
All Aboard	Ginn	Stage 6: Non-fiction	Footprint Detective	9
			Leaves	9
			Canals and Narrow Boats	9
			What Does it Eat?	9
			Wheels	9
		Stage 7: Non-fiction	Clown's Gallery	9
			Putting on a Magic Show	9
			Robot World	9
			Town Animals	9
			What's Cooking?	9
		Stage 8: Non-fiction	Planets, The	9
			Shipwreck	9
			Television: Making a Programme	9
		Stage 8: Sam & Rosie	Mountain Rescue	9
		Stage 9: Play	Names and Games	9
Alphakids	Horwitz Gardner	Extending Level 19	Animal Communications	9
		Extending Level 20	Whales on the World Wide Web	9
		Extending Level 21	Great Tin-rolling Race, The	9
			Pollution	9
			Sour Grapes	9
			Worms at Work	9
		Extending Level 22	Amazing Journeys	9
			Pig's Skin	9
			Present for Dad, A	9
			Under Sail	9
AlphaWorld	Horwitz Gardner	Band 8: Purple	Using Colour	9
Blue Bananas	Mammoth	Amstutz, Andree	Tom's Hats	9
		Bertagna, Julie	Clumsy Clumps and the Baby Moon	9
		Bradman, Tony	Magnificent Mummies, The	9
		Goodhart, Pippa	Happy Sad	9
			Promise You Won't Be Cross	9
			Runaway Fred	9
Book Project	Longman	Fiction Band 4: Cluster E	Anansi at The Pool	9
			Bhalloo the Greedy Bear	9
			Turtle and the Crane, The	9
		Fiction Band 5	Baabra Lamb	9
			New Reader Plays 1	9
			Shadow Dance, The	9
			Webster and the Treacle Toffee	9
		Fiction Band 6	Clever Dog, Webster	9
			Letang and Julie Save the Day	9
			Letang's New Friend	9
			Smugglers of Mourne, The	9
			Trouble for Letang and Julie	9
		Fiction Band 7	Joshua's Junk	9
Book Project Non-fiction A	Longman	Animals	Grass Snakes and Their Young	9
			Robin Redbreasts and Their Young	9
			Toads and Their Young	9
		Babies	Baby Food	9
			Nappies	9
		Food	Knives and Forks and Other Things	9

SERIES	PUBLISHER	SET (OR AUTHOR)	TITLE	BAND
Book Project Non-fiction A	Longman	Food	Party Food	9
			Round the World Cookbook	9
		History of Transport	Aeroplanes Now and Fifty Years Ago	9
			Bicycles Now and Fifty Years Ago	9
			Buses Now and Fifty Years Ago	9
			Cars Now and Fifty Years Ago	9
			Passenger Ships Now and Fifty Years Ago	9
			Trains Now and Fifty Years Ago	9
		Homes	Kitchens Now and Long Ago	9
			Miner's Home, The	9
			Toilets	9
		Reference – 4 Volumes	Encyclopaedia of British Wild Animals	9
		Toys	Dolls Now and Long Ago	9
			Noisy Toys	9
			Toys Around the World	9
Cambridge Reading	CUP	Y2 A: Familiar Settings	Cutting and Sticking	9
		Y2 A: Fantasy Worlds	Big Shrink, The	9
			Treasure Cave, The	9
		Y2 A: Narrative Recount	Tulips for Dad	9
		Y2 A: Poetry	Marvel Paws	9
			Nonsense!	9
		Y2 A: Range of Cultures	Rabbit's Tail	9
		Y2 B: Familiar Settings	Pyjama Party, The	9
		Y2 B: Fantasy Worlds	Magic Sword, The	9
			Peace Ring, The	9
		Y2 B: Narrative Recount	Dancing in Soot	9
		Y2 B: Poetry	Corner of Magic, A	9
			Knickerbocker Number Nine	9
		Y2 C: Familiar Settings	Don't Be Late	9
		Y2: Non-fiction	Camouflage	9
			Codes and Signals	9
		Y2: Playscripts	Big Shrink, The	9
			Dilly and the Goody-Goody	9
			Dilly and the School Play	9
			Dilly and the Wobbly Tooth	9
			Dilly Breaks the Rules	9
Crunchies	Orchard	Colour Crackers	Birthday for Bluebell, A	9
			Fortune for Yo-Yo, A	9
			Long Live Roberto	9
			Medal for Poppy, A	9
			Open Wide, Wilbur!	9
			Phew, Sidney!	9
			Rhode Island Roy	9
			Tiny Tim	9
			We Want William!	9
		Little Horrors	Pumpkin Man, The	9
			Sand Man, The	9
			Swamp Man, The	9
		Raps	Fangtastic Raps	9
			Royal Raps	9
		Seriously Silly Rhymes	Mary, Mary, Fried Canary	9

SERIES	PUBLISHER	SET (OR AUTHOR)	TITLE	BAND
Crunchies	Orchard	Tall Tales	And Pigs Might Fly	9
			King of the Birds, The	9
		Twice Upon a Time	Bad Boys and Naughty Girls	9
			Hairy Toes and Scary Bones	9
			I Spy Pancakes and Pies	9
			If Wishes Were Fishes	9
			Silly Sons and Dozy Daughters	9
			Ugly Dogs and Slimy Frogs	9
Discovery World	Heinemann	Stage E	How to Choose a Pet	9
		Stage F	Science Dictionary	9
Discovery World Links	Heinemann	Stage D	Then and Now	9
			World's Largest Animals	9
		Stage E	Changing Materials	9
			Festival Food	9
			Story of Jeans, The	9
		Stage F	Great Fire of London, The	9
Famous People, Famous Lives	Franklin Watts	Famous Scientists & Inventors	Alexander Graham Bell	9
Find Out About	Franklin Watts		Clay	9
			Paper	9
			Rock and Stone	9
First Explorers	Kingscourt	Level 1	Animal Babies	9
			Going Places	9
			Under Attack	9
			You Are Special	9
		Level 2	Buildings for a Purpose	9
			I Dig Dinosaurs	9
			Rainforest Life	9
Genre Range	Longman	Beginner Poetry	Rhyming Poems	9
		Emergent Poetry	Songs, Alphabet & Playground Rhymes	9
			Story Poems	9
			Tongue Twisters, LimericksÉ	9
Go Facts	A&C Black	Animals	Birds	9
			Insects	9
			Mammals	9
			Reptiles	9
Individual Titles	Frances Lincoln	Allen, Pamela	Brown Bread and Honey	9
	Walker	Blake, Jan	Give Me My Yam!	9
	Puffin	Cole, Babette	Princess Smartypants	9
	Walker	Lewis, Kim	Floss	9
	Franklin Watts	Murphy, Jill	Five Minutes' Peace	9
	Walker	Murphy, Jill	On the Way Home	9
	Walker	Murphy, Jill	Piece of Cake, A	9
	Frances Lincoln	Souhami, Jessica	Leopard's Drum, The	9
	Colour Young Puffin	Strong, Jeremy	Pirate School – Just a Bit of Wind	9
	Colour Young Puffin	Strong, Jeremy	Pirate School – The Birthday Bash	9
	Red Fox	Waite, Judy	Digging for Dinosaurs	9
Info Trail	Longman	Emergent Geography	Are Mountains Like Children?	9
		Emergent History	Did Vikings Eat Chips?	9
			Toilets Through Time	9
			Who Goes on the Bonfire?	9
		Emergent Science	Does Chocolate Grow on Trees?	9

SERIES	PUBLISHER	SET (OR AUTHOR)	TITLE	BAND
Infosteps	Kingscourt	Set 1	Different Places, Different Faces	9
			Forest Giants	9
			Horsepower	9
			Strength in Numbers	9
			Tap into Sap	9
Lighthouse	Ginn	Gold: 1	Amy's Armbands	9
		Gold: 2	Sounds	9
		Gold: 3	Grandpa's Bright Ideas	9
		Gold: 4	Big Bo Peep	9
		Gold: 5	Beanpole Billy	9
		Gold: 6	What Dinah Saw	9
Lightning	Ginn	Brown Level plays	Me, Miss!	9
Literacy Land	Longmans	Genre Range – Competent	Bye, Bye Jasmine	9
			Donut Letters, The	9
			Zoomababy and the Locked Cage	9
		Info Trail – Competent	How to Have a Green Day	9
			How to Remember Absolutely Everything	9
			Romans Go Home!	9
			Would you Like to Live on a Small Island?	9
		Story Street: Step 7	Ben and the Ghost	9
			Monster on the Street, A – Part 1	9
			Monster on the Street, A – Part 2	9
		Story Street: Step 8	All in a Flap	9
			Man-eating Snails	9
			New School, A	9
			Sam Runs Away	9
		Story Street: Step 10	King of the Go-Kart Track	9
			Rat Hunt, The	9
Literacy Links Plus	Kingscourt	Fluent A	Beekeeper, The	9
			He Who Listens	9
			Scare-kid	9
		Fluent B	Bull in a China Shop, A	9
			Dom's Handplant	9
			Duck Magic	9
			Zoe at the Fancy Dress Ball	9
		Fluent C	Little Spider, The	9
			Vicky the High Jumper	9
		Fluent D	Cabbage Princess, The	9
			Grandad	9
			Three Magicians, The	9
			Why Rabbits Have Long Ears	9
Literacy Links Plus Topic	Kingscourt	Fluent A	Animal Fathers	9
			Sandwich Hero, The	9
		Fluent B	Oscar and Tatiana	9
		Fluent D	First Morning, The	9
Literacy World	Heinemann	Stage 1	Twelfth Floor Kids, The	9
My World Non-fiction	Horwitz Gardner		What is a Bear?	9
			What is a Giraffe?	9
			What is a Hippopotamus?	9
			What is a Horse?	9
			What is a Lion?	9

SERIES	PUBLISHER	SET (OR AUTHOR)	TITLE	BAND
My World Non-fiction	Horwitz Gardner		What is a Monkey?	9
			What is a Penguin?	9
			What is a Spider?	9
			What is a Turtle?	9
			What is a Wolf?	9
National Geographic	Rigby	Gold Level	Rice	9
		Purple Level	Fossils	9
			Rain Forest, The	9
		Turquoise Level	Spiders Spin Silk	9
			Water Can Change	9
New Way	Nelson Thornes	Violet Parallel Books	Ugly Duckling, The	9
			Why Flamingoes Have Red Legs	9
Oxford Literacy Web	OUP	Non-fiction: Toys	My Journey Around the World	9
		Poetry Stages: 1–5	I'm Riding on a Giant	9
		Stage 7: Variety	Tale of a Turban, The	9
		Stage 8: Duck Green	Flying Tea Tray, The	9
		Stage 9: Duck Green	Great Stew Disaster, The	9
		Stage 9: Variety	Tessa on TV	9
Oxford Reading Tree	OUP	Citizenship Stories: Stage 9/10	Christmas Fair, The	9
			Clever Invention, A	9
			Quarrel, The	9
			Winning	9
		Cross-curricular Jackdaws	Fruits and Seeds	9
			Seaside, The	9
		Stage 7: More Robins	Long Journey, The	9
			Mum's New Car	9
		Stage 7: Robins	William and the Dog	9
		Stage 8: More Robins	Surprise, The	9
			William's Mistake	9
		Stage 8: Robins	Emergency, The	9
		Stage 9: Magpies	Quest, The	9
		Stage 9: More Robins	Hamid Does His Best	9
			Treasure Hunt, The	9
			William and the Pied Piper	9
		Stage 9: Robins	Photograph, The	9
			Village Show, The	9
		Stage 9: True Stories	High Flier	9
			Underground Railroad, The	9
		TreeTops All Stars: Pack 1	Adventure for Robo-dog, An	9
			Sand Witch, The	9
		TreeTops All Stars: Pack 2	Disgusting Denzil	9
			Eric's Talking Ears	9
		TreeTops All Stars: Pack 3	Ronald the Tough Sheep	9
		TreeTops More All Stars: Pack 2A	Cleaner Genie	9
			Tom Thumb and the Football Team	9
			Town Dog	9
		TreeTops Stage 10/11: Pack B	Great Spaghetti Suit, The	9
			Purple Buttons	9
		TreeTops Stage 10: Playscript	Stupid Trousers	9
		TreeTops Stage 10: Pack A	Boss Dog of Blossom Street, The	9
			Masked Cleaning Ladies of Om, The	9

SERIES	PUBLISHER	SET (OR AUTHOR)	TITLE	BAND
Oxford Reading Tree	OUP	TreeTops Stage 10: Pack A	Masked Cleaning Ladies Save the Day, The	9
			Mr Stofflees and the Painted Tiger	9
		TreeTops Stage 10: Pack C	Dexter's Dinosaurs	9
			Jellyfish Shoes, The	9
			Masked Cleaning Ladies Meet the Pirates, The	9
			Stupid Trousers	9
		TreeTops Stage 10: Pack C	Wrong Letter, The	9
		TreeTops Stage 10: Playscripts	Masked Cleaning Ladies of Om, The	9
		TreeTops Stage 11: Pack A	Flans Across the River	9
		TreeTops Stage 11: Playscripts	Amy the Hedgehog Girl	9
		TreeTops Stage 12: Pack B	Hamper's Great Escape	9
Oxford RT Branch Library	OUP	Oxford Reds: Pack A	Dogs	9
			Frogs and Toads	9
			Sharks	9
		Oxford Reds: Pack B	Bees	9
			Dinosaurs	9
			Spiders	9
			Wolves	9
Oxford RT Rhyme & Analogy	OUP	Story Rhymes: Pack B	Gran, Gran!	9
			How to Kick-start a Dragon	9
			That's Nothing!	9
Pathways to Literacy	Collins	Year 2	Building Bricks and Other Poems	9
			I Want a Party	9
		Year 3	Armband Band, The	9
			Emperor Penguin, The	9
			Mind Bridget	9
			Tell Me Another	9
			Top Step, The	9
Pelican Guided Reading	Longman	Y2 T2	Magical Stories from India	9
PM Non-fiction	Nelson Thornes	Gold Level	Bats	9
			Foxes	9
			Owls	9
			Racoons	9
			Skunks	9
			Tasmanian Devils	9
		Purple Level	Cattle	9
			Chickens	9
			Goats	9
			Horses	9
			Pigs	9
			Sheep	9
PM Storybooks	Nelson Thornes	Gold Set A	Bear's Diet	9
			Clubhouse, The	9
			Luke's Go-Kart	9
			Owls in the Garden	9
			Secret Hideaway, The	9
			Solo Flyer	9
		Gold Set B	Big Balloon Festival, The	9
			Car Trouble	9
			King Midas and the Golden Touch	9
			Patrick and the Leprechaun	9

SERIES	PUBLISHER	SET (OR AUTHOR)	TITLE	BAND
PM Storybooks	Nelson Thornes	Gold Set B	Special Ride, The	9
			Surprise Dinner, The	9
		Gold Set C	Asteroid, The	9
			Dolphins, The	9
			Night Walk, The	9
			Pandas in the Mountains	9
			Picked for the Team	9
			Shooting Star, The	9
PM Traditional Tales	Nelson Thornes	Gold Level	Beauty and the Beast	9
			Cinderella	9
			Jack and the Magic Harp	9
			Rumpelstiltskin	9
			Seven Foolish Fishermen	9
			Snow White and the Seven Dwarfs	9
Rigby Star	Rigby	Gold Level	Emperor's New Clothes, The	9
			Mantu the Elephant	9
			Monster is Coming! The	9
			Rollercoaster	9
			Tiger Hunt	9
Rockets	A&C Black	Anderson, Scoular	Posh Party, The	9
		Anderson, Scoular	Potty Panto, The	9
		Powling, Chris	Rover Goes to School	9
		Powling, Chris	Rover Shows Off	9
		Powling, Chris	Rover the Champion	9
		Powling, Chris	Rover's Birthday	9
		Rodgers, Frank	Crown Jewels, The	9
		Rodgers, Frank	Dragon's Tooth, The	9
		Rodgers, Frank	Lizard the Wizard	9
		Rodgers, Frank	Mr Croc's Walk	9
		Rodgers, Frank	Royal Roar, The	9
		Shulman, Dee	Magenta and the Ghost Babies	9
		Shulman, Dee	Magenta and the Ghost Bride	9
		Shulman, Dee	Magenta and the Ghost School	9
		Shulman, Dee	Magenta and the Scary Ghosts	9
		Smith, Wendy	Circle Magic	9
		Smith, Wendy	Crazy Magic	9
		Smith, Wendy	Magic Hotel	9
		Smith, Wendy	Mouse Magic	9
		Smith, Wendy	Star is Born, A	9
		Smith, Wendy	Sun, Sand and Space	9
		Wallace, Karen	Sandwich Scam, The	9
		Wallace, Karen	Stuff-it-in Specials, The	9
		West, Colin	Grandad's Boneshaker Bicycle	9
		West, Colin	Granny's Jungle Garden	9
		West, Colin	Jenny the Joker	9
		West, Colin	Uncle-and-Auntie Pat	9
Skyrider	Collins	Yellow	Bad Dad List, The	9
			Beating the Drought	9
			Cat Talk	9
			Escape!	9
			Greedy Cat and the Birthday Cake	9

SERIES	PUBLISHER	SET (OR AUTHOR)	TITLE	BAND
Skyrider	Collins	Yellow	I'm So Hungry and Other Plays	9
			Rainbows All Around	9
			Sock Gobbler and Other Stories, The	9
			When the Truck Got Stuck!	9
Spotlight on Fact	Collins	Y2: The Seaside	Places to Visit	9
			Taking Good Holiday Photos	9
Sprinters	Walker	Hayes, Sarah	Easy Peasy	9
		Mark, Jan	Snow Maze, The	9
Star Quest	Rigby	Gold Level	Ice-Cream Factory, The	9
		Turquoise Level	Changing Shape	9
Starters	Walker	Waddell, Martin	Cup Run	9
		Waddell, Martin	Going Up!	9
		West, Colin	Big Wig	9
Stopwatch	A&C Black		Butterfly and Caterpillar	9
			Snail	9
Story Chest	Kingscourt	Stage 6	Cooking Pot	9
			Fiddle-dee-dee	9
			Ghost and the Sausage, The	9
			Grandma's Stick	9
			Pie Thief, The	9
			Tell-tale	9
Storyteller	Kingscourt	Set 9	3, 2, 1...Lift Off!	9
			Bird Watchers	9
			Birds of Prey	9
			Caves	9
			Clever Coyote and Other Wild Dogs	9
			Flutey Family Fruit Cake, The	9
			Hiding Places	9
			Just Hanging Around	9
			Lunch Bunch, The	9
			News on Shoes	9
			No Space to Waste	9
			Pet Tarantula, The	9
			Rupert Goes to School	9
			Sam's Dad	9
			Sculpture	9
			Squirrels	9
			Those Birds!	9
			Trees, Please!	9
Storyworld Bridges	Heinemann	Stage 10	Monster in the Cupboard, The	9
Storyworlds	Heinemann	Stage 9: Fantasy World	Adventure at Sea	9
			Journey into the Earth, The	9
			Magic Carpet, The	9
			Voyage into Space	9
		Stage 9: Our World	Big Barry Baker and the Bullies	9
			Big Barry Baker in Big Trouble	9
			Big Barry Baker on the Stage	9
			Big Barry Baker's Parcel	9
Tristars	Horwitz Gardner	Stage A	Chocolate!	9
			Cook's Catastrophe, The	9
			King Horace's Treasure Hunt	9

SERIES	PUBLISHER	SET (OR AUTHOR)	TITLE	BAND
Tristars	Horwitz Gardner	Stage A	Please Stop Barking	9
			Sneaky Snake, The	9
What's for Lunch?	Franklin Watts	Claire Llewellyn	Bread	9
			Chocolate	9
			Eggs	9
			Honey	9
			Milk	9
			Oranges	9
			Peas	9
			Potatoes	9
			Sweetcorn	9

Band 10 WHITE

NATIONAL CURRICULUM LEVEL 2

Band 10 WHITE

NATIONAL CURRICULUM LEVEL 2

WORKING TOWARDS LEVEL 3: LEARNING OPPORTUNITIES

- Look through a variety of texts with growing independence to predict content, layout and story development
- Read silently most of the time
- Notice the spelling of unfamiliar words and relate to known words
- Sustain interest in longer text, returning to it easily after a break
- Use text more fully as a reference and as a model
- Search for and find information in texts more flexibly
- Show increased awareness of vocabulary and precise meaning
- Express reasoned opinions about what is read, and compare texts
- Offer and discuss interpretations of text and the use of simple poetical and metaphorical language

EXAMPLES OF TEXTS IN BAND 10

RAIN OR SHINE

Explorers Set 1, Kingscourt
1999

ISBN 0 7699 0508 0

Non-fiction with a wide range of text types including procedure, diagrams, text boxes, maps and photographs

Report beginning with general definitions; reader needs to note subtle distinctions between key words

Complex diagram illustrating movement in three dimensions

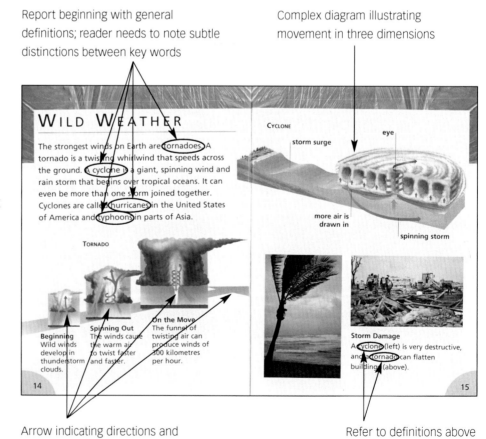

Arrow indicating directions and sequence of movement

Refer to definitions above to appreciate contrast

THE SELFISH GIANT
Leanna Traill
Illustrated by
John Hurford

Literacy Links Plus,
Kingscourt
1990

ISBN 0 7901 0276 5

Metaphorical text with
descriptive passages convey
deeper meaning

Text layout assists fluency as
line breaks follow phrases

Personification for
literary effect

Figurative language to
prompt the reader to
create mental images

Simile for emphasis

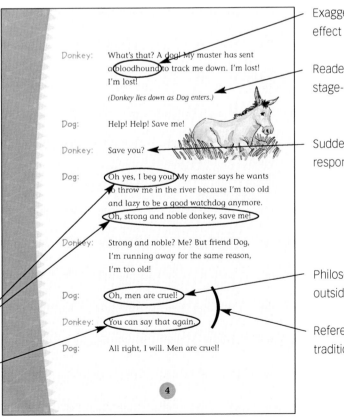

THE BREMENTOWN
MUSICIANS
Eleanor Boylan
Illustrated by
Penny Jensz

Spotlight on Plays,
Collins
2003

ISBN 0 00 7157 44 4

Dramatic script based on
traditional tale

Drama specific language

Reader needs to appreciate
both colloquial and literal
meanings

Exaggeration for dramatic
effect

Reader expected to note
stage-directions silently

Sudden switch in emotional
response

Philosophical observation
outside dialogue

Reference to pantomime
tradition

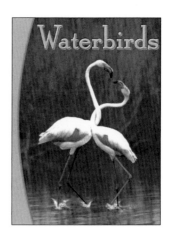

BAND 10
WHITE
EXPOSITORY
Natural science

WATERBIRDS
Infosteps

Avelyn Davidson

Kingscourt (2003)
ISBN 1 877295 55 8

TEACHING OBJECTIVES

- **Y3T1t20** To read information passages, and identify the main points
- **Y3T1t18** To locate information using headings, page numbers, etc
- **Y3T1t18** To locate information, using contents, index, headings, sub-headings, page nos
- **Y3T2w12** To recognise compound words
- **Y3T2w18** To infer the meanings of unknown words from context
- **Y3T2w23** To know the quartiles of a dictionary

TEXT SELECTION

This is an attractive and informative little book in a new non-fiction series. There are brief definitions of what a bird is, how a bird flies, what constitutes a habitat, and how to distinguish different types of birds. There is a brief, clear outline of a migrating bird's year, and a waterbird alphabet – in short, opportunities to work with different types of text layout, use language associated with non-fiction texts, and learn some useful facts about birds.

LINK TO WHOLE-CLASS WORK

Science: *Life processes and living things*. This book fits well with this topic as it demonstrates how animals are suited to their environment; and deals with some ecology issues.

Vocabulary extension: the dictionary and glossary provide access to useful vocabulary such as **migrate, preen, thermal, updraft, wetland**.

TEXT INTRODUCTION

Give a book to each pupil.

Good. Four of you turned straight to the back cover and read the blurb. What type of book do you think it is?
Now take just one minute to look through this book and see how many features of a non-fiction text you can find (contents page, glossary, index, headings, captions, text-boxes, diagrams, map, dictionary). *Well done — you found almost all of them!*
Now read page 4, and find out the seven things that all birds have in common.

STRATEGY CHECK

The next page is called the Features Page. There are four questions listed here. Read these and then read the pages suggested to find the answers. Remember to keep the question in your mind as you are reading, and then remember the answer or note it on a piece of paper.

INDEPENDENT READING

Work with individual pupils, prompting them to check the print with the diagrams and asking them to explain some of the content in their own words.

I like the way you read that through again slowly to check the meaning.
Good — you checked the text with the diagram/map.

RETURN TO THE TEXT

Discuss the four questions, asking children to read out relevant passages. Then ask them to check out the following words using the index and glossary:
preen, colonies, wetlands.

*Turn to the alphabet starting on page 18. Which part of the dictionary will you look in to find **osprey**? Were you right? Read out the description. Now try **yellow-eyed penguin, gannet; loon**.*

FOLLOW-UP AND INDEPENDENT WORK

Direct the children to Discussion Starter 3 on p. 24 and ask them to note down some aspects of water-birds that people have copied to help them swim well.

Locate and write down compound words such as **updrafts, rainforests, grasslands, coastlines, wetlands, waterproof, birdwatching, shellfish, northeast**.

BAND 10
WHITE
NARRATIVE   **In a familiar setting**

JORDAN AND THE NORTHSIDE REPS
PM Library

Stephen Harrison

Illustrations by Al Fiorentino

Nelson Thornes (1999)
ISBN 1 86961 374 0

Story by Stephen Harrison
Illustrations by Al Fiorentino

TEACHING OBJECTIVES

Pupils should be taught
- **Y3T1t2**   how dialogue is presented in stories
- **Y3T1t3**   to be aware of the different voices in stories
- **Y3T1s2**   to take account of grammar and punctuation, e.g. sentences, speech marks, exclamation marks and commas to mark pauses, when reading aloud
- **Y3T1w19** to collect common vocabulary for introducing and concluding dialogue
- **Y3T2w13** to recognise and spell common suffixes and how these influence word meanings, e.g. **-ly**

TEXT SELECTION

The theme deals with Jordan's initial disappointment at not being selected for the soccer team, and the determination and flexibility that subsequently wins him a place alongside his friends. The central character is well-developed and much of the storyline is carried by dialogue between the three boys.

LINK TO WHOLE-CLASS WORK

The recommended range for Year 3, Term 1 is 'stories with familiar settings'. This illustrated text of about 950 words fits well into this category, and is suitable for able readers, particularly boys. There are opportunities for links with PSHE in keeping with team spirit, multi-cultural representation and sexual equality – there are girls selected for the team too!

TEXT INTRODUCTION

Read the title of our new book for today, and leaf through the illustrations. I'm going to ask you to describe the story setting and see if you can work out what happens in the plot.

Ask the children for their predictions, and suggest that they compare their ideas with the story line as they read.

STRATEGY CHECK

There's a lot of dialogue in this story. Think about the tone of voice that the boys would use as you're reading because that will give you clues to how each one is feeling.

INDEPENDENT READING

Work with one child and then another, praising close attention to punctuation and appropriate expression.

Good – you made Liam sound really nervous.
Try reading Jordan's remarks again. He's devastated, and so embarrassed to miss out. Well done – you sounded upset and angry that time!

RETURN TO THE TEXT

Did the plot work out the way you thought it would?
Turn to pages 4–6. There's a lot of dialogue here. What do you notice about the way it is set out on the page? Yes, there's a new paragraph for each speaker.

Select members of the group to take the role of the boys and the selector and read only the direct speech on these two pages as though it was a play.
Prompt for in-character expression and close attention to the punctuation.

FOLLOW-UP AND INDEPENDENT WORK

Go back through the story and write down all the different words that the author uses instead of 'said'.
I found seven.

We did some work on suffixes in class. There are five words in this story that have the suffix -**ly**. Make a list of them and learn how to spell them.

Suggest that the group rehearses a play based on this story and presents it to the class.

SERIES	PUBLISHER	SET (OR AUTHOR)	TITLE	BAND
All Aboard	Ginn	Stage 6: Non-fiction	Planning a Party	10
		Stage 7: Non-fiction	Looking After the Egg	10
		Stage 7: Sam & Rosie	Magic Smell, The	10
		Stage 8: Non-fiction	Tropical Journey, A	10
		Stage 9: Non-fiction	Gardening for Beginners	10
		Stage 9: Non-fiction	Lunchbox	10
		Stage 9: Novel	Stephen and the Family Nose	10
		Stage 9: Poetry	Pocket Full of Pie, A	10
		Stage 10: Non-fiction	Building a House	10
		Stage 10: Play	Old Woman Who Lived in a Vinegar Bottle, The	10
Alphakids	Horwitz Gardner	Extending Level 21	Drag Racing	10
		Extending Level 22	Volcanoes	10
		Extending Level 23	Big Pig's Wig	10
			Graeme Base Writer and Illustrator	10
			Living Together	10
			Making a Torch	10
			Sending Messages	10
			Shooter Shrinker, The	10
Blue Bananas	Mammoth	Stewart, Maddie	Peg	10
			Baby Bear Comes Home	10
			Delilah Digs for Treasure	10
			Dilly and the Goody-Goody	10
			Juggling with Jeremy	10
			Mabel and Max	10
			Midnight in Memphis	10
			Mouse Flute	10
			Nut Map, The	10
			Owl in the House	10
			Rosie and the Robbers	10
Book Project	Longman	Fiction Band 5	Billy Fishbone	10
		Fiction Band 6	New Reader Plays 2	10
		Fiction Band 7	Bumbles, The	10
			Crazy Crocs	10
			Horrible Baby	10
			Jug Ears	10
			New Reader Plays 3	10
			Poupette	10
		Fiction Band 8	B J Dog	10
			Henry Seamouse	10
			Rachel Versus Bonecrusher the Mighty	10
			Rachel and the Difference Thief	10
			Seagull Sweaters	10
Book Project Non-fiction A	Longman	Babies	Baby Equipment	10
			What Babies Wore	10
Book Project Non-fiction B	Longman	Water	Water Experiments	10
Cambridge Reading	CUP	Y2 A: Range of Cultures	How the Animals Got Their Tails	10
		Y2 B: Familiar Settings	Dog Show, The	10
			Special Cake, The	10
		Y2 B: Fantasy Worlds	Jumble Power	10
		Y2 B: Narrative Recount	Haystack, The	10
		Y2 B: Poetry	Lick of the Spoon, A	10

SERIES	PUBLISHER	SET (OR AUTHOR)	TITLE	BAND
Cambridge Reading	CUP	Y2 B: Range of Cultures	Lord Mount Dragon, The	10
			Volcano Woman	10
			Weather Drum, The	10
		Y2: Non-fiction	Animal Communication	10
			Book of Hours, A	10
			Noah's Ark	10
			Tomb of Nebamun, The	10
		Y2: Playscripts	Coyote Girl	10
		Y3 Independent Reading	Garlunk	10
Crunchies	Orchard	Crazy Camelot Capers	Excalibur the Magic Sword	10
			King Arthur and the Mighty Conquest	10
		Raps	Robin Hood Raps	10
		Seriously Silly Rhymes	Little Bo Peep Has Knickers that Bleep	10
		Seriously Silly Stories	Fried Piper of Hamstring, The	10
			Little Red Riding Wolf	10
			Rather Small Turnip, The	10
			Shampoozal	10
Discovery World Links	Heinemann	Stage E	I Love the UK	10
			Jamie's Food Guide	10
		Stage F	Interview with Florence Nightingale, An	10
Explorers	Kingscourt	Set 1	Bright Ideas	10
			Creepy Creatures	10
			Feathers and Flight	10
			Human Body, The	10
			Incredible Creatures	10
			Mammals of the Sea	10
			Native Americans	10
			Rain or Shine	10
			Scaly Things	10
			Sharks and Rays	10
			Sky Watch	10
			Underwater Animals	10
Famous People, Famous Lives	Franklin Watts	Famous Leaders	Captain Scott	10
			Queen Victoria	10
		Famous People	Louis Braille	10
		Famous Scientists & Inventors	George Stephenson	10
			Henry Ford	10
			John Logie Baird	10
			Thomas Edison	10
		Famous Women	Florence Nightingale	10
Find Out About	Franklin Watts		Glass	10
			Metal	10
			Plastic	10
			Wood	10
First Explorers	Kingscourt	Level 1	Earth Materials	10
		Level 2	Forces of Nature	10
			Lights On	10
			Sounds All Round	10
			Spy on Spiders	10
Go Facts	A&C Black	Plants	Plants	10
			Plants as Food	10

SERIES	PUBLISHER	SET (OR AUTHOR)	TITLE	BAND
Individual Titles	Red Fox	Allen, N	Queen's Knickers, The	10
	Puffin	Blundell, Tony	Beware of Girls	10
	Puffin	Dodd, Linley	Scarface Claw	10
	Frances Lincoln	French, Fiona	Anancy and Mr Dry-Bone	10
	Random House	Hedderwick, M	Katie Morag and the Two Grandmothers	10
	Random House	Hedderwick, M	Katie Morag Delivers the Mail	10
	Frances Lincoln	Hoffman, Mary	Amazing Grace	10
	Walker	Hughes, Shirley	Dogger	10
	Wayland	Lewis, Kim	Last Train, The	10
	Wayland	Moses, Brian	Pizza	10
	Frances Lincoln	Onyefulu, Ifeoma	Emeka's Gift	10
	Red Fox	Selway, Martina	Wish You Were Here	10
	Frances Lincoln	Souhami, Jessica	Rama and the Demon King	10
	Collins Jets	Thomson, Pat	Rhyming Russell	10
	Collins Jets	Wallace, Karen	Hiccup on the High Seas, A	10
	Tamarind	Wilkins, Verna	Dave and the Tooth Fairy	10
Info Trail	Longman	Emergent Geography	Millennium Scrapbook, A	10
Infosteps	Kingscourt	Set 1	Gifts from Greece	10
			Insect Army, The	10
			Leading the Way	10
			Living in Two Worlds	10
			No Need for Words	10
			Our Changing Planet	10
			Power-packed Plants	10
			Rock Hunters	10
			Survivors	10
			To Market, To Market	10
			Treats and Eats	10
			Waterbirds	10
Lightning	Ginn	Brown Level N/F	Ask the Experts	10
			Magical Models	10
			You're It! Playground Games	10
		Brown Level, Term 1	Tales from the Playground	10
		Brown Level, Term 3	M.C. Gang Investigates, The	10
Literacy Land	Longmans	Genre Range – Competent	From Sam Summerday	10
			Irish Tale, An	10
			Macdonald Diaries, The	10
			Tons of Lovely Cakes	10
		Genre Range – Fluent	Zoomababy and the Mission to Mars	10
			Zoomababy to the Rescue	10
		Info Trail – Competent	Come on a Desert Safari!	10
			Day in the Life of a Roman Charioteer, A	10
			Five go to Wembley	10
			How to Write a Biography	10
			Leonardo da Vinci: Greatest Genius?	10
			Think About It!	10
			Why Do Cats Purr?	10
		Info Trail – Fluent	How to Build a Wildlife Paradise	10
			How to Prepare a Mummy	10
		Story Street: Step 7	Beyond Strange Street	10
		Story Street: Step 8	More Macdonalds	10

SERIES	PUBLISHER	SET (OR AUTHOR)	TITLE	BAND
Literacy Land	Longmans	Story Street: Step 9	Book Week Goes with a Bang – Part 1	10
			Book Week Goes with a Bang – Part 2	10
		Story Street: Step 10	Blue Game, The	10
			Great Escape, The	10
		Story Street: Step 10	Tea with Grumpyboots	10
			Wizard Wagoo	10
Literacy Links Plus	Kingscourt	Fluent A	Tongues	10
		Fluent B	Lucy Meets a Dragon	10
			Never Bored on Boards	10
			Tom's Handplant	10
		Fluent C	Bringing the Sea Back Home	10
			Cass Becomes a Star	10
			Frog Who Thought He Was a Horse, The	10
			Gribblegrot from Outer Space, The	10
			Selfish Giant, The	10
			Snow Goes to Town	10
			Three Sillies, The	10
		Fluent D	Clouds	10
			I'm a Chef	10
			Rapunzel	10
Literacy Links Plus Topic	Kingscourt	Fluent A	Those Tricky Animals	10
		Fluent B	Dear Diary	10
			Walking	10
		Fluent C	Have You Seen a Javelina?	10
			Honey Tree, The	10
		Fluent D	Emperor and the Nightingale, The	10
Literacy World	Heinemann	Stage 1	How a Book is Made	10
			Incredible Insects	10
			Mrs Dippy and her Amazing Inventions	10
			Nutty as a Noodle Stories	10
			Steggie's Way	10
My World Non-fiction	Horwitz Gardner		What is a Beaver?	10
			What is a Bee?	10
			What is a Beetle?	10
			What is a Bird of Prey?	10
			What is a Builder?	10
			What is a Butterfly?	10
			What is a Crocodile?	10
			What is a Frog?	10
			What is a Hooved Animal?	10
			What is a Travelling Animal?	10
			What is an Animal of Australia?	10
			What is an Animal of the Amazon?	10
			What is an Ape?	10
			What is an Elephant?	10
			What is an Endangered Animal?	10
National Geographic	Rigby	Gold Level	Olympics, The	10
			On Safari	10
			Strange Plants	10
		Purple Level	Magnets	10
		White Level	Divers of the Deep Sea	10

SERIES	PUBLISHER	SET (OR AUTHOR)	TITLE	BAND
National Geographic	Rigby	White Level	Race to the Pole	10
			Up the Amazon	10
Navigator	Rigby	Short Stories – Brown Level	Tale Twisters	10
New Way	Nelson Thornes	Orange Parallel Books	Snow Queen, The	10
			Swan Lake	10
			Happy Prince & The Selfish Giant, The	10
			Hound Gelert & Wookey Witch	10
Oxford Literacy Web	OUP	Playscripts	Magic Pot, The	10
		Stage 9: Variety	Helena and the Wild Man	10
			Pirate Gold	10
			Serve Me, Stefan	10
			Tommy in Trouble	10
		Year 3	Clowns Next Door, The	10
			Dad's Story	10
Oxford Reading Tree	OUP	Citizenship Stories: Stage 9/10	Concert, The	10
			May-Ling's Party	10
		Cross-curricular Jackdaws	Bang the Drum	10
			Emergencies	10
		Jackdaws Anthologies	Anna's Eggs	10
			Catch, The	10
			Karen's Adventure	10
			Kate's Garden	10
			Patrick and the Fox	10
			Spoilt Holiday, The	10
		More Jackdaws Anthologies	Monkey Business	10
			School Play, The	10
			Space Adventure	10
			William and the Spell	10
		Stage 8: True Stories	At the Top of the World	10
		Stage 9: True Stories	Ocean Adventure!	10
		Stage 10: More Robins	Discovery	10
			Ghost Tricks	10
		Stage 10: True Stories	Arctic Hero	10
			King of Football, The	10
			Pioneer Girl	10
		TreeTops All Stars: Pack 2	Doris Bean and the Queen	10
			High Five Henry	10
			Sausage	10
			Yummy Scrummy	10
		TreeTops All Stars: Pack 3	Brer Rabbit's Trickbag	10
			Clever Monkey	10
			Psid and Bolter	10
			Toffee and Marmalade	10
		TreeTops More All Stars: Pack 2A	Badcats	10
			Beastly Basil	10
			Nelly the Monster-sitter	10
		TreeTops More All Stars: Pack 3A	Arabian Nights	10
			Dick Whittington	10
			Huge and Horrible Beast, The	10
			Mary-Anne and the Cat Baby	10
		TreeTops Stage 10/11: True Stories	My Friend Mandela	10

SERIES	PUBLISHER	SET (OR AUTHOR)	TITLE	BAND
Oxford Reading Tree	OUP	TreeTops Stage 10/11: True Stories	Mystery of Cocos Gold, The	10
		TreeTops Stage 10: Pack C	Blackbones Saves the School	10
		TreeTops Stage 11: Pack A	Amy the Hedgehog Girl	10
			Bertha's Secret Battle	10
			Bertie Wiggins' Amazing Ears	10
			Coming Clean	10
			Hard to Please	10
		TreeTops Stage 11: Playscripts	Bertie Wiggins' Amazing Ears	10
		TreeTops Stage 12: True Stories	Fayim's Incredible Journey	10
			Over the Rainbow	10
		TreeTops Stage 12+: Pack F	Cool Clive and the Bubble Trouble	10
			Shelley Holmes, Animal Trainer	10
Oxford RT Branch Library	OUP	Oxford Reds: Pack A	Cars	10
			Rockets	10
			Snakes	10
		Oxford Reds: Pack B	Horses	10
			Whales	10
Oxford RT Rhyme & Analogy	OUP	Story Rhymes: Pack A	Spell Shell, The	10
		Story Rhymes: Pack B	Rockpool Rap	10
Pathways to Literacy	Collins	Year 2	Monkeys	10
			Then and Now	10
		Year 3	Alphabetical Animals	10
			Brave Sea Captain, The	10
			Gold Badge, The	10
			Looking at Birds	10
			Nightmare Neighbours	10
			Sun and Moon	10
			Three Tales from Scotland	10
			Tiger, Tiger	10
			Penny Whistle Pete	10
		Year 3: Non-fiction	Shake, Rattle and Roll	10
		Year 3: Play	Pied Piper, The	10
		Year 4	Just A Touch Of Magic	10
PM Non-fiction	Nelson Thornes	Silver Level	Antarctic Penguins	10
			Antarctic Seals	10
			Caribou (Reindeer)	10
			Polar Bears	10
			Whales	10
			Wolves	10
PM Storybooks	Nelson Thornes	Silver Set A	Fair Swap, A	10
			Kerry	10
			Kerry's Double	10
			Little Adventure, A	10
			My Two Families	10
			Nelson is Kidnapped	10
		Silver Set B	Best Part, The	10
			Dolphin on the Wall, The	10
			Fire and Wind	10
			Skating at Rainbow Lake	10
			Talent Quest, The	10
			Walkathon, The	10

SERIES	PUBLISHER	SET (OR AUTHOR)	TITLE	BAND
PM Storybooks	Nelson Thornes	Silver Set C	Jordan and the Northside Reps	10
			Our Old Friend Bear	10
			Right Place for Jupiter, The	10
			Silver and Prince	10
			Spanish Omelet	10
			Story of William Tell, The	10
PM Traditional Tales	Nelson Thornes	Silver Level	Androcles and the Lion	10
			Bear and the Trolls, The	10
			Dick Whittington	10
			Robin Hood and the Silver Trophy	10
			Sleeping Beauty, The	10
			Strange Shoe, The	10
Rigby Star	Rigby	Gold Level	Magic Jigsaw, The	10
		Star Plus	Always Elephant	10
			Headfirst into the Porridge	10
			Middle of Nowhere, The	10
			Mystery Man, The	10
			Mystery of Mrs Kim, The	10
			School Concert, The	10
			Secret, The	10
		White Level	Charlie the Bridesmaid	10
			Gizmos' Party, The	10
			Gizmos' Trip, The	10
			Little Blue, Big Blue	10
			Picky Prince, The	10
			Singing Princess, The	10
Rockets	A&C Black	Ryan, Margaret	Captain Motley and the Pirate's Crew	10
		Ryan, Margaret	Doris's Brilliant Birthday	10
		Ryan, Margaret	Kevin and the Pirate Test	10
		Ryan, Margaret	Smudger and the Smelly Fish	10
		Smith, Wendy	Space Football	10
		Smith, Wendy	Time Travellers	10
		Wallace, Karen	Minestrone Mob, The	10
		Wallace, Karen	Peanut Prankster, The	10
Skyrider	Collins	Yellow	Big Race, The	10
			Bird in the Basket, The	10
			Canoe Diary	10
			Desert Run, The	10
			Down on the Ice	10
			Ducks Crossing	10
			Letter From Fish Bay, A	10
			Shapes of Water, The	10
			Strange Creatures	10
			What's Living at Your Place?	10
Spotlight on Fact	Collins	Y2: The Seaside	Going on Holiday	10
		Y2: The Seaside	Holidays Then and Now	10
		Y3: Active Earth	Finding Out about Volcanoes	10
			How to make a Rain Gauge	10
			Look Out!	10
Spotlight on Plays	Collins	Age 7+	Bendemolena	10
			Brementown Musicians, The	10

SERIES	PUBLISHER	SET (OR AUTHOR)	TITLE	BAND
Spotlight on Plays	Collins	Age 7+	Hairy Toe, The	10
		Age 8+	Crazy Critters, The	10
Sprinters	Walker	Cross, Gillian	Beware Olga!	10
		French, Vivian	Tillie McGillie's Fantastical Chair	10
		Goodhart, Pippa	Molly and the Beanstalk	10
		Henderson, Kathy	Pappy Mashy	10
		Mark, Jan	Lady Long-legs	10
		Mark, Jan	Taking the Cat's Way Home	10
		McAfee, Annalena	Patrick's Perfect Pet	10
		McBratney, Sam	Art, You're Magic!	10
		McBratney, Sam	Oliver Sundew, Tooth Fairy	10
		Nimmo, Jenny	Ronnie and the Giant Millipede	10
		Pearce, Phillipa	Ghost in Annie's Room, The	10
		Richemont, Enid	Gemma and the Beetle People	10
		Sheldon, Dyan	Elena the Frog	10
		Sheldon, Dyan	Leon Loves Bugs	10
		Sheldon, Dyan	Night to Remember, A	10
		Ure, Jean	Big Head	10
		Waddell, Martin	Ernie and the Fishface Gang	10
		Warburton, Nick	Flora's Fantastic Revenge	10
		Whybrow, Ian	Holly and the Skyboard	10
		Wilkinson, Tony	Hector the Rat	10
Star Quest	Rigby	Star Plus	Jane Goodall	10
		White Level	Count on Your Body	10
			Encyclopaedia of Fantastic Fish	10
			Fish	10
Story Chest	Kingscourt	Stage 7	Big Tease, The	10
			Countdown	10
			Hatupatu and the Birdwoman	10
			Little Brother's Haircut	10
			More! More! More!	10
			Tiddalik	10
Storyteller	Kingscourt	Set 10	Crazy Miss Maisey's Alphabet Pets	10
			Masterpiece, The	10
			Monkey Business	10
			Sea Otters	10
			Storytellers	10
			Sugar and Spice and All Things Nice	10
			Things with Wings	10
			Zoom in!	10
		Set 11	Bats About Bats	10
Storyworld Bridges	Heinemann	Stage 10	Tom's Birthday Treat	10
			Why Tortoise Has a Cracked Shell	10
		Stage 11	Akbar's Dream	10
		Stage 12	Jumble the Puppy	10
Storyworlds	Heinemann	Stage 9: Animal World	Canal Boat Cat	10
			Cherry Blossom Cat	10
			City Cat	10
			Cobra Cat	10
		Stage 9: Once Upon a Time	Hansel and Gretel	10
			Jack and the Beanstalk	10

SERIES	PUBLISHER	SET (OR AUTHOR)	TITLE	BAND
Storyworlds	Heinemann	Stage 9: Once Upon a Time	Little Girl and the Bear, The	10
			Two Giants, The	10
Tristars	Horwitz Gardner	Stage A	Kate Who Was Always Late	10
			Magic Show Review, The	10
			Magic Tricks	10
			Moustachio's Best Magic Trick	10
			Perfect Pirate's Present, The	10
			Petshop Problem, A	10
			Popular Pets	10
			Surprise Party	10
			Who Shares Your Home?	10
		Stage B	Castles	10
			Denny Davidson, Detective	10
			Lost: One Cat	10
			Marvin, The Christmas Cat	10
			R.S.P.C.A.	10
			Riddle of Redstone Castle, The	10
			Riddle of Redstone Ruins, The	10
			Secret Cupboard, The	10
			Trapped Genie, The	10
What's for Lunch?	Franklin Watts	Claire Llewellyn	Banana	10

Band 11 LIME

NATIONAL CURRICULUM LEVEL 3

Band 11 LIME

NATIONAL CURRICULUM LEVEL 3

WORKING WITH LEVEL 3: LEARNING OPPORTUNITIES

- Use experience of reading a variety of material to recognise text type and predict layout and general content
- Read silently most of the time, adjusting speed of reading to suit material and monitoring the precise meaning
- Rerun to make different interpretations of dialogue, more complex sentences, unfamiliar language etc.
- Sustain interest in longer texts, returning easily to them after a break
- Make use of blurbs, chapter headings, glossaries, indexes and procedural texts to search for and locate information quickly and accurately
- Take note and devise ways to remember the meaning and spelling of unfamiliar words
- Express reasoned opinions about what is read, and compare texts
- Investigate and identify the styles and voice of a range of different text types including plays, poetry, narrative, procedural and explanatory texts

EXAMPLES OF TEXTS IN BAND 11

NO TIGHTS FOR GEORGE
June Crebbin
Illustrated by Tony Ross

Sprinters
Walker Books
2002

ISBN 0 7445 5999 5

Humourous short novel in a familiar setting

Illustrations give reader strong support to action and to George's emotional state

Implies that George is shocked and has been put on the spot

George's actions are described to convey what he is thinking

Reader needs to realise that the postman is joking about the school play

Unfamiliar vocabulary

Carefully chosen verb shows postman's annoyance and suspicion

Signal for change of reader's intonation to reflect postman's following (accusatory) comments

> George opened the door. A cheery postman stood on the step. He pulled a pair of green tights out of a carrier bag.
> "Thought you might be needing these, Robin Hood!" he said.
> George gasped. "No thank you," he said. It was all he could think of. He stuck his hands behind his back to stop them taking the tights.

> The postman stopped being cheery. "But they were in this carrier bag," he said, "with this envelope. There's a shopping list on the back but..." The postman turned it over and showed George the front. "This is your address," he said, jabbing the number with his finger.
> George flinched.

Unfamiliar sophisticated term suggesting George's anxiety

Punctuation must be followed carefully as postman's speech is broken into (with description of action)

Pronouns 'he, this, it' need to be interpreted for full comprehension

GOBSTOPPERS

Navigator
Rigby
2002

ISBN 0433 06482 X

Book consists of double page spreads on theme of food

Business letter in formal register associated with written communication

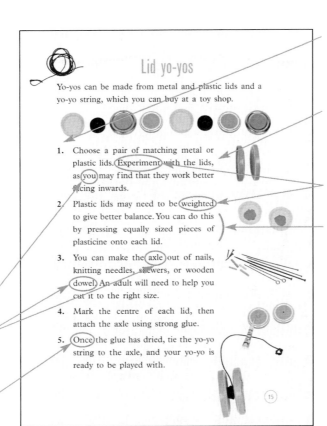

19 Spring Drive
Bridgwater
Somerset
TA19 7AQ

November 13, 2001

Dear Sir/Madam

I am writing to complain about a meal my son and I had at your restaurant yesterday.

My son ordered a pizza. Not only did it take 30 minutes to arrive, but it was dry and over-cooked. Also, his salad was gritty and badly washed. My vegetable stir-fry was tasty but was completely spoilt when I discovered a metal screw among the noodles. When I complained to the waiter about this, he just laughed, and said it must have fallen off the pan.

I feel angry and disappointed. The meal was a disaster from beginning to end, and yet – as you will see from the enclosed receipt – the bill came to over £20. I would welcome an apology and a full refund.

Yours faithfully

Mary Coles
Mary Coles

Reader needs to note layout specific to letter writing

Statement of intent opens letter

Paragraphs distinguish different sections of text

Long sentence with inserted clause. Reader has to sustain meaning over whole sentence

Exaggeration to express outrage

Phrase used exclusively in letter writing

Technical vocabulary

Sophisticated verb tense

YO-YOS
Cathy Hope

PM Non-fiction,
Nelson Thornes
2001

ISBN 1 86961 401 1

Six chapters covering the history and technology of yo-yos and their use

Reader addressed directly

Technical vocabulary not directly supported by illustrations

Meaning 'when' in this context

Lid yo-yos

Yo-yos can be made from metal and plastic lids and a yo-yo string, which you can buy at a toy shop.

1. Choose a pair of matching metal or plastic lids. Experiment with the lids, as you may find that they work better facing inwards.

2. Plastic lids may need to be weighted to give better balance. You can do this by pressing equally sized pieces of plasticine onto each lid.

3. You can make the axle out of nails, knitting needles, skewers, or wooden dowel. An adult will need to help you cut it to the right size.

4. Mark the centre of each lid, then attach the axle using strong glue.

5. Once the glue has dried, tie the yo-yo string to the axle, and your yo-yo is ready to be played with.

15

Procedural text with numbered sequence of actions

Implication is that all instructions should be read before starting

Unusual verb forms

Additional procedure implied

BAND 11

LIME

NON-FICTION
Biography

MAN ON THE MOON
The Story of Neil Armstrong

Oxford Reading Tree True Stories

Christine Butterworth

Oxford University Press (2003)
ISBN 0 19 919541 2

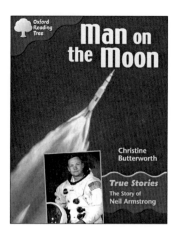

TEACHING OBJECTIVES

Pupils should be taught
- **Y4T1t3** to explore chronology in narrative using written texts, by mapping how much time passes in the course of a story
- **Y3T3t19** to summarise orally in one sentence the content of a passage or text, and the main point it is making
- **Y3T3s6** to investigate through reading how words and phrases can signal time sequences
- **Y3T2w17** to continue the collection of new words from reading
- **Y3T1s3** to take account of the function of verbs in sentences

TEXT SELECTION

Man on the Moon comes from a recently published 32-page biographical series written for 7–8-year-olds. The first two chapters give a very brief outline of Armstrong's background and training, and a description of the Space Race between the USSR and the USA. There is a switch to the present tense in the remaining three chapters to record the Moon Mission and return to Earth.

Colour illustrations and photos are spread liberally through the book and factual information is presented in a clear and straightforward manner. There is a comprehensive glossary and a brief index.

LINK TO WHOLE-CLASS WORK

This book offers an introduction to one of the KS2 Science topics, *The earth and beyond*, through a straightforward biography and a diary-like report. The format would be a useful model for children's topic work, particularly those children already progressing into the Year 4 curriculum.

TEXT INTRODUCTION	I like the way you read the blurb and flicked through the book. There are plenty of clues on the front cover to indicate what sort of book this is. Discuss the terms 'biography' and 'autobiography'. Now look carefully through the book to check what the different sections contain. Good. You noticed that it changes at Chapter 3 into a record of Moon Mission. Yes, the glossary has 19 items; and there's an index too.
STRATEGY CHECK	Turn to pages 4 and 5. Certain words are in bold print. Yes, you can check those words in the glossary as you are reading. Now read the first two chapters, checking the meanings of any words you don't know.
INDEPENDENT READING	As the teacher works with individual children, s/he praises and prompts as appropriate. p. 5 I like the way you broke that word up into syllables (aeronautics) Just re-read that sentence after you used the glossary so that you understand how it fits into the story. What do you think it means by 'the edge of space'? p. 9. Those words in brackets – just read them quietly. Why do you think the author added them?
RETURN TO THE TEXT	Now tell me in just one sentence about the important aeronautical experiences Armstrong had before he became an astronaut. Discuss the verbs on pages 10/11. Identify 'achieved' and 'trained' as past tense; 'was (chosen) to lead', 'was (going) to land' signifying intended action; and the switch to the present tense in Chapter 3: 'gets up', 'eats', 'are driven', 'enter'.
FOLLOW-UP AND INDEPENDENT WORK	Make a time-line on the whiteboard to track Neil Armstrong's childhood and training. Ask the children to locate his birth date, work out the date he went up in the *Tin Goose* and when he got his pilot's licence. Fill in other relevant events up 1969. Ask the children to read the Record of the Moon Mission and write a short dialogue between Armstrong, Michael Collins and Buzz Aldrin as the Eagle descends to the moon's surface and Armstrong takes his first steps on the moon's surface. Suggest that children locate two pairs of words in the glossary that mean the same thing (astronaut/cosmonaut; sputnik/satellite), find out what *NASA* stands for, what 'supersonic' means, and what a test pilot does.

BAND 11

LIME

EXPLANATORY TEXT
Natural science

COMPARING GIRAFFES AND POLAR BEARS
Literacy and Science series

Bobbie Neate

Neate Publishing (2000)
ISBN 1 903634 03 2

TEACHING OBJECTIVES

- **Y3T1t17** To notice differences in the style and structure of fiction and non-fiction
- **Y3T1t18** To locate information using contents, index, headings, sub-headings, page numbers
- **Y3T1t20** To read information pages, and identify main points of gist of text, listing 4 or 5 key points covered
- **Y3T2t14** To identify how written instructions are organised, e.g. diagrams with arrows
- **Y3T3t17** To 'scan' indexes and glossaries to locate information quickly and accurately
- **Y3T2w18** To infer the meaning of unknown words from context

TEXT SELECTION

In this small series, the author 'targets the teaching of literacy and science using interactive strategies'. Flaps on each page of the teacher/parent edition offer suggestions for involving children both in the biological information offered, and also aspects of text, genre, layout, sentence structure and vocabulary.

In comparing two very different mammals, terms such as 'habitat', 'adaptation', 'camouflage', 'food chain' and 'movement' are clearly exemplified and enriched. The text is straightforward and full of interesting detail, and the photographs and diagrams are very clear and pertinent.

LINK TO WHOLE-CLASS WORK

This book has been written explicitly to fit in with the NLS framework for teaching; and with the KS2 science curriculum: *Life processes and living things* and *Humans and other animals*. It has a colour-coded table of contents, glossary, index, list of web sites and details of where to find further information.

TEXT INTRODUCTION

Teacher asks children to examine the front cover and the title page to look for the author's clues to the ways in which giraffes and polar bears might be compared. List children's suggestions about how these two mammals are alike, and how they are different.

Then ask them to turn to pages 6 and 7, read the information on Adaptation and discuss other differences.

STRATEGY CHECK

What do you notice about the language used on these pages (6 and 7)? Why do you think the language is in note form? Yes, there is a lot of information packed into a small amount of space.

Now turn back to the contents page. What do you notice about the way this is organised? (Information is colour-coded blue for bears and orange for giraffes.) Select a section that you would like to find out more about, e.g. habitat, diet, babies, and as you are reading, think about the ways these two animals are alike and how they are different.

INDEPENDENT READING

Teacher works with individual children, prompting for the use of the glossary where appropriate, praising word-solving, and checking their comprehension.

RETURN TO THE TEXT

Teacher may ask each child to summarise the main points of comparison in a section s/he has read.

I have listed some of the special terms used in this book: **camouflage** (pp. 10, 11); **herbivore** (p. 13); **predator** (p. 13); **buoyancy** (p. 6); **insulate** (p. 4); **savannah** (p. 5). Let's try dividing them into syllables and pronouncing them.

Then allocate one word to each child, ask them to read it in context and guess the meaning, check it in the glossary, close the book and explain the meaning to a partner.

FOLLOW-UP AND INDEPENDENT WORK

On pages 12 and 13, there are diagrams of food chains for polar bears and giraffes. Read the pages and then explain in words what the diagrams mean.

Ask children to draw one of the animals and devise fact boxes, e.g. Did you know that the female giraffes have their babies standing up? Did you know that all mammals have seven bones (vertebrae) in their necks?

SERIES	PUBLISHER	SET (OR AUTHOR)	TITLE	BAND
All Aboard	Ginn	Stage 10: Non-fiction	Fun of the Fair, The	11
		Stage 10: Novel	Secrets Tree, The	11
		Stage 10: Poetry	Fox with Moonlit Eyes, A	11
		Stage 10: Short Stories	Three Tales	11
Book Project	Longman	Fiction Band 7	Tales on a Cold Dark Night	11
		Fiction Band 8	Kung Fu Katy and the Horrors	11
			Plays 4 for New Readers	11
			Sand Tiger, The	11
Book Project Non-fiction B	Longman	Water	Reference Book of Water and Weather	11
			Water Fun	11
			Water is a Solid, Liquid and Gas	11
Cambridge Reading	CUP	Y3 Independent Reading	Best Present Ever, The	11
			Captain Cool and the Ice Queen	11
			Carnival	11
			How to Trick a Tiger	11
			Ollie	11
			Proper Princess Test, The	11
			Pussy Cat, Pussy Cat	11
			Rachel's Mysterious Drawings	11
		Y4 Independent Reading	Captain Cool and the Robogang	11
			Clyde's Leopard	11
			Don't Do That	11
			Great-Grandma's Dancing Dress	11
			Harry and the Megabyte Brain	11
			Leaving the Island	11
Crunchies	Orchard	Raps	Great Greek Myth Raps	11
			Groovy Greek Hero Raps	11
			Mega Greek Myth Raps	11
			Mighty Greek Myth Raps	11
			Monster Raps	11
			Scary Raps	11
		Seriously Silly Stories	Billy Beast	11
			Cinderboy	11
			Daft Jack and the Beanstalk	11
			Eco-Wolf and the Three Pigs	11
			Emperor's Underwear, The	11
			Rumply Crumply Stinky Pin	11
Discovery World Links	Heinemann	Stage F	Circuit Challenge	11
			World Atlas	11
Famous People, Famous Lives	Franklin Watts	Famous Scientists & Inventors	James Watt	11
			Louis Pasteur	11
		Famous Women	Mary Seacole	11
First Explorers	Kingscourt	Level 2	Bugs Don't Bug Me	11
			Erosion and Weathering	11
			Why Things Move	11
Go Facts	A&C Black	Plants	Flowers	11
			Trees	11
Individual Titles	Frances Lincoln	Anholt, Laurence	Degas and the Little Dancer	11
	Puffin	Horse, Harry	Last Polar Bears, The	11
	Puffin	Kroll, Virginia	Masai and I	11
	Collins Colour Jets	Mark, Jan	Under the Red Elephant	11

SERIES	PUBLISHER	SET (OR AUTHOR)	TITLE	BAND
Individual Titles	Collins Jumbo Jets	Rayner, Shoo	We Won the Lottery	11
	Macdonald	Reeves, James	Rapunzel	11
Infosteps	Kingscourt	Set 1	Gadgets and Gismos	11
			Ocean Explorers	11
			Our Place in Space	11
Lightning	Ginn	Brown Level, Term 2	Legends of the Lake	11
Literacy and Science	Neate Publishing	7–9-yr-olds	Basic Dictionary of Plants and Gardening, A	11
			Comparing Giraffes and Polar Bears	11
Literacy Land	Longmans	Genre Range – Competent	Caribbean Tale, A	11
			Collectors, The	11
			Jewish Tale, A	11
			Poems are Crazy	11
			Poems are Noisy	11
			Poems are Quiet	11
		Genre Range – Fluent	Two Asian Tales	11
			Two European Tales	11
			Two Folk Tales	11
			Zoomababy and the World Cup	11
		Info Trail – Competent	Death of the Dinosaurs	11
			Dr Jenner and the Cow Pox	11
			From Pictures to Words: The Story of Writing	11
			Poles Apart	11
		Info Trail – Fluent	Darwin's Voyage of Discovery	11
			King's Dinner, The	11
			Surviving the Volcano	11
		Story Street: Step 8	Soup with Obby	11
		Story Street: Step 9	Baby Day, The	11
			Barbecue, The	11
			Down the Rushing River	11
			Sam's New Flat	11
		Story Street: Step 11	French Adventures Part 1	11
			French Adventures Part 2	11
			Old Friends, New Friends	11
			Taming Tessa	11
			Tree House, The	11
			Up the Dizzy Mountain	11
Literacy Links Plus	Kingscourt	Fluent C	Crunch, Munch, Lunch!	11
		Fluent D	Baba Yaga	11
			Charlie	11
			Rabbits	11
Literacy Links Plus Topic	Kingscourt	Fluent B	1 Potato, 2 Potato	11
			I'm an Artist	11
		Fluent C	Silent World, A	11
Literacy World	Heinemann	Comets	Goat-skin Lad, The	11
			Quackers	11
		Stage 1	Search for Tutankhamen, The	11
National Geographic	Rigby	White Level	Volcanoes	11
Navigator	Rigby	Non-fiction: Brown Level	Gobstoppers	11
			Welcome to Planet Earth	11
			Zoom in	11
		Short Stories – Brown Level	Tricksters	11

SERIES	PUBLISHER	SET (OR AUTHOR)	TITLE	BAND
Oxford Literacy Web	OUP	Playscripts	Golden Arrow, The	11
			Thor's Hammer	11
		Stage 8: Variety	First Leaf Festival	11
			Grizzlegrump's Revenge	11
			Una's Spelling Test	11
		Stage 9: Variety	Wise Girl, The	11
Oxford Reading Tree	OUP	Cross-curricular Jackdaws	Fire! Fire!	11
			Puzzling Shapes	11
		Jackdaws Anthologies	Danger At Sea	11
			In the Snow	11
			William and the Ghost	11
			William and the Mouse	11
		More Jackdaws Anthologies	Chimney Sweep, The	11
			Island, The	11
			Jokers, The	11
			Playroom, The	11
			Secret Cave, The	11
			Snow Storm, The	11
		Stage 11: True Stories	Born to Dance	11
			Man on the Moon	11
			Titanic Survivor	11
		TreeTops All Stars: Pack 3	The Jam Street Puzzle	11
		TreeTops More All Stars: Pack 3A	Dancing the Night Away	11
			Duperball	11
		TreeTops Stage 10/11: Pack B	Dangerous Trainers	11
			Hilda's Big Chance	11
			Janey's Giants	11
			Odd Job for Bob and Benny, An	11
		TreeTops Stage 10/11: True Stories	Sea Empress Disaster	11
		TreeTops Stage 12: Pack B	Blue Shoes	11
			Clive Keeps his Cool	11
			Lie Detector, The	11
			Robbie Woods and his Merry Men	11
			Scrapman	11
		TreeTops Stage 12: Pack C	Cool Clive and the Little Pest	11
			Here Comes Trouble	11
			Pass the Ball, Grandad	11
			Shelley Holmes, Ace Detective	11
			Snooty Prune	11
			Terrible Birthday Present, The	11
		TreeTops Stage 12: Playscripts	Blue Shoes	11
			Lie Detector, The	11
		TreeTops Stage 12: True Stories	Cup Winners	11
		TreeTops Stage 12+: Pack D	Dads Win Prizes	11
			Doohickey and the Robot	11
			Kid Wonder and the Terrible Truth	11
			Kitten in Daisy Street, A	11
			Me and My Newt	11
			Scrapman and Scrapcat	11
		TreeTops Stage 12+: Pack F	Doughnut Dilemma	11
			Kid Wonder and the Half-Hearted Hero	11

SERIES	PUBLISHER	SET (OR AUTHOR)	TITLE	BAND
Oxford Reading Tree	OUP	TreeTops Stage 12+: Pack F	Kid Wonder and the Sticky Skyscraper	11
			Scrapman and the Incredible Flying Machine	11
		TreeTops Stage 12–14: Pack A	Billy's Luck	11
			Call 999!	11
			Cool Clive	11
			Front Page Story	11
			Pet Squad	11
		TreeTops Stage 13: Pack B	Case of the Smiling Shark, The	11
			Goalie's Secret, The	11
			I Wish, I Wish	11
			Personality Potion, The	11
			Ultimate Trainers, The	11
			Waiting for Goldie	11
		TreeTops Stage 13: Pack C	Black Dan	11
			Bones	11
			Goalie from Nowhere, The	11
			Monster in the Wardrobe, The	11
			Revenge of Captain Blood, The	11
			Spooky!	11
		TreeTops Stage 13: Playscripts	Personality Potion, The	11
			Spooky!	11
		TreeTops Stage 13+: Pack D	Anti-Bully Machine, The	11
			Case of the Walking Trousers, The	11
			Cat Out of the Bag	11
			Quest for the Golden See-Saw, The	11
			Star Struck	11
			True Diary of Carly Ann Potter, The	11
		TreeTops Stage 14: Pack B	Danny's Secret Fox	11
			Night of the Ticklers, The	11
			Okay Spanner, You Win!	11
Oxford RT Rhyme & Analogy	OUP	Story Rhymes: Pack B	My Home	11
Pathways to Literacy	Collins	Year 2	Snug as a Bug	11
		Year 3	City of Fire	11
			Hive and the Mulberry Tree, The	11
			Scrub-A-Dub	11
			Stick in the Mud	11
Pelican Guided Reading	Longman	Y3 T2	Poems to Perform	11
PM Chapter Books	Nelson Thornes	Emerald Set A	Creature of Cassidy's Creek, The	11
			Falcon, The	11
			MacTavish's Creature	11
			Queen of the Pool	11
			Secret, The	11
			Tall Tales	11
		Emerald Set B	Alfred the Curious	11
			Crystal Unicorn, The	11
			Junkyard Dog, The	11
			Medal for Molly, A	11
			Super-Tuned!	11
			Trouble with Oatmeal, The	11
PM Non-fiction	Nelson Thornes	Emerald	All About Yo-Yos	11
			Bicycle Book	11

SERIES	PUBLISHER	SET (OR AUTHOR)	TITLE	BAND
PM Non-fiction	Nelson Thornes	Emerald	Kites	11
			Pushcart Team	11
			Skateboarding	11
			Snowboarding Diary	11
Rigby Star	Rigby	Star Plus	Mammoth Mistake, A	11
			Quork Attack	11
Skyrider	Collins	Yellow	Measuring the Weather	11
			Saving the Yellow Eye	11
			There's No Place Like Home	11
			What's Cooking?	11
Spotlight on Fact	Collins	Y2: The Seaside	Our Digital Holiday	11
			Which Holiday?	11
		Y3: Active Earth	Art for Everyone	11
			Bridge for Nearport, A	11
			Digging for Dinosaurs	11
Spotlight on Plays	Collins	Age 8+	Short Pants	11
Sprinters	Walker	Allen, Judy	Auntie Billie's Greatest Invention	11
		Allen, Judy	Most Brilliant Trick Ever, The	11
		Blake, Jon	Little Stupendo	11
		Blake, Jon	Little Stupendo Flies High	11
		Blake, Jon	Little Stupendo Rides Again	11
		Cheshire, Sam	Me and My Big Mouse	11
		Crebbin, June	Emmelina and the Monster	11
		Crebbin, June	No Tights for George!	11
		Crebbin, June	Tarquin the Wonder Horse	11
		Cross, Gillian	Posh Watson	11
		Fine, Anne	Care of Henry	11
		Fine, Anne	Haunting of Pip Parker, The	11
		Gates, Susan	Beware the Killer Coat	11
		Gates, Susan	Return of the Killer Coat	11
		Jungman, Ann	Little Luis and the Bad Bandit	11
		King-Smith, Dick	Finger-eater, The	11
		Llewellyn, Sam	Magic Boathouse, The	11
		Llewellyn, Sam	Polecat Café, The	11
		McNaughton, Colin	Jolly Roger	11
		Morgan, Alison	Biggest Birthday Card in the World, The	11
		Pilling, Ann	Baked Bean Kids, The	11
		Rix, Jamie	Free the Whales	11
		Ryan, Margaret	Millie Morgan, Pirate	11
		Ure, Jean	Captain Cranko and the Crybaby	11
		Waddell, Martin	Cup Final Kid	11
Star Quest	Rigby	Star Plus	Using the River	11
Storyteller	Kingscourt	Set 11	And the Winner is...	11
			How Not to Catch the Moon	11
			Magic Shoes, The	11
			Seiko the Watchdog	11
			Spider and Buffalo	11
			Turtles, Tortoises and Terrapins	11
Storyworld Bridges	Heinemann	Stage 10	Jake, Ace Detective	11
Storyworld Bridges	Heinemann	Stage 11	Standing Tall	11
			Storm at Sea	11

SERIES	PUBLISHER	SET (OR AUTHOR)	TITLE	BAND
Storyworld Bridges	Heinemann	Stage 11	Wrong Words, The	11
		Stage 12	Deep Water	11
			Greyfriars Bobby	11
			Star Striker	11
			Body Systems	11
			Brand New Ideas	11
The News	Horwitz Gardner		Changing Earth	11
			Clues to Crime	11
			Day and Night	11
			Eat to Win	11
			Endangered or Extinct!	11
			Ends of the Earth	11
			Energy and Me	11
			Firefighters	11
			Hamburger Heaven	11
			Let the Games Begin	11
			Making Myths	11
			Minibeasts	11
			On the Move	11
			Sport Rules	11
			Sports for You	11
			Talk Back	11
			Underwater	11
			Who Shot the Movies?	11
Tristars	Horwitz Gardner	Stage A	Keeping Time	11
		Stage B	Aircraft Adventure	11
			Grandma's Flying Adventure	11
			Ocean Flight Adventure	11
			Tales, Fables and Rhymes	11
			Today, August 17, 1929	11
			Weird and Wacky Inventions	11

Titles in alphabetical order

TITLE	SERIES	PUBLISHER	SET (OR AUTHOR)	BAND
1 Potato, 2 Potato	Literacy Links Plus Topic	Kingscourt	Fluent B	11
3, 2, 1… Lift Off!	Storyteller	Kingscourt	Set 9	9
A				
Absolutely Brilliant Crazy Party, The	Pelican Big Books	Longman	Body, Wendy	7
Adventure at Sea	Storyworlds	Heinemann	Stage 9: Fantasy World	9
Adventure for Robo-dog, An	Oxford Reading Tree	OUP	TreeTops All Stars: Pack 1	9
Adventures of the Robber Pig	Storyteller	Kingscourt	Set 8	8
Aeroplanes Now and Fifty Years Ago	Book Project Non-fiction A	Longman	History of Transport	9
After the Storm	AlphaWorld	Horwitz Gardner	Band 6: Orange	6
Ahhh, Said The Stork	Individual Titles	Pan Ch P/backs	Rose, Gerald	6
Aircraft Adventure	Tristars	Horwitz Gardner	Stage B	11
Akbar's Dream	Storyworld Bridges	Heinemann	Stage 11	10
Alex Brychta	Oxford Reading Tree	OUP	Stage 8: True Stories	8
Alexander Graham Bell	Famous People, Famous Lives	Franklin Watts	Famous Scientists & Inventors	9
Alfred the Curious	PM Chapter Books	Nelson Thornes	Emerald Set B	11
Ali Hassan and the Donkey	Storyworlds	Heinemann	Stage 8: Once Upon a Time	7
Alien Landing	Info Trail	Longman	Emergent Geography	8
Alison Wendlebury	Literacy Links Plus	Kingscourt	Fluent B	8
All Aboard	Pathways to Literacy	Collins	Year 2	8
All About Yo-Yos	PM Non-fiction	Nelson Thornes	Emerald	11
All By Myself	Cambridge Reading	CUP	Y1 B: Narrative Recount	7
All in a Flap	Literacy Land	Longmans	Story Street: Step 8	9
All Join in	Individual Titles	Red Fox	Blake, Quentin	8
All Kinds of Dolls	Oxford Literacy Web	OUP	Non-fiction: Toys	7
Along the Seashore	Spotlight on Fact	Collins	Y2: The Seaside	7
Alphabetical Animals	Pathways to Literacy	Collins	Year 3	10
Always Elephant	Rigby Star	Rigby	Star Plus	10
Amazing Ants	Alphakids Plus	Horwitz Gardner	Transitional Level 17	6
Amazing Grace	Individual Titles	Frances Lincoln	Hoffman, Mary	10
Amazing Journeys	Alphakids	Horwitz Gardner	Extending Level 22	9
Amazing Plants	AlphaWorld	Horwitz Gardner	Band 8: Purple	8
Amazing Tricks	Storyteller	Kingscourt	Set 7	7
Amy the Hedgehog Girl	Oxford Reading Tree	OUP	TreeTops Stage 11: Pack A	10
Amy the Hedgehog Girl	Oxford Reading Tree	OUP	TreeTops Stage 11: Playscripts	9
Amy's Armbands	Lighthouse	Ginn	Gold: 1	9
Anancy and Mr Dry-Bone	Individual Titles	Frances Lincoln	French, Fiona	10
Anansi at The Pool	Book Project	Longman	Fiction Band 4: Cluster E	9
And Pigs Might Fly	Crunchies	Orchard	Tall Tales	9
And the Winner is…	Storyteller	Kingscourt	Set 11	11
Androcles and the Lion	PM Traditional Tales	Nelson Thornes	Silver Level	10
Animal Armour	National Geographic	Rigby	Orange Level	7
Animal Babies	First Explorers	Kingscourt	Level 1	9
Animal Band, The	PM Traditional Tales	Nelson Thornes	Purple Level	8
Animal Builders	Alphakids	Horwitz Gardner	Transitional Level 17	7
Animal Close-ups	AlphaWorld	Horwitz Gardner	Band 8: Purple	8
Animal Communication	Cambridge Reading	CUP	Y2: Non-fiction	10
Animal Communications	Alphakids	Horwitz Gardner	Extending Level 19	9
Animal Diggers	Alphakids	Horwitz Gardner	Transitional Level 16	6
Animal Fathers	Literacy Links Plus Topic	Kingscourt	Fluent A	9
Animal Life Cycles	Discovery World Links	Heinemann	Stage F	8
Animal Rescue	Discovery World Links	Heinemann	Stage D	6

TITLE	SERIES	PUBLISHER	SET (OR AUTHOR)	BAND
Animal Senses	Cambridge Reading	CUP	Y1: Non-fiction	7
Animal Sets	Literacy and Science	Neate Publishing	4–7 yr olds	8
Animal Tails	Lighthouse	Ginn	Orange: 2	6
Animal Wrestlers, The	Cambridge Reading	CUP	Y1 C: Range of Cultures	7
Animals That Sting	Alphakids Plus	Horwitz Gardner	Transitional Level 16	8
Anna's Eggs	Oxford Reading Tree	OUP	Jackdaws Anthologies	10
Annie and the Pirates	Alphakids	Horwitz Gardner	Extending Level 20	8
Ant and the Grasshopper, The	Literacy Links Plus	Kingscourt	Fluent D	6
Ant City	PM Storybooks	Nelson Thornes	Turquoise Set C	7
Antarctic Penguins	PM Non-fiction	Nelson Thornes	Silver Level	10
Antarctic Seals	PM Non-fiction	Nelson Thornes	Silver Level	10
Anti-Bully Machine, The	Oxford Reading Tree	OUP	TreeTops Stage 13+: Pack D	11
Apples!	Cambridge Reading	CUP	Bridging Books	7
Arabian Nights	Oxford Reading Tree	OUP	TreeTops More All Stars: Pack 3A	10
Arctic Hero	Oxford Reading Tree	OUP	Stage 10: True Stories	10
Are Mountains Like Children?	Info Trail	Longman	Emergent Geography	9
Are You My Mother?	Beginner Books	Collins	Eastman, P D	6
Armband Band, The	Pathways to Literacy	Collins	Year 3	9
Art for Everyone	Spotlight on Fact	Collins	Y3: Active Earth	11
Art, You're Magic!	Sprinters	Walker	McBratney, Sam	10
Ask the Experts	Lightning	Ginn	Brown Level N/F	10
Asteroid, The	PM Storybooks	Nelson Thornes	Gold Set C	9
At the Top of the World	Oxford Reading Tree	OUP	Stage 8: True Stories	10
Atul's Christmas Hamster	Cambridge Reading	CUP	Y1 C: Narrative Recount	7
Auntie Billie's Greatest Invention	Sprinters	Walker	Allen, Judy	11
Awumpalema	Literacy Links Plus	Kingscourt	Fluent A	8
B				
B J Dog	Book Project	Longman	Fiction Band 8	10
Baabra Lamb	Book Project	Longman	Fiction Band 5	9
Baba Yaga	Literacy Links Plus	Kingscourt	Fluent D	11
Baby Bear Comes Home	Blue Bananas	Mammoth		10
Baby Day, The	Literacy Land	Longmans	Story Street: Step 9	11
Baby Equipment	Book Project Non-fiction A	Longman	Babies	10
Baby Food	Book Project Non-fiction A	Longman	Babies	9
Bad Bears and Good Bears	Crunchies	Orchard	Twice Upon a Time	8
Bad Boys and Naughty Girls	Crunchies	Orchard	Twice Upon a Time	9
Bad Dad List, The	Skyrider	Collins	Yellow	9
Bad Day, Good Day	Oxford RT Rhyme & Analogy	OUP	Story Rhymes: Pack A	8
Badcats	Oxford Reading Tree	OUP	TreeTops More All Stars: Pack 2A	10
Baked Bean Kids, The	Sprinters	Walker	Pilling, Ann	11
Bakery, The	Alphakids	Horwitz Gardner	Transitional Level 13	6
Banana	What's for Lunch?	Franklin Watts	Claire Llewellyn	10
Bang the Drum	Oxford Reading Tree	OUP	Cross-curricular Jackdaws	10
Barbecue, The	Literacy Land	Longmans	Story Street: Step 9	11
Basic Dictionary of Plants and Gardening, A	Literacy and Science	Neate Publishing	7–9 yr olds	11
Bats	PM Non-fiction	Nelson Thornes	Gold Level	9
Bats About Bats	Storyteller	Kingscourt	Set 11	10
Beanbag	Literacy Links Plus Topic	Kingscourt	Fluent B	8
Beanpole Billy	Lighthouse	Ginn	Gold: 5	9
Bear and the Trolls, The	PM Traditional Tales	Nelson Thornes	Silver Level	10
Bears' Christmas, The	Beginner Books	Collins	Berenstain, Stan & Jan	8

TITLE	SERIES	PUBLISHER	SET (OR AUTHOR)	BAND
Bear's Diet	PM Storybooks	Nelson Thornes	Gold Set A	9
Bear's Lunch, The	Individual Titles	Puffin	Allen, Pamela	6
Bears' Picnic, The	Beginner Books	Collins	Berenstain, Stan & Jan	8
Beastly Basil	Oxford Reading Tree	OUP	TreeTops More All Stars: Pack 2A	10
Beating the Drought	Skyrider	Collins	Yellow	9
Beauty and the Beast	PM Traditional Tales	Nelson Thornes	Gold Level	9
Because a Little Bug Went Ka-choo!	Beginner Books	Collins	Stone, Rosetta	6
Beds	Book Project Non-fiction A	Longman	Homes	8
Bee In My Bonnet, A	Pathways to Literacy	Collins	Year 3	6
Beekeeper, The	Literacy Links Plus	Kingscourt	Fluent A	9
Beep Goes My Belly Button	Oxford Literacy Web	OUP	Poetry Stages: 1–5	7
Bees	Oxford RT Branch Library	OUP	Oxford Reds: Pack B	9
Ben and the Ghost	Literacy Land	Longmans	Story Street: Step 7	9
Bendemolena	Spotlight on Plays	Collins	Age 7+	10
Ben's Amazing Birthday	Cambridge Reading	CUP	Y2 A: Narrative Recount	8
Ben's Get Well Cards	Genre Range	Longman	Emergent Letters	6
Berenstain Bears & Missing Dinosaur Bone	Beginner Books	Collins	Berenstain, Stan & Jan	8
Bertha's Secret Battle	Oxford Reading Tree	OUP	TreeTops Stage 11: Pack A	10
Bertie and the Bear	Individual Titles	Picture Puffin	Allen, Pamela	6
Bertie Wiggins' Amazing Ears	Oxford Reading Tree	OUP	TreeTops Stage 11: Pack A	10
Bertie Wiggins' Amazing Ears	Oxford Reading Tree	OUP	TreeTops Stage 11: Playscripts	10
Best Birthday Present, The	Literacy Links Plus	Kingscourt	Fluent C	8
Best Nest, The	Beginner Books	Collins	Eastman, P D	7
Best Part, The	PM Storybooks	Nelson Thornes	Silver Set B	10
Best Pet, The	Lighthouse	Ginn	Purple: 3	8
Best Present Ever, The	Cambridge Reading	CUP	Y3 Independent Reading	11
Betty Boots	Alphakids	Horwitz Gardner	Extending Level 18	7
Beware of Girls	Individual Titles	Puffin	Blundell, Tony	10
Beware Olga!	Sprinters	Walker	Cross, Gillian	10
Beware the Killer Coat	Sprinters	Walker	Gates, Susan	11
Beyond Strange Street	Literacy Land	Longmans	Story Street: Step 7	10
Bhalloo the Greedy Bear	Book Project	Longman	Fiction Band 4: Cluster E	9
Bicycle Book	PM Non-Fiction	Nelson Thornes	Emerald	11
Bicycles Now and Fifty Years Ago	Book Project Non-fiction A	Longman	History of Transport	9
Big Bad Bill	All Aboard	Ginn	Stage 6: Patt & Rhyme	6
Big Bad Raps	Crunchies	Orchard	Raps	8
Big Ball of String, A	Beginner Books	Collins	Holland, Marion	8
Big Balloon Festival, The	PM Storybooks	Nelson Thornes	Gold Set B	9
Big Barry Baker and the Bullies	Storyworlds	Heinemann	Stage 9: Our World	9
Big Barry Baker in Big Trouble	Storyworlds	Heinemann	Stage 9: Our World	9
Big Barry Baker on the Stage	Storyworld Plays	Heinemann	Stage 9	8
Big Barry Baker on the Stage	Storyworlds	Heinemann	Stage 9: Our World	9
Big Barry Baker's Parcel	Storyworlds	Heinemann	Stage 9: Our World	9
Big Bo Peep	Lighthouse	Ginn	Gold: 4	9
Big Catch, The	Literacy Links Plus Topic	Kingscourt	Fluent C	8
Big Dog and Little Dog Visit the Moon	Blue Bananas	Mammoth	Young, Selina	8
Big Dog, Little Dog	Beginner Books	Collins	Eastman, P D	6
Big Dog, The	Alphakids	Horwitz Gardner	Transitional Level 14	6
Big Head	Sprinters	Walker	Ure, Jean	10
Big Pig's Wig	Alphakids	Horwitz Gardner	Extending Level 23	10
Big Race, The	Skyrider	Collins	Yellow	10

TITLE	SERIES	PUBLISHER	SET (OR AUTHOR)	BAND
Big Shrink, The	Cambridge Reading	CUP	Y2 A: Fantasy Worlds	9
Big Shrink, The	Cambridge Reading	CUP	Y2: Playscripts	9
Big Tease, The	Story Chest	Kingscourt	Stage 7	10
Big Wide-Mouthed Frog, The	Individual Titles	Walker	Larranaga, Ana Martin	6
Big Wig	Starters	Walker	West, Colin	9
Big, Bad Cook, The	Literacy Links Plus Topic	Kingscourt	Fluent A	6
Biggest and Smallest	All Aboard	Ginn	Stage 5: Non-fiction	6
Biggest Birthday Card in the World, The	Sprinters	Walker	Morgan, Alison	11
Biggest Tree, The	PM Storybooks	Nelson Thornes	Orange Set A	6
Bike for Brad, A	PM Storybooks	Nelson Thornes	Purple Set B	8
Bike Lesson, The	Beginner Books	Collins	Berenstain, Stan & Jan	6
Billy Beast	Crunchies	Orchard	Seriously Silly Stories	11
Billy Fishbone	Book Project	Longman	Fiction Band 5	10
Billy's Luck	Oxford Reading Tree	OUP	TreeTops Stage 12–14: Pack A	11
Bird Hide, The	Alphakids	Horwitz Gardner	Extending Level 20	7
Bird in the Basket, The	Skyrider	Collins	Yellow	10
Bird in the Bush, A	Oxford Literacy Web	OUP	Stage 7: Duck Green	7
Bird Watchers	Storyteller	Kingscourt	Set 9	9
Birds	Go Facts	A&C Black	Animals	9
Bird's Eye View	PM Storybooks	Nelson Thornes	Turquoise Set B	7
Birds of Prey	Storyteller	Kingscourt	Set 9	9
Birthday for Bluebell, A	Crunchies	Orchard	Colour Crackers	9
Birthday Treasure Hunt, The	Info Trail	Longman	Emergent Geography	8
Black Dan	Oxford Reading Tree	OUP	TreeTops Stage 13: Pack C	11
Blackbones Saves the School	Oxford Reading Tree	OUP	TreeTops Stage 10: Pack C	10
Blue Eye, The	Oxford Reading Tree	OUP	Stage 9: More Magpies	8
Blue Game, The	Literacy Land	Longmans	Story Street: Step 10	10
Blue Jackal, The	Genre Range	Longman	Emergent Trad Tales	6
Blue Moo	Book Project	Longman	Fiction Band 5	7
Blue Shoes	Oxford Reading Tree	OUP	TreeTops Stage 12: Pack B	11
Blue Shoes	Oxford Reading Tree	OUP	TreeTops Stage 12: Playscripts	11
Bobby Glow-Worm	All Aboard	Ginn	Stage 8: Sam & Rosie	8
Body Parts	Literacy and Science	Neate Publishing	4–7 yr olds	8
Body Systems	The News	Horwitz Gardner		11
Bones	Oxford Reading Tree	OUP	TreeTops Stage 13: Pack C	11
Book of Hours, A	Cambridge Reading	CUP	Y2: Non-fiction	10
Book Week Goes with a Bang – Part 1	Literacy Land	Longmans	Story Street: Step 9	10
Book Week Goes with a Bang – Part 2	Literacy Land	Longmans	Story Street: Step 9	10
Boring Old Bed	Lighthouse	Ginn	Turquoise: 2	7
Boris the Brainiest Baby	Crunchies	Orchard	The One And Only	8
Born to Dance	Oxford Reading Tree	OUP	Stage 11: True Stories	11
Boss Dog of Blossom Street, The	Oxford Reading Tree	OUP	TreeTops Stage 10: Pack A	9
Boxes	Literacy Links Plus	Kingscourt	Early C	6
Boy and His Donkey, A	Literacy Links Plus Topic	Kingscourt	Fluent A	6
Boy Who Cried Wolf, The	PM Traditional Tales	Nelson Thornes	Purple Level	8
Boy Who Talked to the Birds, The	Oxford Literacy Web	OUP	Stage 7: Variety	7
Boy Who Went to the North Wind, The	Literacy Links Plus	Kingscourt	Fluent D	7
Brand New Ideas	The News	Horwitz Gardner		11
Brand-new Butterfly, A	Literacy Links Plus	Kingscourt	Early C	6
Brave Little Tailor, The	PM Traditional Tales	Nelson Thornes	Turquoise Level	7
Brave Sea Captain, The	Pathways to Literacy	Collins	Year 3	10

TITLE	SERIES	PUBLISHER	SET (OR AUTHOR)	BAND
Bread	What's for Lunch?	Franklin Watts	Claire Llewellyn	9
Brementown Musicians, The	Spotlight on Plays	Collins	Age 7+	10
Brer Rabbit's Trickbag	Oxford Reading Tree	OUP	TreeTops All Stars: Pack 3	10
Bridge for Nearport, A	Spotlight on Fact	Collins	Y3: Active Earth	11
Bridge, The	Cambridge Reading	CUP	Y1: Non-fiction	7
Bright Ideas	Explorers	Kingscourt	Set 1	10
Bringing the Sea Back Home	Literacy Links Plus	Kingscourt	Fluent C	10
Broad Bean	Stopwatch	A&C Black		7
Broken Roof, The	Oxford Reading Tree	OUP	Stage 7: Owls	7
Bronwen The Brave	Pathways to Literacy	Collins	Year 2	8
Brown Bears	PM Non-fiction	Nelson Thornes	Turquoise Level	8
Brown Bread and Honey	Individual Titles	Frances Lincoln	Allen, Pamela	9
Bruno the Bravest Man	Crunchies	Orchard	The One And Only	7
Bubbles	Cambridge Reading	CUP	Y1: Non-fiction	8
Budgies	PM Non-fiction	Nelson Thornes	Orange Level	6
Bugs Don't Bug Me	First Explorers	Kingscourt	Level 2	11
Building a House	All Aboard	Ginn	Stage 10: Non-fiction	10
Building Bricks and Other Poems	Pathways to Literacy	Collins	Year 2	9
Buildings for a Purpose	First Explorers	Kingscourt	Level 2	9
Bull in a China Shop, A	Literacy Links Plus	Kingscourt	Fluent B	9
Bully, The	Oxford Reading Tree	OUP	Stage 7: More Owls	7
Bumbles, The	Book Project	Longman	Fiction Band 7	10
Bun, The	Storyteller	Kingscourt	Set 7	7
Buses Now and Fifty Years Ago	Book Project Non-fiction A	Longman	History of Transport	9
Busy Beavers, The	PM Storybooks	Nelson Thornes	Orange Set C	6
But Martin!	Individual Titles	Transworld	Counsel, June	8
But Where is the Green Parrot?	Individual Titles	Pan Ch P/backs	Zacharias, Thomas	8
Butterflies	All Aboard	Ginn	Stage 3: Non-fiction	6
Butterfly and Caterpillar	Stopwatch	A&C Black		9
Butterfly, the Bird, the Beetle and Me, The	Alphakids	Horwitz Gardner	Transitional Level 15	6
Bye, Bye Jasmine	Literacy Land	Longmans	Genre Range – Competent	9
C				
Cabbage Princess, The	Literacy Links Plus	Kingscourt	Fluent D	9
Cabin in the Hills, The	PM Storybooks	Nelson Thornes	Turquoise Set A	7
Call 999!	Oxford Reading Tree	OUP	TreeTops Stage 12–14: Pack A	11
Camels and their Cousins	Storyteller	Kingscourt	Set 8	8
Camille and the Sunflowers	Individual Titles	Frances Lincoln	Anholt, Lawrence	8
Camouflage	Cambridge Reading	CUP	Y2: Non-fiction	9
Camping with Claudine	Literacy Links Plus	Kingscourt	Fluent B	8
Canal Boat Cat	Storyworlds	Heinemann	Stage 9: Animal World	10
Canals and Narrow Boats	All Aboard	Ginn	Stage 6: Non-fiction	9
Canoe Diary	Skyrider	Collins	Yellow	10
Captain Cool and the Ice Queen	Cambridge Reading	CUP	Y3 Independent Reading	11
Captain Cool and the Robogang	Cambridge Reading	CUP	Y4 Independent Reading	11
Captain Cranko and the Crybaby	Sprinters	Walker	Ure, Jean	11
Captain Motley and the Pirate's Crew	Rockets	A&C Black	Ryan, Margaret	10
Captain Scott	Famous People, Famous Lives	Franklin Watts	Famous Leaders	10
Car Trouble	PM Storybooks	Nelson Thornes	Gold Set B	9
Care of Henry	Sprinters	Walker	Fine, Anne	11
Careful Crocodile, The	PM Storybooks	Nelson Thornes	Orange Set C	6
Caribbean Tale, A	Literacy Land	Longmans	Genre Range – Competent	11

TITLE	SERIES	PUBLISHER	SET (OR AUTHOR)	BAND
Caribou (Reindeer)	PM Non-fiction	Nelson Thornes	Silver Level	10
Carnival	Cambridge Reading	CUP	Y3 Independent Reading	11
Cars	Oxford RT Branch Library	OUP	Oxford Reds: Pack A	10
Cars Now and Fifty Years Ago	Book Project Non-fiction A	Longman	History of Transport	9
Case of the Smiling Shark, The	Oxford Reading Tree	OUP	TreeTops Stage 13: Pack B	11
Case of the Walking Trousers, The	Oxford Reading Tree	OUP	TreeTops Stage 13+: Pack D	11
Cass Becomes a Star	Literacy Links Plus	Kingscourt	Fluent C	10
Castles	Tristars	Horwitz Gardner	Stage B	10
Cat and Dog	Alphakids	Horwitz Gardner	Extending Level 19	8
Cat and Dog	Individual Titles	Walker	Lloyd, D & Scruton, C	6
Cat and Rat Fall Out	Lighthouse	Ginn	Turquoise: 4	7
Cat Concert	Literacy Links Plus	Kingscourt	Fluent A	7
Cat in the Hat, The	Beginner Books	Collins	Seuss, Dr	7
Cat Out of the Bag	Oxford Reading Tree	OUP	TreeTops Stage 13+: Pack D	11
Cat Talk	Skyrider	Collins	Yellow	9
Catch, The	Oxford Reading Tree	OUP	Jackdaws Anthologies	10
Cats	PM Non-fiction	Nelson Thornes	Orange Level	6
Cattle	PM Non-fiction	Nelson Thornes	Purple Level	9
Caves	Storyteller	Kingscourt	Set 9	9
Changing Earth	The News	Horwitz Gardner		11
Changing Materials	Discovery World Links	Heinemann	Stage E	9
Changing Shape	Star Quest	Rigby	Turquoise Level	9
Chano	Literacy Links Plus Topic	Kingscourt	Fluent A	8
Charlie	Literacy Links Plus	Kingscourt	Fluent D	11
Charlie the Bridesmaid	Rigby Star	Rigby	White Level	10
Chatting	Individual Titles	Walker	Hughes, Shirley	6
Cherokee Little People, The	Rigby Star	Rigby	Purple Level	8
Cherry Blossom Cat	Storyworlds	Heinemann	Stage 9: Animal World	10
Chicken and Egg	Stopwatch	A&C Black		7
Chicken Little	Literacy Links Plus	Kingscourt	Traditional Tales	7
Chicken-Licken	PM Traditional Tales	Nelson Thornes	Orange Level	6
Chickens	PM Non-fiction	Nelson Thornes	Purple Level	9
Chimney Sweep, The	Oxford Reading Tree	OUP	More Jackdaws Anthologies	11
Chinese Adventure	Oxford Reading Tree	OUP	Stage 7: More Owls	7
Chinese New Year, The	Cambridge Reading	CUP	Y1 C: Range of Cultures	7
Chloe the Chameleon	Rigby Star	Rigby	Orange Level	6
Chocolate	What's for Lunch?	Franklin Watts	Claire Llewellyn	9
Chocolate!	Tristars	Horwitz Gardner	Stage A	9
Christmas Adventure	Oxford Reading Tree	OUP	Stage 6: More Owls	6
Christmas Fair, The	Oxford Reading Tree	OUP	Citizenship Stories: Stage 9/10	9
Cinderboy	Crunchies	Orchard	Seriously Silly Stories	11
Cinderella	Pelican Big Books	Longman	Cullimore, Stan	8
Cinderella	PM Traditional Tales	Nelson Thornes	Gold Level	9
Circle Magic	Rockets	A&C Black	Smith, Wendy	9
Circuit Challenge	Discovery World Links	Heinemann	Stage F	11
City Cat	Storyworlds	Heinemann	Stage 9: Animal World	10
City of Fire	Pathways to Literacy	Collins	Year 3	11
Classroom Animals	AlphaWorld	Horwitz Gardner	Band 7: Turquoise	7
Clay	Find Out About	Franklin Watts		9
Clay Creatures	Star Quest	Rigby	Orange Level	6
Clay Dog, The	Lighthouse	Ginn	Turquoise: 5	7

TITLE	SERIES	PUBLISHER	SET (OR AUTHOR)	BAND
Cleaner Genie	Oxford Reading Tree	OUP	TreeTops More All Stars: Pack 2A	9
Clever Coyote and Other Wild Dogs	Storyteller	Kingscourt	Set 9	9
Clever Dog, Webster	Book Project	Longman	Fiction Band 6	9
Clever Invention, A	Oxford Reading Tree	OUP	Citizenship Stories: Stage 9/10	9
Clever Monkey	Oxford Reading Tree	OUP	TreeTops All Stars: Pack 3	10
Clive Keeps his Cool	Oxford Reading Tree	OUP	TreeTops Stage 12: Pack B	11
Clouds	Literacy Links Plus	Kingscourt	Fluent D	10
Clown's Gallery	All Aboard	Ginn	Stage 7: Non-fiction	9
Clowns Next Door, The	Oxford Literacy Web	OUP	Year 3	10
Clubhouse, The	PM Storybooks	Nelson Thornes	Gold Set A	9
Clues to Crime	The News	Horwitz Gardner		11
Clumsy Clumps and the Baby Moon	Blue Bananas	Mammoth	Bertagna, Julie	9
Clyde's Leopard	Cambridge Reading	CUP	Y4 Independent Reading	11
Coastlines	Alphakids Plus	Horwitz Gardner	Transitional Level 15	8
Cobra Cat	Storyworlds	Heinemann	Stage 9: Animal World	10
Codes and Signals	Cambridge Reading	CUP	Y2: Non-fiction	9
Collectors, The	Literacy Land	Longmans	Genre Range – Competent	11
Colours Around Us	Literacy and Science	Neate Publishing	4–7 yr olds	8
Come on a Desert Safari!	Literacy Land	Longmans	Info Trail – Competent	10
Come to My Party!	Info Trail	Longman	Emergent Geography	6
Coming Clean	Oxford Reading Tree	OUP	TreeTops Stage 11: Pack A	10
Comparing Giraffes and Polar Bears	Literacy and Science	Neate Publishing	7–9 yr olds	11
Concert, The	Oxford Reading Tree	OUP	Citizenship Stories: Stage 9/10	10
Construction Toys	Book Project Non-fiction A	Longman	Toys	8
Cooking Pot	Story Chest	Kingscourt	Stage 6	9
Cook's Catastrophe, The	Tristars	Horwitz Gardner	Stage A	9
Cool Clive	Oxford Reading Tree	OUP	TreeTops Stage 12–14: Pack A	11
Cool Clive and the Bubble Trouble	Oxford Reading Tree	OUP	TreeTops Stage 12+: Pack F	10
Cool Clive and the Little Pest	Oxford Reading Tree	OUP	TreeTops Stage 12: Pack C	11
Corn	National Geographic	Rigby	Turquoise Level	8
Corner of Magic, A	Cambridge Reading	CUP	Y2 B: Poetry	9
Cosmo for Captain	Oxford Reading Tree	OUP	TreeTops All Stars: Pack 1	8
Count on Your Body	Star Quest	Rigby	White Level	10
Countdown	Story Chest	Kingscourt	Stage 7	10
Coyote Girl	Cambridge Reading	CUP	Y2: Playscripts	10
Coyote, Fox, and Wolf Tales	Storyteller	Kingscourt	Set 8	8
Crabs	Alphakids Plus	Horwitz Gardner	Transitional Level 16	7
Crazy Critters, The	Spotlight on Plays	Collins	Age 8+	10
Crazy Crocs	Book Project	Longman	Fiction Band 7	10
Crazy Magic	Rockets	A&C Black	Smith, Wendy	9
Crazy Miss Maisey's Alphabet Pets	Storyteller	Kingscourt	Set 10	10
Creature of Cassidy's Creek, The	PM Chapter Books	Nelson Thornes	Emerald Set A	11
Creepy Creatures	Explorers	Kingscourt	Set 1	10
Crocodile Watching	Alphakids Plus	Horwitz Gardner	Transitional Level 15	7
Crocodile's Bag	Storyteller	Kingscourt	Set 7	7
Crosby Crocodile's Disguise	Literacy Links Plus	Kingscourt	Fluent D	8
Crown Jewels, The	Rockets	A&C Black	Rodgers, Frank	9
Crunch, Munch, Lunch!	Literacy Links Plus	Kingscourt	Fluent C	11
Crystal Unicorn, The	PM Chapter Books	Nelson Thornes	Emerald Set B	11
Cup Final Kid	Sprinters	Walker	Waddell, Martin	11
Cup Run	Starters	Walker	Waddell, Martin	9

TITLE	SERIES	PUBLISHER	SET (OR AUTHOR)	BAND
Cup Winners	Oxford Reading Tree	OUP	TreeTops Stage 12: True Stories	11
Cutting and Sticking	Cambridge Reading	CUP	Y2 A: Familiar Settings	9
D				
Dad's Grand Plan	Oxford Reading Tree	OUP	Stage 6 & 7: More Owls B	6
Dad's Promise	Cambridge Reading	CUP	Y2 A: Narrative Recount	8
Dad's Story	Oxford Literacy Web	OUP	Year 3	10
Dads Win Prizes	Oxford Reading Tree	OUP	TreeTops Stage 12+: Pack D	11
Daft Jack and the Beanstalk	Crunchies	Orchard	Seriously Silly Stories	11
Dancing Dudley	Alphakids Plus	Horwitz Gardner	Transitional Level 17	6
Dancing in Soot	Cambridge Reading	CUP	Y2 B: Narrative Recount	9
Dancing the Night Away	Oxford Reading Tree	OUP	TreeTops More All Stars: Pack 3A	11
Dancing to the River	Cambridge Reading	CUP	Y2 A: Range of Cultures	8
Danger At Sea	Oxford Reading Tree	OUP	Jackdaws Anthologies	11
Dangerous Trainers	Oxford Reading Tree	OUP	TreeTops Stage 10/11: Pack B	11
Danny's Secret Fox	Oxford Reading Tree	OUP	TreeTops Stage 14: Pack B	11
Darwin's Voyage of Discovery	Literacy Land	Longmans	Info Trail – Fluent	11
Dave and the Tooth Fairy	Individual Titles	Tamarind	Wilkins, Verna	10
Day and Night	The News	Horwitz Gardner		11
Day in London, A	Oxford Reading Tree	OUP	Stage 8: Magpies	8
Day in London, A	Oxford Reading Tree	OUP	Stage 8: Playscripts	7
Day in the Life of a Roman Charioteer, A	Literacy Land	Longmans	Info Trail – Competent	10
Day in the Life of a Victorian Child, A	Discovery World	Heinemann	Stage C	8
Day Poppy Said "Yes!", The	Book Project	Longman	Fiction Band 5	7
Day Poppy Went Out, The	Book Project	Longman	Fiction Band 6	7
Daylight Robbery	Oxford Literacy Web	OUP	Stage 9: Duck Green	7
Dear Daddy…	Pelican Big Books	Longman	Dupasquier, Philippe	6
Dear Diary	Literacy Links Plus Topic	Kingscourt	Fluent B	10
Dear Grandma	Storyteller	Kingscourt	Set 6	6
Death of the Dinosaurs	Literacy Land	Longmans	Info Trail – Competent	11
Deep Water	Storyworld Bridges	Heinemann	Stage 12	11
Deer and the Crocodile, The	Literacy Links Plus	Kingscourt	Early D	6
Degas and the Little Dancer	Individual Titles	Frances Lincoln	Anholt, Laurence	11
Delilah Digs for Treasure	Blue Bananas	Mammoth		10
Denny Davidson, Detective	Tristars	Horwitz Gardner	Stage B	10
Desert Run, The	Skyrider	Collins	Yellow	10
Detective Tilak	All Aboard	Ginn	Stage 8: Sam & Rosie	8
Dexter's Dinosaurs	Oxford Reading Tree	OUP	TreeTops Stage 10: Pack C	9
Diary of a Honey Bee	Literacy Links Plus	Kingscourt	Fluent A	7
Dick Whittington	Oxford Reading Tree	OUP	TreeTops More All Stars: Pack 3A	10
Dick Whittington	PM Traditional Tales	Nelson Thornes	Silver Level	10
Did a Hamster Go into Space?	Info Trail	Longman	Beginner History	7
Did Vikings Eat Chips?	Info Trail	Longman	Emergent History	9
Different Places, Different Faces	Infosteps	Kingscourt	Set 1	9
Digging for Dinosaurs	Individual Titles	Red Fox	Waite, Judy	9
Digging for Dinosaurs	Spotlight on Fact	Collins	Y3: Active Earth	11
Dilly and the Goody-Goody	Blue Bananas	Mammoth		10
Dilly and the Goody-Goody	Cambridge Reading	CUP	Y2: Playscripts	9
Dilly and the School Play	Cambridge Reading	CUP	Y2: Playscripts	9
Dilly and the Wobbly Tooth	Cambridge Reading	CUP	Y2: Playscripts	9
Dilly Breaks the Rules	Cambridge Reading	CUP	Y2: Playscripts	9
Ding Dong Bell, Whats That Funny Smell?	Crunchies	Orchard	Seriously Silly Rhymes	8

TITLE	SERIES	PUBLISHER	SET (OR AUTHOR)	BAND
Dinosaur (whole text)	Cambridge Reading	CUP	Y1: Non-fiction	8
Dinosaur Alphabet	Oxford Literacy Web	OUP	Non-fiction: Animals	7
Dinosaur Chase	PM Storybooks	Nelson Thornes	Orange Set A	6
Dinosaur Danger!	Oxford Literacy Web	OUP	Stage 8: Duck Green	7
Dinosaurs	Oxford RT Branch Library	OUP	Oxford Reds: Pack B	9
Dinosaur's Cold, The	Literacy Links Plus	Kingscourt	Early D	6
Discovery	Oxford Reading Tree	OUP	Stage 10: More Robins	10
Disgusting Denzil	Oxford Reading Tree	OUP	TreeTops All Stars: Pack 2	9
Divers of the Deep Sea	National Geographic	Rigby	White Level	10
Do All Rivers Go to the Sea?	Info Trail	Longman	Beginner Geography	7
Does Cheese Come From Cows?	Info Trail	Longman	Beginner Science	8
Does Chocolate Grow on Trees?	Info Trail	Longman	Emergent Science	9
Dog Called Bear, A	PM Storybooks	Nelson Thornes	Purple Set A	8
Dog from Outer Space, The	Lighthouse	Ginn	Orange: 6	6
Dog Show, The	Cambridge Reading	CUP	Y2 B: Familiar Settings	10
Dogger	Individual Titles	Walker	Hughes, Shirley	10
Dogs	Oxford RT Branch Library	OUP	Oxford Reds: Pack A	9
Dogs	PM Non-fiction	Nelson Thornes	Orange Level	6
Dogstar	Literacy Links Plus	Kingscourt	Fluent B	7
Dolls Now and Long Ago	Book Project Non-fiction A	Longman	Toys	9
Dolphin on the Wall, The	PM Storybooks	Nelson Thornes	Silver Set B	10
Dolphins, The	PM Storybooks	Nelson Thornes	Gold Set C	9
Dom's Handplant	Literacy Links Plus	Kingscourt	Fluent B	9
Donkey That Sneezed, The	Oxford RT Branch Library	OUP	Traditional Tales	6
Don't Be a Beetroot!	Info Trail	Longman	Emergent Science	7
Don't Be Late	Cambridge Reading	CUP	Y2 C: Familiar Settings	9
Don't Be Silly	Oxford Reading Tree	OUP	Stage 6 & 7: More Owls B	6
Don't Do That	Cambridge Reading	CUP	Y4 Independent Reading	11
Don't Worry	Literacy Links Plus	Kingscourt	Fluent A	7
Donut Letters, The	Literacy Land	Longmans	Genre Range – Competent	9
Doohickey and the Robot	Oxford Reading Tree	OUP	TreeTops Stage 12+: Pack D	11
Doris Bean and the Queen	Oxford Reading Tree	OUP	TreeTops All Stars: Pack 2	10
Doris's Brilliant Birthday	Rockets	A&C Black	Ryan, Margaret	10
Dormouse Pot, The	Oxford Literacy Web	OUP	Stage 9: Duck Green	7
Doughnut Dilemma	Oxford Reading Tree	OUP	TreeTops Stage 12+: Pack F	11
Down in the Woods	Storyteller	Kingscourt	Set 6	6
Down on the Ice	Skyrider	Collins	Yellow	10
Down the Rushing River	Literacy Land	Longmans	Story Street: Step 9	11
Dr Jenner and the Cow Pox	Literacy Land	Longmans	Info Trail – Competent	11
Drag Racing	Alphakids	Horwitz Gardner	Extending Level 21	10
Dragon Test, The	Starters	Walker	Crebbin, June	8
Dragon Who Had the Measles, The	Literacy Links Plus	Kingscourt	Fluent A	7
Dragonflies and Their Young	Book Project Non-fiction A	Longman	Animals	8
Dragon's Tooth, The	Rockets	A&C Black	Rodgers, Frank	9
Drat that Cat!	Cambridge Reading	CUP	Bridging Books	7
Dream Catchers	Storyteller	Kingscourt	Set 8	8
Dream Team, The	Lighthouse	Ginn	Orange: 7	6
Dress-up Parade, The	Alphakids	Horwitz Gardner	Transitional Level 17	7
Duck	Individual Titles	Walker	Lloyd, David	7
Duck in The Hat, The	Pelican Big Books	Longman	Waddell, Martin	6
Duck Magic	Literacy Links Plus	Kingscourt	Fluent B	9

TITLE	SERIES	PUBLISHER	SET (OR AUTHOR)	BAND
Ducks Crossing	Skyrider	Collins	Yellow	10
Dump, The	Oxford Reading Tree	OUP	Stage 6: Robins	7
Duperball	Oxford Reading Tree	OUP	TreeTops More All Stars: Pack 3A	11
Dutch Adventure	Oxford Reading Tree	OUP	Stage 9: More Magpies	7
E				
Earth Materials	First Explorers	Kingscourt	Level 1	10
Easy Peasy	Sprinters	Walker	Hayes, Sarah	9
Eat to Win	The News	Horwitz Gardner		11
Eco-Wolf and the Three Pigs	Crunchies	Orchard	Seriously Silly Stories	11
Eggs	What's for Lunch?	Franklin Watts	Claire Llewellyn	9
Egyptian Adventure	Oxford Reading Tree	OUP	Stage 8: More Magpies	8
Elena the Frog	Sprinters	Walker	Sheldon, Dyan	10
Elephant Diary	Oxford Literacy Web	OUP	Non-fiction: Animals	7
Elephant Walk	Storyteller	Kingscourt	Set 8	8
Elephants	PM Non-fiction	Nelson Thornes	Turquoise Level	8
Elves and the Shoemaker, The	Alphakids	Horwitz Gardner	Transitional Level 14	6
Elves and the Shoemaker, The	PM Traditional Tales	Nelson Thornes	Turquoise Level	7
Elves and the Shoemaker, The	Storyworlds	Heinemann	Stage 7: Once Upon a Time	6
Elves and the Shoemakers, The	Rigby Star	Rigby	Purple Level	8
Emeka's Gift	Individual Titles	Frances Lincoln	Onyefulu, Ifeoma	10
Emergencies	Oxford Reading Tree	OUP	Cross-curricular Jackdaws	10
Emergency, The	Oxford Reading Tree	OUP	Stage 8: Robins	9
Emma's Problem	Literacy Links Plus	Kingscourt	Early C	7
Emmelina and the Monster	Sprinters	Walker	Crebbin, June	11
Emperor and the Nightingale, The	Literacy Links Plus Topic	Kingscourt	Fluent D	10
Emperor Penguin, The	Pathways to Literacy	Collins	Year 3	9
Emperor's New Clothes, The	Rigby Star	Rigby	Gold Level	9
Emperor's Underwear, The	Crunchies	Orchard	Seriously Silly Stories	11
Encyclopaedia of British Wild Animals	Book Project Non-fiction A	Longman	Reference – 4 Volumes	9
Encyclopaedia of Fantastic Fish	Star Quest	Rigby	White Level	10
Endangered or Extinct!	The News	Horwitz Gardner		11
Ends of the Earth	The News	Horwitz Gardner		11
Energy and Me	The News	Horwitz Gardner		11
Enjoy! Enjoy!	Alphakids	Horwitz Gardner	Transitional Level 17	7
Eric's Talking Ears	Oxford Reading Tree	OUP	TreeTops All Stars: Pack 2	9
Ernie and the Fishface Gang	Sprinters	Walker	Waddell, Martin	10
Erosion and Weathering	First Explorers	Kingscourt	Level 2	11
Escape!	Skyrider	Collins	Yellow	9
Everyday Forces	Discovery World	Heinemann	Stage E	7
Evil Genie, The	Oxford Reading Tree	OUP	Stage 8: More Magpies	8
Excalibur the Magic Sword	Crunchies	Orchard	Crazy Camelot Capers	10
Eyes	AlphaWorld	Horwitz Gardner	Band 7: Turquoise	7
F				
Fabulous Freckles	Literacy Links Plus Topic	Kingscourt	Fluent C	7
Fair Swap, A	PM Storybooks	Nelson Thornes	Silver Set A	10
Falcon, The	PM Chapter Books	Nelson Thornes	Emerald Set A	11
Families	Storyteller	Kingscourt	Set 6	6
Fangtastic Raps	Crunchies	Orchard	Raps	9
Farmer Skiboo	Oxford Reading Tree	OUP	TreeTops All Stars: Pack 1	8
Fascinating Faces	Literacy Links Plus Topic	Kingscourt	Early C	6
Fast Food for Butterflies	Storyteller	Kingscourt	Set 7	7

TITLE	SERIES	PUBLISHER	SET (OR AUTHOR)	BAND
Fastest Gazelle, The	Literacy Links Plus	Kingscourt	Early D	6
Fayim's Incredible Journey	Oxford Reading Tree	OUP	TreeTops Stage 12: True Stories	10
Feathers	Storyteller	Kingscourt	Set 8	8
Feathers and Flight	Explorers	Kingscourt	Set 1	10
Feet	Info Trail	Longman	Beginner Science	7
Festival Food	Discovery World Links	Heinemann	Stage E	9
Fiddle-dee-dee	Story Chest	Kingscourt	Stage 6	9
Finding Out about Volcanoes	Spotlight on Fact	Collins	Y3: Active Earth	10
Finest in the Land, The	Oxford Reading Tree	OUP	Stage 9: More Magpies	8
Finger-eater, The	Sprinters	Walker	King-Smith, Dick	11
Finish the Story, Dad	Individual Titles	Walker	Smee, Nicola	8
Fire and Wind	PM Storybooks	Nelson Thornes	Silver Set B	10
Fire! Fire!	Oxford Reading Tree	OUP	Cross-curricular Jackdaws	11
Fire! Fire!	Storyteller	Kingscourt	Set 8	8
Firefighters	The News	Horwitz Gardner		11
First Leaf Festival	Oxford Literacy Web	OUP	Stage 8: Variety	11
First Morning, The	Literacy Links Plus Topic	Kingscourt	Fluent D	9
Fish	Star Quest	Rigby	White Level	10
Fish Out of Water, A	Beginner Books	Collins	Palmer, Helen	7
Fisherman and His Wife, The	Literacy Links Plus	Kingscourt	Traditional Tales	8
Five go to Wembley	Literacy Land	Longmans	Info Trail – Competent	10
Five Minutes' Peace	Individual Titles	Franklin Watts	Murphy, Jill	9
Fizzkid Liz	Rigby Star	Rigby	Orange Level	6
Flans Across the River	Oxford Reading Tree	OUP	TreeTops Stage 11: Pack A	9
Flood!	Oxford Reading Tree	OUP	Stage 8: More Magpies	7
Flora's Fantastic Revenge	Sprinters	Walker	Warburton, Nick	10
Florence Nightingale	Famous People, Famous Lives	Franklin Watts	Famous Women	10
Floss	Individual Titles	Walker	Lewis, Kim	9
Flowers	Go Facts	A&C Black	Plants	11
Flutey Family Fruit Cake, The	Storyteller	Kingscourt	Set 9	9
Flyers	Rigby Star	Rigby	Turquoise Level	7
Flying Carpet, The	Oxford Reading Tree	OUP	Stage 8: Magpies	8
Flying Carpet, The	Oxford Reading Tree	OUP	Stage 8: Playscripts	7
Flying Fingers	Literacy Links Plus Topic	Kingscourt	Fluent B	8
Flying Football, The	Cambridge Reading	CUP	Bridging Books	6
Flying Machine, The	Oxford Reading Tree	OUP	Stage 9: More Magpies	7
Flying Machines	Alphakids Plus	Horwitz Gardner	Early Level 11	6
Flying Tea Tray, The	Oxford Literacy Web	OUP	Stage 8: Duck Green	9
Food for All	First Explorers	Kingscourt	Level 1	8
Food for Animals	AlphaWorld	Horwitz Gardner	Band 7: Turquoise	8
Food for Festivals	Pelican Big Books	Longman	Witherington, Anne	8
Footprint Detective	All Aboard	Ginn	Stage 6 : Non-fiction	9
Forces of Nature	First Explorers	Kingscourt	Level 2	10
Forest Giants	Infosteps	Kingscourt	Set 1	9
Forest, The	Cambridge Reading	CUP	Y1: Non-fiction	7
Forgotten Princess, The	Literacy Links Plus Topic	Kingscourt	Fluent D	8
Fortune for Yo-Yo, A	Crunchies	Orchard	Colour Crackers	9
Fossils	National Geographic	Rigby	Purple Level	9
Fowler's Family Tree	Storyteller	Kingscourt	Set 7	7
Fox with Moonlit Eyes, A	All Aboard	Ginn	Stage 10: Poetry	11
Foxes	PM Non-fiction	Nelson Thornes	Gold Level	9

TITLE	SERIES	PUBLISHER	SET (OR AUTHOR)	BAND
Free the Whales	Sprinters	Walker	Rix, Jamie	11
French Adventures – Part 1	Literacy Land	Longmans	Story Street: Step 11	11
French Adventures – Part 2	Literacy Land	Longmans	Story Street: Step 11	11
Fried Piper of Hamstring, The	Crunchies	Orchard	Seriously Silly Stories	10
Friends Are Forever	Literacy Links Plus	Kingscourt	Fluent A	7
Fright in the Night, A	Oxford Reading Tree	OUP	Stage 6: More Owls	6
Frog and Toad Are Friends	Individual Titles	Egmont	Lobel, Arnold	7
Frog and Toad Together	Individual Titles	Egmont	Lobel, Arnold	8
Frog Day	Storyteller	Kingscourt	Set 8	8
Frog Prince, The	Storyworlds	Heinemann	Stage 7: Once Upon a Time	6
Frog Princess, The	Literacy Links Plus	Kingscourt	Early D	6
Frog Who Thought He Was a Horse, The	Literacy Links Plus	Kingscourt	Fluent C	10
Froggy Tale, A	Literacy Links Plus Topic	Kingscourt	Fluent A	8
Frogs and Toads	All Aboard	Ginn	Stage 8: Non-fiction	8
Frogs and Toads	Oxford RT Branch Library	OUP	Oxford Reds: Pack A	9
From a Bean to a Bar	Lighthouse	Ginn	Turquoise: 3	7
From Pictures to Words: The Story of Writing	Literacy Land	Longmans	Info Trail – Competent	11
From Sam Summerday	Literacy Land	Longmans	Genre Range – Competent	10
Front Page Story	Oxford Reading Tree	OUP	TreeTops Stage 12–14: Pack A	11
Fruits and Seeds	Oxford Reading Tree	OUP	Cross-curricular Jackdaws	9
Fun of the Fair, The	All Aboard	Ginn	Stage 10: Non-fiction	11
Fun Run, The	All Aboard	Ginn	Stage 5 Set B: Sam & Rosie	6
Funnybones	Individual Titles	Little Mammoth	Ahlberg, Allan	7
G				
Gadgets and Gismos	Infosteps	Kingscourt	Set 1	11
Gallo and Zorro	Literacy Links Plus	Kingscourt	Early D	8
Gardening for Beginners	All Aboard	Ginn	Stage 9: Non-fiction	10
Garlunk	Cambridge Reading	CUP	Y3 Independent Reading	10
Gemma and the Beetle People	Sprinters	Walker	Richemont, Enid	10
George Stephenson	Famous People, Famous Lives	Franklin Watts	Famous Scientists & Inventors	10
Getting Around	Alphakids Plus	Horwitz Gardner	Transitional Level 13	6
Ghost and the Sausage, The	Story Chest	Kingscourt	Stage 6	9
Ghost in Annie's Room, The	Sprinters	Walker	Pearce, Phillipa	10
Ghost Tricks	Oxford Reading Tree	OUP	Stage 10: More Robins	10
Ghostyshocks and the Three Scares	Crunchies	Orchard	Seriously Silly Stories	8
Giant and the Frippit, The	Rigby Star	Rigby	Orange Level	6
Giant Jumperee, The	Rigby Star	Rigby	Turquoise Level	7
Gifts from Greece	Infosteps	Kingscourt	Set 1	10
Ginger, Where Are You?	Pathways to Literacy	Collins	Year 2	8
Gingerbread Man, The	Literacy Links Plus	Kingscourt	Traditional Tales	6
Gingerbread Man, The	PM Traditional Tales	Nelson Thornes	Orange Level	6
Give Me My Yam!	Individual Titles	Walker	Blake, Jan	9
Gizmos' Party, The	Rigby Star	Rigby	White Level	10
Gizmos' Trip, The	Rigby Star	Rigby	White Level	10
Glass	Find Out About	Franklin Watts		10
Goalie from Nowhere, The	Oxford Reading Tree	OUP	TreeTops Stage 13: Pack C	11
Goalie's Secret, The	Oxford Reading Tree	OUP	TreeTops Stage 13: Pack B	11
Goats	PM Non-fiction	Nelson Thornes	Purple Level	9
Goat-skin Lad, The	Literacy World	Heinemann	Comets	11
Gobstoppers	Navigator	Rigby	Non-fiction: Brown Level	11
Going on Holiday	Spotlight on Fact	Collins	Y2: The Seaside	10

TITLE	SERIES	PUBLISHER	SET (OR AUTHOR)	BAND
Going Places	First Explorers	Kingscourt	Level 1	9
Going to School	Cambridge Reading	CUP	Y1 B: Narrative Recount	7
Going Up!	Starters	Walker	Waddell, Martin	9
Go-kart Race, The	Oxford Reading Tree	OUP	Stage 6: More Owls	6
Gold Badge, The	Pathways to Literacy	Collins	Year 3	10
Golden Arrow, The	Oxford Literacy Web	OUP	Playscripts	11
Goldfish	PM Non-fiction	Nelson Thornes	Orange Level	6
Goldilocks and the Three Bears	Individual Titles	OUP	Beck, Ian	7
Goldilocks and the Three Bears	PM Traditional Tales	Nelson Thornes	Turquoise Level	7
Good Dog	Book Project	Longman	Fiction Band 6	8
Goodness Gracious!	Literacy Links Plus	Kingscourt	Early C	7
Gorgo Meets Her Match	PM Storybooks	Nelson Thornes	Purple Set C	8
Gorillas	Alphakids Plus	Horwitz Gardner	Early Level 11	6
Gotcha Smile, The	Individual Titles	Orchard	Mitchell, R P	7
Grabber	Pathways to Literacy	Collins	Year 2	6
Grabbing Bird, The	Cambridge Reading	CUP	Y2 A: Fantasy Worlds	8
Grace and Family	Individual Titles	Frances Lincoln	Hoffman, M & Binch, C	8
Gracie's Cat	Cambridge Reading	CUP	Y1 C: Narrative Recount	7
Graeme Base Writer and Illustrator	Alphakids	Horwitz Gardner	Extending Level 23	10
Gran, Gran!	Oxford RT Rhyme & Analogy	OUP	Story Rhymes: Pack B	9
Grandad	Literacy Links Plus	Kingscourt	Fluent D	9
Grandad's Boneshaker Bicycle	Rockets	A&C Black	West, Colin	9
Grandad's Mask	PM Storybooks	Nelson Thornes	Turquoise Set C	7
Grandma's Flying Adventure	Tristars	Horwitz Gardner	Stage B	11
Grandma's Memories	Literacy Links Plus	Kingscourt	Early B	6
Grandma's Stick	Story Chest	Kingscourt	Stage 6	9
Grandpa's Birthday	Literacy Links Plus	Kingscourt	Fluent A	7
Grandpa's Bright Ideas	Lighthouse	Ginn	Gold: 3	9
Granny Garcia's Gifts	Storyteller	Kingscourt	Set 7	7
Granny's Jungle Garden	Rockets	A&C Black	West, Colin	9
Grass Snakes and Their Young	Book Project Non-fiction A	Longman	Animals	9
Great Day for Up!	Beginner Books	Collins	Seuss, Dr	6
Great Escape, The	Literacy Land	Longmans	Story Street: Step 10	10
Great Fire of London, The	Discovery World Links	Heinemann	Stage F	9
Great Greek Myth Raps	Crunchies	Orchard	Raps	11
Great Lorenzo, The	All Aboard	Ginn	Stage 6: Sam & Rosie	6
Great Sebastian, The	Alphakids	Horwitz Gardner	Extending Level 19	7
Great Spaghetti Suit, The	Oxford Reading Tree	OUP	TreeTops Stage 10/11: Pack B	9
Great Stew Disaster, The	Oxford Literacy Web	OUP	Stage 9: Duck Green	9
Great Tin-rolling Race, The	Alphakids	Horwitz Gardner	Extending Level 21	9
Greatest Show on Earth, The	Individual Titles	Walker	Prater, John	7
Great-Grandma's Dancing Dress	Cambridge Reading	CUP	Y4 Independent Reading	11
Greedy Cat and the Birthday Cake	Skyrider	Collins	Yellow	9
Greedy Guts and Belly Busters	Crunchies	Orchard	Twice Upon a Time	8
Greedy King, The	Lighthouse	Ginn	Orange: 3	6
Green Dragons, The	PM Storybooks	Nelson Thornes	Purple Set B	8
Green Eggs and Ham	Beginner Books	Collins	Seuss, Dr	6
Green Island	Oxford Reading Tree	OUP	Stage 9: Magpies	8
Gregor, The Grumblesome Giant	Literacy Links Plus	Kingscourt	Early C	6
Gregorie Peck	Book Project	Longman	Fiction Band 5	7
Greyfriars Bobby	Storyworld Bridges	Heinemann	Stage 12	11

TITLE	SERIES	PUBLISHER	SET (OR AUTHOR)	BAND
Gribblegrot from Outer Space, The	Literacy Links Plus	Kingscourt	Fluent C	10
Grizzlegrump's Revenge	Oxford Literacy Web	OUP	Stage 8: Variety	11
Groovy Greek Hero Raps	Crunchies	Orchard	Raps	11
Growing Up in Australia	Book Project Non-fiction A	Longman	Children Around the World	7
Growing Up in Canada	Book Project Non-fiction A	Longman	Children Around the World	7
Growing Up in Denmark	Book Project Non-fiction A	Longman	Children Around the World	7
Growing Up in Japan	Book Project Non-fiction A	Longman	Children Around the World	7
Growing Up in South Africa	Book Project Non-fiction A	Longman	Children Around the World	7
Growing Up in Sri Lanka	Book Project Non-fiction A	Longman	Children Around the World	7
Grown-ups Make You Grumpy	Lighthouse	Ginn	Turquoise: 1	7
Guinea Pigs	PM Non-fiction	Nelson Thornes	Orange Level	6
H				
Hailstorm, The	PM Storybooks	Nelson Thornes	Turquoise Set B	7
Hair Book, The	Bright and Early Books	Collins	Tether, Graham	6
Hairy Maclary from Donaldson's Dairy	Individual Titles	Picture Puffin	Dodd, Lynley	8
Hairy Toe, The	Spotlight on Plays	Collins	Age 7+	10
Hairy Toes and Scary Bones	Crunchies	Orchard	Twice Upon a Time	9
Hal the Highwayman	Starters	Walker	Crebbin, June	8
Half for You, Half for Me	Literacy Links Plus	Kingscourt	Early D	6
Hamburger Heaven	The News	Horwitz Gardner		11
Hamid Does His Best	Oxford Reading Tree	OUP	Stage 9: More Robins	9
Hamper's Great Escape	Oxford Reading Tree	OUP	TreeTops Stage 12: Pack B	9
Hand, Hand, Fingers, Thumb	Bright and Early Books	Collins	Perkins, Al	7
Handle with Care	First Explorers	Kingscourt	Level 2	8
Hansel and Gretel	Storyworlds	Heinemann	Stage 9: Once Upon a Time	10
Happily Ever After	Storyteller	Kingscourt	Set 8	8
Happy Prince & The Selfish Giant, The	New Way	Nelson Thornes	Orange Platform Books	10
Happy Sad	Blue Bananas	Mammoth	Goodhart, Pippa	9
Harbour, The (whole text)	Cambridge Reading	CUP	Y1: Non-fiction	8
Hard to Please	Oxford Reading Tree	OUP	TreeTops Stage 11: Pack A	10
Hare and the Tortoise, The	Literacy Links Plus	Kingscourt	Fluent B	8
Hare and the Tortoise, The	PM Traditional Tales	Nelson Thornes	Purple Level	8
Harold the Hairiest Man	Crunchies	Orchard	The One And Only	8
Harry and the Megabyte Brain	Cambridge Reading	CUP	Y4 Independent Reading	11
Harry, the Dirty Dog	Individual Titles	Red Fox	Zion, G	8
Has it Gone Off?	Book Project Non-fiction A	Longman	Food	7
Hat Came Back, The	Literacy Links Plus Topic	Kingscourt	Fluent C	6
Hat Chat	Storyteller	Kingscourt	Set 7	7
Hattie Hates Hats	Pathways to Literacy	Collins	Year 2	7
Hatupatu and the Birdwoman	Story Chest	Kingscourt	Stage 7	10
Haunting of Pip Parker, The	Sprinters	Walker	Fine, Anne	11
Have a Go, Sam	All Aboard	Ginn	Stage 5 Set B: Sam & Rosie	6
Have You Seen a Javelina?	Literacy Links Plus Topic	Kingscourt	Fluent C	10
Haystack, The	Cambridge Reading	CUP	Y2 B: Narrative Recount	10
He Bear, She Bear	Bright and Early Books	Collins	Berenstain, Stan & Jan	7
He Who Listens	Literacy Links Plus	Kingscourt	Fluent A	9
Headfirst into the Porridge	Rigby Star	Rigby	Star Plus	10
Hector the Rat	Sprinters	Walker	Wilkinson, Tony	10
Helena and the Wild Man	Oxford Literacy Web	OUP	Stage 9: Variety	10
Henry Ford	Famous People, Famous Lives	Franklin Watts	Famous Scientists & Inventors	10
Henry Seamouse	Book Project	Longman	Fiction Band 8	10

TITLE	SERIES	PUBLISHER	SET (OR AUTHOR)	BAND
Hen's Eggs	Book Project Non-fiction A	Longman	Food	8
Here Comes Trouble	Oxford Reading Tree	OUP	TreeTops Stage 12: Pack C	11
Hiccup on the High Seas, A	Individual Titles	Collins Jets	Wallace, Karen	10
Hiding Places	Storyteller	Kingscourt	Set 9	9
High Five Henry	Oxford Reading Tree	OUP	TreeTops All Stars: Pack 2	10
High Flier	Oxford Reading Tree	OUP	Stage 9: True Stories	9
Hilda's Big Chance	Oxford Reading Tree	OUP	TreeTops Stage 10/11: Pack B	11
Hippos	PM Non-fiction	Nelson Thornes	Turquoise Level	8
Hippo's Hiccups	Literacy Links Plus	Kingscourt	Early C	6
History of Football, The	Info Trail	Longman	Emergent History	8
Hive and the Mulberry Tree, The	Pathways to Literacy	Collins	Year 3	11
Holiday, The	Oxford Reading Tree	OUP	Stage 10: Robins	8
Holidays Then and Now	Spotlight on Fact	Collins	Y2: The Seaside	10
Holly and the Skyboard	Sprinters	Walker	Whybrow, Ian	10
Home for Bonnie, A	Star Quest	Rigby	Turquoise Level	7
Honey	What's for Lunch?	Franklin Watts	Claire Llewellyn	9
Honey Tree, The	Literacy Links Plus Topic	Kingscourt	Fluent C	10
Hop on Pop	Beginner Books	Collins	Seuss, Dr	6
Horrible Baby	Book Project	Longman	Fiction Band 7	10
Horse in the House	Blue Bananas	Mammoth	Morse, Brian	7
Horsepower	Infosteps	Kingscourt	Set 1	9
Horses	Oxford RT Branch Library	OUP	Oxford Reds: Pack B	10
Horses	PM Non-fiction	Nelson Thornes	Purple Level	9
Hot Dog Harris	Crunchies	Orchard	Colour Crackers	8
Hot Surprise, A	Rigby Star	Rigby	Orange Level	6
Hot-air Balloons	Alphakids	Horwitz Gardner	Extending Level 18	8
Hound Gelert & Wookey Witch	New Way	Nelson Thornes	Orange Platform Books	10
Housework	Book Project Non-fiction A	Longman	Homes	8
How a Book is Made	Literacy World	Heinemann	Stage 1	10
How Babies Grow	Book Project Non-fiction A	Longman	Babies	8
How Bat Learned to Fly	Storyteller	Kingscourt	Set 6	6
How Big is it?	Lighthouse	Ginn	Turquoise: 6	7
How Fire Came to Earth	Literacy Links Plus	Kingscourt	Early D	7
How My Bike Was Made	Oxford Literacy Web	OUP	Non-fiction: Toys	7
How Not to Catch the Moon	Storyteller	Kingscourt	Set 11	11
How the Animals Got Their Tails	Cambridge Reading	CUP	Y2 A: Range of Cultures	10
How the Camel Got His Hump	Storyteller	Kingscourt	Set 6	6
How to Build a Wildlife Paradise	Literacy Land	Longmans	Info Trail – Fluent	10
How to Choose a Pet	Discovery World	Heinemann	Stage E	9
How to Grow a Nasturtium	Discovery World Links	Heinemann	Stage C	8
How to Have a Green Day	Literacy Land	Longmans	Info Trail – Competent	9
How to Kick-start a Dragon	Oxford RT Rhyme & Analogy	OUP	Story Rhymes: Pack B	9
How to Look After a Rat	Info Trail	Longman	Emergent Science	6
How to make a Rain Gauge	Spotlight on Fact	Collins	Y3: Active Earth	10
How to Make Toys from the Past	Oxford Literacy Web	OUP	Non-fiction: Toys	6
How to Prepare a Mummy	Literacy Land	Longmans	Info Trail – Fluent	10
How to Read the Sky	Info Trail	Longman	Beginner Geography	6
How to Remember Absolutely Everything	Literacy Land	Longmans	Info Trail – Competent	9
How to Trick a Tiger	Cambridge Reading	CUP	Y3 Independent Reading	11
How to Write a Biography	Literacy Land	Longmans	Info Trail – Competent	10
How Turtle Got His Shell	Rigby Star	Rigby	Orange Level	6

TITLE	SERIES	PUBLISHER	SET (OR AUTHOR)	BAND
How Turtle Raced Beaver	Literacy Links Plus	Kingscourt	Early D	7
Huge and Horrible Beast, The	Oxford Reading Tree	OUP	TreeTops More All Stars: Pack 3A	10
Human Body, The	Explorers	Kingscourt	Set 1	10
Hunt for Gold, The	Oxford Reading Tree	OUP	Stage 7: More Owls	7
Hunting in the Dark	Alphakids Plus	Horwitz Gardner	Transitional Level 15	6
I				
I Can Read with My Eyes Shut	Beginner Books	Collins	Seuss, Dr	6
I Dig Dinosaurs	First Explorers	Kingscourt	Level 2	9
I Don't Want to Say YES!	Blue Bananas	Mammoth	Mooney, Bel	6
I Have a Question, Grandma	Literacy Links Plus	Kingscourt	Early D	6
I Love the UK	Discovery World Links	Heinemann	Stage E	10
I Spy Pancakes and Pies	Crunchies	Orchard	Twice Upon a Time	9
I Want a Party	Pathways to Literacy	Collins	Year 2	9
I Wish, I Wish	Oxford Reading Tree	OUP	TreeTops Stage 13: Pack B	11
Ice-Cream Factory, The	Star Quest	Rigby	Gold Level	9
If I Were Invisible…	Alphakids	Horwitz Gardner	Extending Level 18	7
If Wishes Were Fishes	Crunchies	Orchard	Twice Upon a Time	9
I'll Teach My Dog 100 Words	Bright and Early Books	Collins	Frith, Michael	7
I'm a Chef	Literacy Links Plus	Kingscourt	Fluent D	10
I'm an Artist	Literacy Links Plus Topic	Kingscourt	Fluent B	11
I'm Riding on a Giant	Oxford Literacy Web	OUP	Poetry Stages: 1–5	9
I'm So Hungry and Other Plays	Skyrider	Collins	Yellow	9
In the Afternoon	PM Non-fiction	Nelson Thornes	Green Level	6
In the Mirror	Cambridge Reading	CUP	Y2 A: Poetry	8
In the Morning	PM Non-fiction	Nelson Thornes	Green Level	6
In the Snow	Oxford Reading Tree	OUP	Jackdaws Anthologies	11
Incredible Creatures	Explorers	Kingscourt	Set 1	10
Incredible Insects	Literacy World	Heinemann	Stage 1	10
Insect Army, The	Infosteps	Kingscourt	Set 1	10
Insects	Alphakids	Horwitz Gardner	Transitional Level 14	6
Insects	Go Facts	A&C Black	Animals	9
Interview with Florence Nightingale, An	Discovery World Links	Heinemann	Stage F	10
Irish Tale, An	Literacy Land	Longmans	Genre Range – Competent	10
Is Lightning Most Frightening?	Info Trail	Longman	Emergent Geography	6
Is Simba Happy in the Zoo?	Info Trail	Longman	Emergent Science	6
Is the Wise Owl Wise?	Rigby Star	Rigby	Turquoise Level	7
Island, The	Oxford Reading Tree	OUP	More Jackdaws Anthologies	11
It's About Time	Storyteller	Kingscourt	Set 7	7
It's Not Easy Being a Bunny	Beginner Books	Collins	Sadler, Marilyn	6
J				
Jack and Chug	PM Storybooks	Nelson Thornes	Orange Set A	6
Jack and the Beanstalk	Literacy Links Plus	Kingscourt	Traditional Tales	6
Jack and the Beanstalk	Oxford RT Branch Library	OUP	Traditional Tales	6
Jack and the Beanstalk	Storyworld Plays	Heinemann	Stage 9	8
Jack and the Beanstalk	Storyworlds	Heinemann	Stage 9: Once Upon a Time	10
Jack and the Magic Harp	PM Traditional Tales	Nelson Thornes	Gold Level	9
Jade Emperor and the Four Dragons, The	Lighthouse	Ginn	Purple: 4	8
Jake, Ace Detective	Storyworld Bridges	Heinemann	Stage 10	11
James Watt	Famous People, Famous Lives	Franklin Watts	Famous Scientists & Inventors	11
Jamie's Food Guide	Discovery World Links	Heinemann	Stage E	10
Jane Goodall	Star Quest	Rigby	Star Plus	10

TITLE	SERIES	PUBLISHER	SET (OR AUTHOR)	BAND
Janey's Giants	Oxford Reading Tree	OUP	TreeTops Stage 10/11: Pack B	11
Jellyfish Shoes, The	Oxford Reading Tree	OUP	TreeTops Stage 10: Pack C	9
Jenny the Joker	Rockets	A&C Black	West, Colin	9
Jessica in the Dark	PM Storybooks	Nelson Thornes	Orange Set B	6
Jewish Tale, A	Literacy Land	Longmans	Genre Range – Competent	11
Jigsaw Puzzle, The	Oxford Reading Tree	OUP	Stage 7: More Owls	7
Jilly's Days	Book Project	Longman	Fiction Band 6	7
Jo the Model Maker	Lighthouse	Ginn	Orange: 5	6
Johann and the Birds	Alphakids	Horwitz Gardner	Extending Level 22	8
John Logie Baird	Famous People, Famous Lives	Franklin Watts	Famous Scientists & Inventors	10
Jojo Makes the Team	Literacy Land	Longmans	Story Street: Step 7	8
Joke Machine, The	Oxford Reading Tree	OUP	Stage 6 & 7: More Owls B	7
Jokers, The	Oxford Reading Tree	OUP	More Jackdaws Anthologies	11
Jolly Hungry Jack	Lighthouse	Ginn	Orange: 4	6
Jolly Roger	Sprinters	Walker	McNaughton, Colin	11
Jonathan Buys a Present	PM Storybooks	Nelson Thornes	Turquoise Set A	7
Jordan and the Northside Reps	PM Storybooks	Nelson Thornes	Silver Set C	10
Jordan's Catch	PM Storybooks	Nelson Thornes	Purple Set C	8
Jordan's Lucky Day	PM Storybooks	Nelson Thornes	Turquoise Set C	7
Josh and the Beanstalk	Oxford Literacy Web	OUP	Stage 9: Duck Green	8
Joshua's Junk	Book Project	Longman	Fiction Band 7	9
Journey into the Earth, The	Storyworlds	Heinemann	Stage 9: Fantasy World	9
Jug Ears	Book Project	Longman	Fiction Band 7	10
Juggling with Jeremy	Blue Bananas	Mammoth		10
Jumble Power	Cambridge Reading	CUP	Y2 B: Fantasy Worlds	10
Jumble the Puppy	Storyworld Bridges	Heinemann	Stage 12	10
Jumping Jack	Rigby Star	Rigby	Purple Level	8
Jungle Shorts	Oxford Reading Tree	OUP	TreeTops Stage 10: Pack A	8
Junkyard Dog, The	PM Chapter Books	Nelson Thornes	Emerald Set B	11
Just A Touch Of Magic	Pathways to Literacy	Collins	Year 4	10
Just Hanging Around	Storyteller	Kingscourt	Set 9	9
Just My Luck	Literacy Links Plus	Kingscourt	Early C	7
Just One Guinea Pig	PM Storybooks	Nelson Thornes	Orange Set B	6
K				
Kangaroos	All Aboard	Ginn	Stage 6: Patt & Rhyme	7
Kangaroos	PM Non-fiction	Nelson Thornes	Turquoise Level	8
Karen's Adventure	Oxford Reading Tree	OUP	Jackdaws Anthologies	10
Kate and the Crocodile	Oxford Reading Tree	OUP	Stage 8: Woodpeckers	7
Kate and the Sheep	Oxford Reading Tree	OUP	Stage 8: Robins	8
Kate Who Was Always Late	Tristars	Horwitz Gardner	Stage A	10
Kate's Garden	Oxford Reading Tree	OUP	Jackdaws Anthologies	10
Katie Morag and the Two Grandmothers	Individual Titles	Random House	Hedderwick, M	10
Katie Morag Delivers the Mail	Individual Titles	Random House	Hedderwick, M	10
Keep Your Hamster Happy	Oxford Literacy Web	OUP	Non-fiction: Animals	7
Keeping Secrets	Blue Bananas	Mammoth	Koralek, Jenny	7
Keeping Time	Tristars	Horwitz Gardner	Stage A	11
Kerry	PM Storybooks	Nelson Thornes	Silver Set A	10
Kerry's Double	PM Storybooks	Nelson Thornes	Silver Set A	10
Kevin and the Pirate Test	Rockets	A&C Black	Ryan, Margaret	10
Key Trouble	Oxford Reading Tree	OUP	Stage 9: More Magpies	7
Kid Wonder and the Half-Hearted Hero	Oxford Reading Tree	OUP	TreeTops Stage 12+: Pack F	11

TITLE	SERIES	PUBLISHER	SET (OR AUTHOR)	BAND
Kid Wonder and the Sticky Skyscraper	Oxford Reading Tree	OUP	TreeTops Stage 12+: Pack F	11
Kid Wonder and the Terrible Truth	Oxford Reading Tree	OUP	TreeTops Stage 12+: Pack D	11
Kidnappers, The	Oxford Reading Tree	OUP	Stage 8: Magpies	6
Kidnappers, The	Oxford Reading Tree	OUP	Stage 8: Playscripts	6
King Arthur and the Mighty Conquest	Crunchies	Orchard	Crazy Camelot Capers	10
King Grumpyguts	Book Project	Longman	Fiction Band 5	8
King Horace's Treasure Hunt	Tristars	Horwitz Gardner	Stage A	9
King Midas and the Golden Touch	PM Storybooks	Nelson Thornes	Gold Set B	9
King of Football, The	Oxford Reading Tree	OUP	Stage 10: True Stories	10
King of the Birds, The	Crunchies	Orchard	Tall Tales	9
King of the Birds, The	Rigby Star	Rigby	Purple Level	8
King of the Go-Kart Track	Literacy Land	Longmans	Story Street: Step 10	9
King, the Mice and the Cheese, The	Beginner Books	Collins	Gurney, Nancy	8
King's Dinner, The	Literacy Land	Longmans	Info Trail – Fluent	11
King's Ears, The	Oxford Literacy Web	OUP	Stage 7: Variety	7
King's Pudding, The	Literacy Links Plus Topic	Kingscourt	Early C	6
King's Socks, The	Oxford RT Rhyme & Analogy	OUP	Story Rhymes: Pack B	8
Kipper and the Giant	Oxford Reading Tree	OUP	Stage 6: Owls	6
Kitchens Now and Long Ago	Book Project Non-fiction A	Longman	Homes	9
Kites	AlphaWorld	Horwitz Gardner	Band 8: Purple	8
Kites	Oxford Literacy Web	OUP	Non-fiction: Toys	7
Kites	PM Non-Fiction	Nelson Thornes	Emerald	11
Kitten in Daisy Street, A	Oxford Reading Tree	OUP	TreeTops Stage 12+: Pack D	11
Knickerbocker Number Nine	Cambridge Reading	CUP	Y2 B: Poetry	9
Knit, Knit, Knit, Knit	Literacy Links Plus	Kingscourt	Fluent A	6
Knitting for Penguins	Storyteller	Kingscourt	Set 7	8
Knives and Forks and Other Things	Book Project Non-fiction A	Longman	Food	9
Knock, Knock! Who's There?	Crunchies	Orchard	Twice Upon a Time	8
Knucklebones	Info Trail	Longman	Beginner History	7
Korka the Mighty Elf	Rigby Star	Rigby	Turquoise Level	7
Kung Fu Katy and the Horrors	Book Project	Longman	Fiction Band 8	11
L				
Lady Long-legs	Sprinters	Walker	Mark, Jan	10
Ladybird	Stopwatch	A&C Black		8
Land of the Dinosaurs	Oxford Reading Tree	OUP	Stage 6: Owls	6
Last Polar Bears, The	Individual Titles	Puffin	Horse, Harry	11
Last Train, The	Individual Titles	Wayland	Lewis, Kim	10
Last Word, The	Alphakids Plus	Horwitz Gardner	Transitional Level 15	6
Laughing Princess, The	Oxford Reading Tree	OUP	Stage 6: More Owls	6
Leading the Way	Infosteps	Kingscourt	Set 1	10
Leaves	All Aboard	Ginn	Stage 6 : Non-fiction	9
Leaving the Island	Cambridge Reading	CUP	Y4 Independent Reading	11
Legends of the Lake	Lightning	Ginn	Brown Level, Term 2	11
Leon Loves Bugs	Sprinters	Walker	Sheldon, Dyan	10
Leonardo da Vinci: Greatest Genius?	Literacy Land	Longmans	Info Trail – Competent	10
Leopard's Drum, The	Individual Titles	Frances Lincoln	Souhami, Jessica	9
Let the Games Begin	The News	Horwitz Gardner		11
Letang and Julie Save the Day	Book Project	Longman	Fiction Band 6	9
Letang's New Friend	Book Project	Longman	Fiction Band 6	9
Letter From Fish Bay, A	Skyrider	Collins	Yellow	10
Letters From Lucy	Pathways to Literacy	Collins	Year 2	8

TITLE	SERIES	PUBLISHER	SET (OR AUTHOR)	BAND
Lick of the Spoon, A	Cambridge Reading	CUP	Y2 B: Poetry	10
Lie Detector, The	Oxford Reading Tree	OUP	TreeTops Stage 12: Pack B	11
Lie Detector, The	Oxford Reading Tree	OUP	TreeTops Stage 12: Playscripts	11
Lights On	First Explorers	Kingscourt	Level 2	10
Lion Talk	Storyteller	Kingscourt	Set 6	6
Lions and Tigers	PM Non-fiction	Nelson Thornes	Turquoise Level	8
Lion's Roar, The	All Aboard	Ginn	Stage 6: Patt & Rhyme	7
Litter Queen, The	Oxford Reading Tree	OUP	Stage 9: Magpies	7
Little Adventure, A	PM Storybooks	Nelson Thornes	Silver Set A	10
Little Blue, Big Blue	Rigby Star	Rigby	White Level	10
Little Bo Peep Has Knickers that Bleep	Crunchies	Orchard	Seriously Silly Rhymes	10
Little Brother's Haircut	Story Chest	Kingscourt	Stage 7	10
Little Dinosaur Escapes	PM Storybooks	Nelson Thornes	Turquoise Set B	7
Little Girl and Her Beetle, The	Literacy Links Plus	Kingscourt	Fluent B	7
Little Girl and the Bear, The	Storyworlds	Heinemann	Stage 9: Once Upon a Time	10
Little Half Chick	Literacy Links Plus Topic	Kingscourt	Early D	6
Little Luis and the Bad Bandit	Sprinters	Walker	Jungman, Ann	11
Little Red Hen, The	Cambridge Reading	CUP	Y1: Playscripts	6
Little Red Hen, The	PM Traditional Tales	Nelson Thornes	Orange Level	6
Little Red Riding Hood	PM Traditional Tales	Nelson Thornes	Turquoise Level	7
Little Red Riding Hood	Storyworlds	Heinemann	Stage 8: Once Upon a Time	7
Little Red Riding Wolf	Crunchies	Orchard	Seriously Silly Stories	10
Little Spider, The	Literacy Links Plus	Kingscourt	Fluent C	9
Little Stupendo	Sprinters	Walker	Blake, Jon	11
Little Stupendo Flies High	Sprinters	Walker	Blake, Jon	11
Little Stupendo Rides Again	Sprinters	Walker	Blake, Jon	11
Living in Two Worlds	Infosteps	Kingscourt	Set 1	10
Living Together	Alphakids	Horwitz Gardner	Extending Level 23	10
Lizard the Wizard	Rockets	A&C Black	Rodgers, Frank	9
Lizzie's Lizard	Storyteller	Kingscourt	Set 7	7
Lonely Giant, The	Literacy Links Plus	Kingscourt	Fluent B	7
Lonely Troll, The	Alphakids	Horwitz Gardner	Transitional Level 17	7
Long Journey, The	Oxford Reading Tree	OUP	Stage 7: More Robins	9
Long Live Roberto	Crunchies	Orchard	Colour Crackers	9
Look Inside	Storyteller	Kingscourt	Set 8	8
Look Out for Your Tail	Literacy Links Plus	Kingscourt	Fluent C	8
Look Out!	Spotlight on Fact	Collins	Y3: Active Earth	10
Look Up	First Explorers	Kingscourt	Level 1	8
Looking After Chickens	Alphakids	Horwitz Gardner	Transitional Level 15	6
Looking After the Egg	All Aboard	Ginn	Stage 7: Non-fiction	10
Looking After Their Young	Alphakids	Horwitz Gardner	Extending Level 18	8
Looking at Birds	Pathways to Literacy	Collins	Year 3	10
Looking at Teddy Bears	Pelican Big Books	Longman	Purkis, Sallie	7
Looking Like Plants	Alphakids Plus	Horwitz Gardner	Transitional Level 12	6
Lord Mount Dragon, The	Cambridge Reading	CUP	Y2 B: Range of Cultures	10
Lord Scarecrow	All Aboard	Ginn	Stage 6: Sam & Rosie	6
Lost in the Forest	PM Storybooks	Nelson Thornes	Orange Set C	6
Lost in the Jungle	Oxford Reading Tree	OUP	Stage 7: Owls	7
Lost in the Park	Alphakids	Horwitz Gardner	Transitional Level 13	6
Lost Key, The	Oxford Reading Tree	OUP	Stage 7: Owls	7
Lost: One Cat	Tristars	Horwitz Gardner	Stage B	10

TITLE	SERIES	PUBLISHER	SET (OR AUTHOR)	BAND
Loudest Sneeze, The	Alphakids	Horwitz Gardner	Transitional Level 16	6
Louis Braille	Famous People, Famous Lives	Franklin Watts	Famous People	10
Louis Pasteur	Famous People, Famous Lives	Franklin Watts	Famous Scientists & Inventors	11
Lucy Meets a Dragon	Literacy Links Plus	Kingscourt	Fluent B	10
Luke's Go-Kart	PM Storybooks	Nelson Thornes	Gold Set A	9
Lunch Bunch, The	Storyteller	Kingscourt	Set 9	9
Lunchbox	All Aboard	Ginn	Stage 9: Non-fiction	10
M				
M.C. Gang Investigates, The	Lightning	Ginn	Brown Level, Term 3	10
Mabel and Max	Blue Bananas	Mammoth		10
Macdonald Diaries, The	Literacy Land	Longmans	Genre Range – Competent	10
MacTavish's Creature	PM Chapter Books	Nelson Thornes	Emerald Set A	11
Magenta and the Ghost Babies	Rockets	A&C Black	Shulman, Dee	9
Magenta and the Ghost Bride	Rockets	A&C Black	Shulman, Dee	9
Magenta and the Ghost School	Rockets	A&C Black	Shulman, Dee	9
Magenta and the Scary Ghosts	Rockets	A&C Black	Shulman, Dee	9
Magic Boathouse, The	Sprinters	Walker	Llewellyn, Sam	11
Magic Carpet, The	Storyworlds	Heinemann	Stage 9: Fantasy World	9
Magic Doctor, The	Oxford RT Branch Library	OUP	Traditional Tales	8
Magic Hotel	Rockets	A&C Black	Smith, Wendy	9
Magic Jigsaw, The	Rigby Star	Rigby	Gold Level	10
Magic Number, The	Oxford Literacy Web	OUP	Stage 9: Duck Green	8
Magic Porridge Pot, The	Oxford Reading Tree	OUP	TreeTops All Stars: Pack 1	8
Magic Pot, The	Oxford Literacy Web	OUP	Playscripts	10
Magic Shoes, The	Storyteller	Kingscourt	Set 11	11
Magic Show Review, The	Tristars	Horwitz Gardner	Stage A	10
Magic Smell, The	All Aboard	Ginn	Stage 7: Sam & Rosie	10
Magic Sword, The	Cambridge Reading	CUP	Y2 B: Fantasy Worlds	9
Magic Tricks	Tristars	Horwitz Gardner	Stage A	10
Magical Models	Lightning	Ginn	Brown Level N/F	10
Magical Stories from India	Pelican Guided Reading	Longman	Y2 T2	9
Magnets	National Geographic	Rigby	Purple Level	10
Magnets	Star Quest	Rigby	Gold Level	8
Magnificent Mummies, The	Blue Bananas	Mammoth	Bradman, Tony	9
Make a Book Book, The	Pathways to Literacy	Collins	Year 2	7
Make a Bottle Garden	Lighthouse	Ginn	Purple: 2	8
Making a Torch	Alphakids	Horwitz Gardner	Extending Level 23	10
Making Caterpillars and Butterflies	Literacy Links Plus	Kingscourt	Early C	6
Making Myths	The News	Horwitz Gardner		11
Making Pots with Dad	Alphakids Plus	Horwitz Gardner	Transitional Level 14	6
Making Puppets	Book Project Non-fiction A	Longman	Toys	8
Mammals	Go Facts	A&C Black	Animals	9
Mammals of the Sea	Explorers	Kingscourt	Set 1	10
Mammoth Mistake, A	Rigby Star	Rigby	Star Plus	11
Man on the Moon	Oxford Reading Tree	OUP	Stage 11: True Stories	11
Man-eating Snails	Literacy Land	Longmans	Story Street: Step 8	9
Mantu the Elephant	Rigby Star	Rigby	Gold Level	9
Maps	Discovery World	Heinemann	Stage E	7
Marble Patch, The	PM Storybooks	Nelson Thornes	Purple Set C	8
Marvel Paws	Cambridge Reading	CUP	Y2 A: Poetry	9
Marvin, The Christmas Cat	Tristars	Horwitz Gardner	Stage B	10

TITLE	SERIES	PUBLISHER	SET (OR AUTHOR)	BAND
Mary Seacole	Famous People, Famous Lives	Franklin Watts	Famous Women	11
Mary, Mary, Fried Canary	Crunchies	Orchard	Seriously Silly Rhymes	9
Mary-Anne and the Cat Baby	Oxford Reading Tree	OUP	TreeTops More All Stars: Pack 3A	10
Masai and I	Individual Titles	Puffin	Kroll, Virginia	11
Masked Cleaning Ladies Meet the Pirates, The	Oxford Reading Tree	OUP	TreeTops Stage 10: Pack C	9
Masked Cleaning Ladies of Om, The	Oxford Reading Tree	OUP	TreeTops Stage 10: Pack A	9
Masked Cleaning Ladies of Om, The	Oxford Reading Tree	OUP	TreeTops Stage 10: Playscripts	9
Masked Cleaning Ladies Save the Day, The	Oxford Reading Tree	OUP	TreeTops Stage 10: Pack A	9
Masterpiece, The	Storyteller	Kingscourt	Set 10	10
Materials	Individual Titles	Heinemann	Bryant-Mole, Karen	8
May-Ling's Party	Oxford Reading Tree	OUP	Citizenship Stories: Stage 9/10	10
Me and My Big Mouse	Sprinters	Walker	Cheshire, Sam	11
Me and My Newt	Oxford Reading Tree	OUP	TreeTops Stage 12+: Pack D	11
Me, Miss!	Lightning	Ginn	Brown Level plays	9
Measuring the Weather	Skyrider	Collins	Yellow	11
Medal for Molly, A	PM Chapter Books	Nelson Thornes	Emerald Set B	11
Medal for Poppy, A	Crunchies	Orchard	Colour Crackers	9
Meet Me at the Water Hole	Storyteller	Kingscourt	Set 6	6
Mega Greek Myth Raps	Crunchies	Orchard	Raps	11
Metal	Find Out About	Franklin Watts		10
Mice	Literacy Links Plus	Kingscourt	Early D	6
Mice	PM Non-fiction	Nelson Thornes	Orange Level	6
Micky the Muckiest Boy	Crunchies	Orchard	The One And Only	7
Middle of Nowhere, The	Rigby Star	Rigby	Star Plus	10
Midnight in Memphis	Blue Bananas	Mammoth		10
Mighty Greek Myth Raps	Crunchies	Orchard	Raps	11
Mighty Machines	National Geographic	Rigby	Green Level	6
Milk	What's for Lunch?	Franklin Watts	Claire Llewellyn	9
Millennium Scrapbook, A	Info Trail	Longman	Emergent Geography	10
Millie Morgan, Pirate	Sprinters	Walker	Ryan, Margaret	11
Millie's Party	Blue Bananas	Mammoth	Stewart, Paul	8
Mind Bridget	Pathways to Literacy	Collins	Year 3	9
Miner's Home, The	Book Project Non-fiction A	Longman	Homes	9
Minestrone Mob, The	Rockets	A&C Black	Wallace, Karen	10
Miniature Toys	Book Project Non-fiction A	Longman	Toys	8
Minibeast Encyclopaedia	Discovery World	Heinemann	Stage C	8
Minibeasts	The News	Horwitz Gardner		11
Mirror Island	Oxford Reading Tree	OUP	Stage 6 & 7: More Owls B	6
Misha Disappears	Literacy Links Plus	Kingscourt	Fluent D	8
Miss Blossom	Pathways to Literacy	Collins	Year 2	6
Miss Jump the Jockey	Individual Titles	Puffin	Ahlberg, Allan	7
Miss Ross is Cross	Oxford Literacy Web	OUP	Stage 9: Duck Green	7
Mitch to the Rescue	PM Storybooks	Nelson Thornes	Orange Set B	6
Mog and the Baby	Individual Titles	Collins Pict Lions	Kerr, Judith	7
Molly and the Beanstalk	Sprinters	Walker	Goodhart, Pippa	10
Moneypenny and the Pond	Oxford Literacy Web	OUP	Stage 8: Variety	8
Moneypenny Goes Camping	Oxford Literacy Web	OUP	Stage 8: Variety	8
Moneypenny's Big Walk	Oxford Literacy Web	OUP	Stage 8: Variety	8
Monkey and Fire	Literacy Links Plus	Kingscourt	Early D	7
Monkey Business	Oxford Reading Tree	OUP	More Jackdaws Anthologies	10
Monkey Business	Storyteller	Kingscourt	Set 10	10

TITLE	SERIES	PUBLISHER	SET (OR AUTHOR)	BAND
Monkey Tricks	PM Storybooks	Nelson Thornes	Turquoise Set A	7
Monkeys	Pathways to Literacy	Collins	Year 2	10
Monkeys and Apes	PM Non-fiction	Nelson Thornes	Turquoise Level	8
Monster Eyeballs	Blue Bananas	Mammoth	Wilson, Jacqueline	6
Monster in the Cave, The	Lighthouse	Ginn	Turquoise: 7	7
Monster in the Cupboard, The	Storyworld Bridges	Heinemann	Stage 10	9
Monster in the Wardrobe, The	Oxford Reading Tree	OUP	TreeTops Stage 13: Pack C	11
Monster is Coming! The	Rigby Star	Rigby	Gold Level	9
Monster of Mirror Mountain, The	Literacy Links Plus	Kingscourt	Fluent C	8
Monster on the Street, A – Part 1	Literacy Land	Longmans	Story Street: Step 7	9
Monster on the Street, A – Part 2	Literacy Land	Longmans	Story Street: Step 7	9
Monster Raps	Crunchies	Orchard	Raps	11
Moon and the Mirror, The	Literacy Links Plus Topic	Kingscourt	Fluent C	8
Moonlit Owl, The	Cambridge Reading	CUP	Y1 B: Narrative Recount	7
Moppet on the Run	PM Storybooks	Nelson Thornes	Purple Set A	8
More Macdonalds	Literacy Land	Longmans	Story Street: Step 8	10
More! More! More!	Story Chest	Kingscourt	Stage 7	10
Morning Star	Literacy Links Plus	Kingscourt	Fluent A	8
Most Brilliant Trick Ever, The	Sprinters	Walker	Allen, Judy	11
Motorway, The	Oxford Reading Tree	OUP	Stage 7: More Owls	7
Mountain Rescue	All Aboard	Ginn	Stage 8: Sam & Rosie	9
Mouse Flute	Blue Bananas	Mammoth		10
Mouse Magic	Rockets	A&C Black	Smith, Wendy	9
Mouse Stone, The	Lighthouse	Ginn	Purple: 5	8
Moustachio's Best Magic Trick	Tristars	Horwitz Gardner	Stage A	10
Mr Archimedes' Bath	Individual Titles	Picture Puffin	Allen, Pamela	8
Mr Croc's Clock	Rockets	A&C Black	Rodgers, Frank	8
Mr Croc's Silly Sock	Rockets	A&C Black	Rodgers, Frank	8
Mr Croc's Walk	Rockets	A&C Black	Rodgers, Frank	9
Mr Stofflees and the Painted Tiger	Oxford Reading Tree	OUP	TreeTops Stage 10: Pack A	9
Mrs Dippy and her Amazing Inventions	Literacy World	Heinemann	Stage 1	10
Mrs Pepperpot's Pet	Literacy Links Plus	Kingscourt	Fluent B	8
Muddled Monsters, The	Rockets	A&C Black	Anderson, Scoular	8
Muffin is Trapped	PM Storybooks	Nelson Thornes	Purple Set B	8
Mum's New Car	Oxford Reading Tree	OUP	Stage 7: More Robins	9
Mungle Flap, The	Oxford RT Rhyme & Analogy	OUP	Story Rhymes: Pack A	7
My Cat Likes to Hide in Boxes	Individual Titles	Picture Puffin	Sutton, Eve	7
My Diary by Fairy Godmother	Alphakids	Horwitz Gardner	Extending Level 20	8
My Friend Mandela	Oxford Reading Tree	OUP	TreeTops Stage 10/11: True Stories	10
My Grandpa Plants the Rainforest	Alphakids Plus	Horwitz Gardner	Transitional Level 17	7
My Home	Oxford RT Rhyme & Analogy	OUP	Story Rhymes: Pack B	11
My Journey Around the World	Oxford Literacy Web	OUP	Non-fiction: Toys	9
My Secret Pet	Pathways to Literacy	Collins	Year 2	6
My Shells	Alphakids	Horwitz Gardner	Transitional Level 16	6
My Street	Alphakids	Horwitz Gardner	Transitional Level 16	6
My Toys, Gran's Toys	Oxford Literacy Web	OUP	Non-fiction: Toys	6
My Two Families	PM Storybooks	Nelson Thornes	Silver Set A	10
Mystery Man, The	Rigby Star	Rigby	Star Plus	10
Mystery of Cocos Gold, The	Oxford Reading Tree	OUP	TreeTops Stage 10/11: True Stories	10
Mystery of Mrs Kim, The	Rigby Star	Rigby	Star Plus	10

TITLE	SERIES	PUBLISHER	SET (OR AUTHOR)	BAND
N				
Names and Games	All Aboard	Ginn	Stage 9: Play	9
Nappies	Book Project Non-fiction A	Longman	Babies	9
Native Americans	Explorers	Kingscourt	Set 1	10
Natural Disasters	Alphakids	Horwitz Gardner	Extending Level 19	8
Nelly the Monster-sitter	Oxford Reading Tree	OUP	TreeTops More All Stars: Pack 2A	10
Nelson Gets a Fright	PM Storybooks	Nelson Thornes	Purple Set A	8
Nelson is Kidnapped	PM Storybooks	Nelson Thornes	Silver Set A	10
Nelson the Baby Elephant	PM Storybooks	Nelson Thornes	Turquoise Set A	7
Nesting Place, The	PM Storybooks	Nelson Thornes	Turquoise Set C	7
Nests and Shelters	First Explorers	Kingscourt	Level 1	8
Never Bored on Boards	Literacy Links Plus	Kingscourt	Fluent B	10
New Reader Plays 1	Book Project	Longman	Fiction Band 5	9
New Reader Plays 2	Book Project	Longman	Fiction Band 6	10
New Reader Plays 3	Book Project	Longman	Fiction Band 7	10
New School for Megan, A	PM Storybooks	Nelson Thornes	Purple Set B	8
New School, A	Literacy Land	Longmans	Story Street: Step 8	9
News on Shoes	Storyteller	Kingscourt	Set 9	9
Newts	All Aboard	Ginn	Stage 5: Non-fiction	8
Nibbles	Cambridge Reading	CUP	Bridging Books	8
Night of the Ticklers, The	Oxford Reading Tree	OUP	TreeTops Stage 14: Pack B	11
Night to Remember, A	Sprinters	Walker	Sheldon, Dyan	10
Night Walk, The	PM Storybooks	Nelson Thornes	Gold Set C	9
Nightmare Neighbours	Pathways to Literacy	Collins	Year 3	10
No Need for Words	Infosteps	Kingscourt	Set 1	10
No Space to Waste	Storyteller	Kingscourt	Set 9	9
No Tights for George!	Sprinters	Walker	Crebbin, June	11
Noah's Ark	Cambridge Reading	CUP	Y2: Non-fiction	10
Nognapped	All Aboard	Ginn	Stage 9: Short Stories	8
Noisy Toys	Book Project Non-fiction A	Longman	Toys	9
Nonsense!	Cambridge Reading	CUP	Y2 A: Poetry	9
Number Plates	PM Storybooks	Nelson Thornes	Turquoise Set B	7
Nut Map, The	Blue Bananas	Mammoth		10
Nutty as a Noodle Stories	Literacy World	Heinemann	Stage 1	10
Nyamia and the Bag of Gold	Book Project	Longman	Fiction Band 7	7
O				
Ocean Adventure!	Oxford Reading Tree	OUP	Stage 9: True Stories	10
Ocean Explorers	Infosteps	Kingscourt	Set 1	11
Ocean Flight Adventure	Tristars	Horwitz Gardner	Stage B	11
Odd Job for Bob and Benny, An	Oxford Reading Tree	OUP	TreeTops Stage 10/11: Pack B	11
Off to the Shop	Storyteller	Kingscourt	Set 6	6
Oh, Columbus!	Literacy Links Plus	Kingscourt	Fluent B	8
Oi! Get Off Our Train	Individual Titles	Red Fox	Burningham, John	7
Okay Spanner, You Win!	Oxford Reading Tree	OUP	TreeTops Stage 14: Pack B	11
Old Friends, New Friends	Literacy Land	Longmans	Story Street: Step 11	11
Old Hat New Hat	Individual Titles	Harper Collins	Berenstain, Stan	6
Old King Cole Played in Goal	Crunchies	Orchard	Seriously Silly Rhymes	7
Old Vase, The	Oxford Reading Tree	OUP	Stage 7: Robins	8
Old Woman Who Lived in a Vinegar Bottle, The	All Aboard	Ginn	Stage 10: Play	10
Oliver Sundew, Tooth Fairy	Sprinters	Walker	McBratney, Sam	10
Ollie	Cambridge Reading	CUP	Y3 Independent Reading	11

TITLE	SERIES	PUBLISHER	SET (OR AUTHOR)	BAND
Olympics, The	National Geographic	Rigby	Gold Level	10
On Safari	National Geographic	Rigby	Gold Level	10
On the Move	First Explorers	Kingscourt	Level 1	8
On the Move	The News	Horwitz Gardner		11
On the Way Home	Individual Titles	Walker	Murphy, Jill	9
Once There Were Giants	Individual Titles	Walker	Waddell, Martin	7
One Puzzled Parrot	Pathways to Literacy	Collins	Year 2	6
Only an Octopus	Literacy Links Plus	Kingscourt	Early C	6
Oogly Gum Chasing Game, The	Literacy Links Plus	Kingscourt	Fluent B	7
Open Wide, Wilbur!	Crunchies	Orchard	Colour Crackers	9
Oranges	What's for Lunch?	Franklin Watts	Claire Llewellyn	9
Oscar and Tatiana	Literacy Links Plus Topic	Kingscourt	Fluent B	9
Oscar Got the Blame	Individual Titles	Red Fox	Ross, Tony	6
Osprey	Cambridge Reading	CUP	Y1: Non-fiction	6
Our Changing Planet	Infosteps	Kingscourt	Set 1	10
Our Digital Holiday	Spotlight on Fact	Collins	Y2: The Seaside	11
Our Old Friend Bear	PM Storybooks	Nelson Thornes	Silver Set C	10
Our Place in Space	Infosteps	Kingscourt	Set 1	11
Outing, The	Oxford Reading Tree	OUP	Stage 6: Owls	7
Over on the Farm	Individual Titles	Random House	Gunson, Christopher	7
Over the Rainbow	Oxford Reading Tree	OUP	TreeTops Stage 12: True Stories	10
Over the Stile and Into the Sack	Crunchies	Orchard	Twice Upon a Time	8
Owl	Pathways to Literacy	Collins	Year 2	7
Owl Babies	Individual Titles	Walker	Waddell, Martin	8
Owl in the House	Blue Bananas	Mammoth		10
Owls	PM Non-fiction	Nelson Thornes	Gold Level	9
Owls in the Garden	PM Storybooks	Nelson Thornes	Gold Set A	9
Ozlo's Beard	Lighthouse	Ginn	Purple: 1	8
P				
Packing for A Holiday	Spotlight on Fact	Collins	Y2: The Seaside	7
Painting with Poster Paint	All Aboard	Ginn	Stage 8: Non-fiction	8
Pandas in the Mountains	PM Storybooks	Nelson Thornes	Gold Set C	9
Pandora's Box	Storyteller	Kingscourt	Set 8	8
Paper	Find Out About	Franklin Watts		9
Pappy Mashy	Sprinters	Walker	Henderson, Kathy	10
Parachutes	Storyteller	Kingscourt	Set 7	7
Parrot Talk	Cambridge Reading	CUP	Y2 A: Familiar Settings	8
Party Food	Book Project Non-fiction A	Longman	Food	9
Pass the Ball, Grandad	Oxford Reading Tree	OUP	TreeTops Stage 12: Pack C	11
Passenger Ships Now and Fifty Years Ago	Book Project Non-fiction A	Longman	History of Transport	9
Patrick	Individual Titles	Harper Collins	Blake, Quentin	8
Patrick and the Fox	Oxford Reading Tree	OUP	Jackdaws Anthologies	10
Patrick and the Leprechaun	PM Storybooks	Nelson Thornes	Gold Set B	9
Patrick's Perfect Pet	Sprinters	Walker	McAfee, Annalena	10
Peace Ring, The	Cambridge Reading	CUP	Y2 B: Fantasy Worlds	9
Peanut Prankster, The	Rockets	A&C Black	Wallace, Karen	10
Peanuts	Star Quest	Rigby	Purple Level	7
Peanuts	What's for Lunch?	Franklin Watts	Claire Llewellyn	8
Peas	What's for Lunch?	Franklin Watts	Claire Llewellyn	9
Pedal Power	Star Quest	Rigby	Purple Level	8
Pedlar's Caps, The	PM Storybooks	Nelson Thornes	Purple Set A	8

TITLE	SERIES	PUBLISHER	SET (OR AUTHOR)	BAND
Peg	Blue Bananas	Mammoth	Stewart, Maddie	10
Penny Whistle Pete	Pathways to Literacy	Collins	Year 3: Fiction	10
People and Places	First Explorers	Kingscourt	Level 2	8
People Live in the Desert	National Geographic	Rigby	Green Level	6
Percy the Pink	Starters	Walker	West, Colin	8
Perfect Pirate's Present, The	Tristars	Horwitz Gardner	Stage A	10
Perfect Pizza, The	Rigby Star	Rigby	Turquoise Level	7
Perfect Pizza, The	Rockets	A&C Black	Anderson, Scoular	8
Personality Potion, The	Oxford Reading Tree	OUP	TreeTops Stage 13: Pack B	11
Personality Potion, The	Oxford Reading Tree	OUP	TreeTops Stage 13: Playscripts	11
Pet Squad	Oxford Reading Tree	OUP	TreeTops Stage 12–14: Pack A	11
Pet Tarantula, The	Storyteller	Kingscourt	Set 9	9
Petshop Problem, A	Tristars	Horwitz Gardner	Stage A	10
Phew, Sidney!	Crunchies	Orchard	Colour Crackers	9
Philippa and the Dragon	Literacy Links Plus	Kingscourt	Early C	6
Photograph, The	Oxford Reading Tree	OUP	Stage 9: Robins	9
Picked for the Team	PM Storybooks	Nelson Thornes	Gold Set C	9
Picky Prince, The	Rigby Star	Rigby	White Level	10
Pie Thief, The	Story Chest	Kingscourt	Stage 6	9
Piece of Cake, A	Individual Titles	Walker	Murphy, Jill	9
Pied Piper of Hamelin, The	Oxford RT Branch Library	OUP	Traditional Tales	8
Pied Piper, The	Pathways to Literacy	Collins	Year 3: Play	10
Pied Piper, The	Storyworlds	Heinemann	Stage 7: Once Upon a Time	6
Pig in the Pond, The	Individual Titles	Walker	Waddell, Martin	7
Pigs	PM Non-fiction	Nelson Thornes	Purple Level	9
Pig's Skin	Alphakids	Horwitz Gardner	Extending Level 22	9
Pioneer Girl	Oxford Reading Tree	OUP	Stage 10: True Stories	10
Pipe Down, Prudle!	Crunchies	Orchard	Colour Crackers	8
Pirate Gold	Oxford Literacy Web	OUP	Stage 9: Variety	10
Pirate School – Just a Bit of Wind	Individual Titles	Colour Young Puffin	Strong, Jeremy	9
Pirate School – The Birthday Bash	Individual Titles	Colour Young Puffin	Strong, Jeremy	9
Pit-a-Pat-a-Parrot	Oxford Literacy Web	OUP	Poetry Stages: 1–5	6
Pizza	Individual Titles	Wayland	Moses, Brian	10
Pizza For Dinner	Literacy Links Plus	Kingscourt	Early C	6
Places to Visit	Spotlight on Fact	Collins	Y2: The Seaside	9
Planets, The	All Aboard	Ginn	Stage 8: Non-fiction	9
Planning a Party	All Aboard	Ginn	Stage 6: Non-fiction	10
Plants	Go Facts	A&C Black	Plants	10
Plants All Round	First Explorers	Kingscourt	Level 1	8
Plants as Food	Go Facts	A&C Black	Plants	10
Plastic	Find Out About	Franklin Watts		10
Platypus	Individual Titles	Viking	Riddell, Chris	8
Playroom, The	Oxford Reading Tree	OUP	More Jackdaws Anthologies	11
Plays 4 for New Readers	Book Project	Longman	Fiction Band 8	11
Please Do Not Drop Your Jelly Beans	Storyteller	Kingscourt	Set 7	7
Please Don't Sneeze!	Storyteller	Kingscourt	Set 6	7
Please Stop Barking	Tristars	Horwitz Gardner	Stage A	9
Plum Magic	All Aboard	Ginn	Stage 6: Sam & Rosie	6
Pocket Full of Pie, A	All Aboard	Ginn	Stage 9: Poetry	10
Pocket Money	Oxford Reading Tree	OUP	Stage 8: More Magpies	8
Poems are Crazy	Literacy Land	Longmans	Genre Range – Competent	11

TITLE	SERIES	PUBLISHER	SET (OR AUTHOR)	BAND
Poems are Noisy	Literacy Land	Longmans	Genre Range – Competent	11
Poems are Quiet	Literacy Land	Longmans	Genre Range – Competent	11
Poems to Perform	Pelican Guided Reading	Longman	Y3 T2	11
Polar Bears	PM Non-fiction	Nelson Thornes	Silver Level	10
Polecat Caf…, The	Sprinters	Walker	Llewellyn, Sam	11
Poles Apart	Rigby Star	Rigby	Purple Level	8
Poles Apart	Literacy Land	Longmans	Info Trail – Competent	11
Pollution	Alphakids	Horwitz Gardner	Extending Level 21	9
Polly the Most Poetic Person	Crunchies	Orchard	The One And Only	8
Ponds and Rivers	First Explorers	Kingscourt	Level 1	8
Pookie and Joe	Literacy Links Plus Topic	Kingscourt	Fluent D	7
Popular Pets	Tristars	Horwitz Gardner	Stage A	10
Posh Party, The	Rockets	A&C Black	Anderson, Scoular	9
Posh Watson	Sprinters	Walker	Cross, Gillian	11
Potatoes	What's for Lunch?	Franklin Watts	Claire Llewellyn	9
Potty Panto, The	Rockets	A&C Black	Anderson, Scoular	9
Poupette	Book Project	Longman	Fiction Band 7	10
Power-packed Plants	Infosteps	Kingscourt	Set 1	10
Precious Potter	Crunchies	Orchard	Colour Crackers	8
Predators	Alphakids	Horwitz Gardner	Transitional Level 16	7
Present for Dad, A	Alphakids	Horwitz Gardner	Extending Level 22	9
Present for Our Teacher, A	AlphaWorld	Horwitz Gardner	Band 6: Orange	6
Princess Jo	Alphakids Plus	Horwitz Gardner	Transitional Level 17	6
Princess Smartypants	Individual Titles	Puffin	Cole, Babette	9
Promise You Won't Be Cross	Blue Bananas	Mammoth		9
Proper Bike, A	Oxford Reading Tree	OUP	Stage 9: Robins	8
Proper Princess Test, The	Cambridge Reading	CUP	Y3 Independent Reading	11
Psid and Bolter	Oxford Reading Tree	OUP	TreeTops All Stars: Pack 3	10
Pterosaur's Long Flight	PM Storybooks	Nelson Thornes	Orange Set B	6
Pumpkin House, The	Literacy Links Plus	Kingscourt	Fluent B	7
Pumpkin Man, The	Crunchies	Orchard	Little Horrors	9
Puppy Chase, The	Cambridge Reading	CUP	Bridging Books	6
Purple Buttons	Oxford Reading Tree	OUP	TreeTops Stage 10/11: Pack B	9
Pushcart Team	PM Non-Fiction	Nelson Thornes	Emerald	11
Puss-in-Boots	Literacy Links Plus	Kingscourt	Traditional Tales	8
Puss-in-Boots	PM Traditional Tales	Nelson Thornes	Purple Level	8
Pussy Cat, Pussy Cat	Cambridge Reading	CUP	Y3 Independent Reading	11
Putting on a Magic Show	All Aboard	Ginn	Stage 7: Non-fiction	9
Puzzling Shapes	Oxford Reading Tree	OUP	Cross-curricular Jackdaws	11
Pyjama Party, The	Cambridge Reading	CUP	Y2 B: Familiar Settings	9
Pyjama Party, The	Cambridge Reading	CUP	Y2: Playscripts	8
Q				
Quackers	Literacy World	Heinemann	Comets	11
Quarrel, The	Oxford Reading Tree	OUP	Citizenship Stories: Stage 9/10	9
Queen of the Pool	PM Chapter Books	Nelson Thornes	Emerald Set A	11
Queen Victoria	Famous People, Famous Lives	Franklin Watts	Famous Leaders	10
Queen's Knickers, The	Individual Titles	Red Fox	Allen, N	10
Queen's Parrot, The	Literacy Links Plus	Kingscourt	Early D	6
Quest for the Golden See-Saw, The	Oxford Reading Tree	OUP	TreeTops Stage 13+: Pack D	11
Quest, The	Oxford Reading Tree	OUP	Stage 9: Magpies	9
Quork Attack	Rigby Star	Rigby	Star Plus	11

TITLE	SERIES	PUBLISHER	SET (OR AUTHOR)	BAND
R				
R.S.P.C.A.	Tristars	Horwitz Gardner	Stage B	10
Rabbits	Literacy Links Plus	Kingscourt	Fluent D	11
Rabbits and Their Young	Book Project Non-fiction A	Longman	Animals	8
Rabbit's Surprise Birthday	Rigby Star	Rigby	Purple Level	8
Rabbit's Tail	Cambridge Reading	CUP	Y2 A: Range of Cultures	9
Race to Green End, The	PM Storybooks	Nelson Thornes	Turquoise Set C	7
Race to the Pole	National Geographic	Rigby	White Level	10
Rachel Versus Bonecrusher the Mighty	Book Project	Longman	Fiction Band 8	10
Rachel and the Difference Thief	Book Project	Longman	Fiction Band 8	10
Rachel's Mysterious Drawings	Cambridge Reading	CUP	Y3 Independent Reading	11
Racing Pigeons	All Aboard	Ginn	Stage 5: Non-fiction	6
Racoons	PM Non-fiction	Nelson Thornes	Gold Level	9
Rain Arrow, The	Pathways to Literacy	Collins	Year 2	7
Rain Forest, The	National Geographic	Rigby	Purple Level	9
Rain or Shine	Explorers	Kingscourt	Set 1	10
Rainbow Adventure, The	Oxford Reading Tree	OUP	Stage 8: Magpies	8
Rainbow Machine, The	Oxford Reading Tree	OUP	Stage 8: Playscripts	7
Rainbows All Around	Skyrider	Collins	Yellow	9
Rainforest Life	First Explorers	Kingscourt	Level 2	9
Rama and the Demon King	Individual Titles	Frances Lincoln	Souhami, Jessica	10
Rapunzel	Individual Titles	Macdonald	Reeves, James	11
Rapunzel	Literacy Links Plus	Kingscourt	Fluent D	10
Rat for Mouse, A	Literacy Land	Longmans	Story Street: Step 7	8
Rat Hunt, The	Literacy Land	Longmans	Story Street: Step 10	9
Rather Small Turnip, The	Crunchies	Orchard	Seriously Silly Stories	10
Real Princess, The	Alphakids	Horwitz Gardner	Extending Level 19	8
Rebecca and the Concert	PM Storybooks	Nelson Thornes	Orange Set C	6
Red Fox Dances	Individual Titles	Walker	Baron, Alan	7
Red Planet	Oxford Reading Tree	OUP	Stage 7: Owls	7
Red Riding Hood	Pathways to Literacy	Collins	Year 2	6
Reference Book of Water and Weather	Book Project Non-fiction B	Longman	Water	11
Reptiles	Go Facts	A&C Black	Animals	9
Rescue!	Lighthouse	Ginn	Purple: 6	8
Rescue!	Oxford Reading Tree	OUP	Stage 9: More Magpies	8
Rescuing Nelson	PM Storybooks	Nelson Thornes	Turquoise Set B	7
Return of the Killer Coat	Sprinters	Walker	Gates, Susan	11
Revenge of Captain Blood, The	Oxford Reading Tree	OUP	TreeTops Stage 13: Pack C	11
Rhode Island Roy	Crunchies	Orchard	Colour Crackers	9
Rhyming Poems	Genre Range	Longman	Beginner Poetry	9
Rhyming Princess, The	Storyteller	Kingscourt	Set 8	8
Rhyming Russell	Individual Titles	Collins Jets	Thomson, Pat	10
Rice	Literacy Links Plus Topic	Kingscourt	Early D	6
Rice	National Geographic	Rigby	Gold Level	9
Rice	What's for Lunch?	Franklin Watts	Claire Llewellyn	8
Rice Cakes	Literacy Links Plus	Kingscourt	Early D	6
Riddle of Redstone Castle, The	Tristars	Horwitz Gardner	Stage B	10
Riddle of Redstone Ruins, The	Tristars	Horwitz Gardner	Stage B	10
Riding High	PM Storybooks	Nelson Thornes	Purple Set C	8
Riding to Craggy Rock	PM Storybooks	Nelson Thornes	Turquoise Set C	7
Riff-Raff Rabbit	Blue Bananas	Mammoth	Ritchie, Alison	7

TITLE	SERIES	PUBLISHER	SET (OR AUTHOR)	BAND
Right Place for Jupiter, The	PM Storybooks	Nelson Thornes	Silver Set C	10
Rise and Shine	Individual Titles	Hodder Wayland	Godwin, Sam	8
Road Safety	Discovery World Links	Heinemann	Stage D	7
Road Signs	All Aboard	Ginn	Stage 4: Non-fiction	7
Robbie Woods and his Merry Men	Oxford Reading Tree	OUP	TreeTops Stage 12: Pack B	11
Robert, the Rose Horse	Beginner Books	Collins	Heilbroner, Joan	6
Robin Hood	Oxford Reading Tree	OUP	Stage 6: Owls	6
Robin Hood and the Silver Trophy	PM Traditional Tales	Nelson Thornes	Silver Level	10
Robin Hood Raps	Crunchies	Orchard	Raps	10
Robin Redbreasts and Their Young	Book Project Non-fiction A	Longman	Animals	9
Robodog and the Big Dig, The	Individual Titles	Colour Young Puffin	Rodgers, Frank	8
Robot World	All Aboard	Ginn	Stage 7: Non-fiction	9
Rock and Stone	Find Out About	Franklin Watts		9
Rock Hunters	Infosteps	Kingscourt	Set 1	10
Rockets	Oxford RT Branch Library	OUP	Oxford Reds: Pack A	10
Rockpool Rap	Oxford RT Rhyme & Analogy	OUP	Story Rhymes: Pack B	10
Roller Blade Run, The	PM Storybooks	Nelson Thornes	Purple Set A	8
Roller Blades for Luke	PM Storybooks	Nelson Thornes	Orange Set C	6
Roller Coaster	All Aboard	Ginn	Stage 5: Non-fiction	7
Rollercoaster	Rigby Star	Rigby	Gold Level	9
Roman Adventure	Oxford Reading Tree	OUP	Stage 7: More Owls	7
Romans Go Home!	Literacy Land	Longmans	Info Trail – Competent	9
Ronald the Tough Sheep	Oxford Reading Tree	OUP	TreeTops All Stars: Pack 3	9
Ronnie and the Giant Millipede	Sprinters	Walker	Nimmo, Jenny	10
Rosie and the Robbers	Blue Bananas	Mammoth		10
Rosie Moon	Alphakids	Horwitz Gardner	Extending Level 18	6
Rosie's House	Literacy Links Plus	Kingscourt	Fluent C	7
Rotten Apples	Oxford Reading Tree	OUP	Stage 6: More Owls	6
Round the World Cookbook	Book Project Non-fiction A	Longman	Food	9
Rover Goes to School	Rockets	A&C Black	Powling, Chris	9
Rover Shows Off	Rockets	A&C Black	Powling, Chris	9
Rover the Champion	Rockets	A&C Black	Powling, Chris	9
Rover's Birthday	Rockets	A&C Black	Powling, Chris	9
Royal Raps	Crunchies	Orchard	Raps	9
Royal Roar, The	Rockets	A&C Black	Rodgers, Frank	9
Ruby the Rudest Girl	Crunchies	Orchard	The One And Only	7
Rumpelstiltskin	Literacy Links Plus	Kingscourt	Traditional Tales	7
Rumpelstiltskin	PM Traditional Tales	Nelson Thornes	Gold Level	9
Rumply Crumply Stinky Pin	Crunchies	Orchard	Seriously Silly Stories	11
Runaway Cakes and Skipalong Pots	Crunchies	Orchard	Twice Upon a Time	7
Runaway Fred	Blue Bananas	Mammoth		9
Rupert Goes to School	Storyteller	Kingscourt	Set 9	9
S				
Sally's Surprise Garden	Literacy Links Plus Topic	Kingscourt	Early C	6
Salmon's Journey, The	Oxford Literacy Web	OUP	Non-fiction: Animals	8
Sam and the Firefly	Beginner Books	Collins	Eastman, P D	7
Sam Runs Away	Literacy Land	Longmans	Story Street: Step 8	9
Sam's Dad	Storyteller	Kingscourt	Set 9	9
Sam's New Flat	Literacy Land	Longmans	Story Street: Step 9	11
Sam's Snacks	Cambridge Reading	CUP	Bridging Books	7
Sand Man, The	Crunchies	Orchard	Little Horrors	9

TITLE	SERIES	PUBLISHER	SET (OR AUTHOR)	BAND
Sand Tiger, The	Book Project	Longman	Fiction Band 8	11
Sand Witch, The	Oxford Reading Tree	OUP	TreeTops All Stars: Pack 1	9
Sandwich Hero, The	Literacy Links Plus Topic	Kingscourt	Fluent A	9
Sandwich Scam, The	Rockets	A&C Black	Wallace, Karen	9
Sarah and the Barking Dog	PM Storybooks	Nelson Thornes	Orange Set B	6
Sarah's Pet	Storyteller	Kingscourt	Set 7	7
Sausage	Oxford Reading Tree	OUP	TreeTops All Stars: Pack 2	10
Sausage and the Little Visitor	Rockets	A&C Black	Morgan, Michaela	7
Sausage and the Spooks	Rockets	A&C Black	Morgan, Michaela	7
Sausage in Trouble	Rockets	A&C Black	Morgan, Michaela	7
Save Floppy!	Oxford Reading Tree	OUP	Stage 8: More Magpies	8
Saving the Yellow Eye	Skyrider	Collins	Yellow	11
Saving Up	AlphaWorld	Horwitz Gardner	Band 6: Orange	6
Scaly Things	Explorers	Kingscourt	Set 1	10
Scare-kid	Literacy Links Plus	Kingscourt	Fluent A	9
Scarface Claw	Individual Titles	Puffin	Dodd, Linley	10
Scary Raps	Crunchies	Orchard	Raps	11
Scat, Cat!	Oxford RT Rhyme & Analogy	OUP	Story Rhymes: Pack A	8
School Concert, The	Rigby Star	Rigby	Star Plus	10
School Days, Cool Days	Storyteller	Kingscourt	Set 8	8
School for Sausage	Rockets	A&C Black	Morgan, Michaela	7
School News, The	Alphakids	Horwitz Gardner	Transitional Level 16	6
School Play, The	Oxford Reading Tree	OUP	More Jackdaws Anthologies	10
Science Dictionary	Discovery World	Heinemann	Stage F	9
Scots Pine, The	Cambridge Reading	CUP	Y1: Non-fiction	7
Scrapman	Oxford Reading Tree	OUP	TreeTops Stage 12: Pack B	11
Scrapman and Scrapcat	Oxford Reading Tree	OUP	TreeTops Stage 12+: Pack D	11
Scrapman and the Incredible Flying Machine	Oxford Reading Tree	OUP	TreeTops Stage 12+: Pack F	11
Scrub-A-Dub	Pathways to Literacy	Collins	Year 3	11
Sculpture	Storyteller	Kingscourt	Set 9	9
Sea Empress Disaster	Oxford Reading Tree	OUP	TreeTops Stage 10/11:True Stories	11
Sea Otters	Storyteller	Kingscourt	Set 10	10
Sea Stars	Alphakids	Horwitz Gardner	Transitional Level 17	6
Seagull Sweaters	Book Project	Longman	Fiction Band 8	10
Seahorses	Alphakids Plus	Horwitz Gardner	Transitional Level 14	6
Search for Tutankhamen, The	Literacy World	Heinemann	Stage 1	11
Seashore Crabs	Alphakids Plus	Horwitz Gardner	Transitional Level 16	7
Seaside, The	Oxford Reading Tree	OUP	Cross-curricular Jackdaws	9
Seat Belt Song, The	PM Storybooks	Nelson Thornes	Turquoise Set B	7
Sebastian Tidies Up	Alphakids	Horwitz Gardner	Extending Level 18	7
Sebastian's Special Present	Alphakids	Horwitz Gardner	Transitional Level 15	7
Secret Cave, The	Oxford Reading Tree	OUP	More Jackdaws Anthologies	11
Secret Cupboard, The	Tristars	Horwitz Gardner	Stage B	10
Secret Hideaway, The	PM Storybooks	Nelson Thornes	Gold Set A	9
Secret Plans, The	Oxford Reading Tree	OUP	Stage 10: Robins	8
Secret, The	PM Chapter Books	Nelson Thornes	Emerald Set A	11
Secret, The	Rigby Star	Rigby	Star Plus	10
Secrets Tree, The	All Aboard	Ginn	Stage 10: Novel	11
Seeds on the Move	AlphaWorld	Horwitz Gardner	Band 7: Turquoise	6
Seiko the Watchdog	Storyteller	Kingscourt	Set 11	11
Selfish Giant, The	Literacy Links Plus	Kingscourt	Fluent C	10

TITLE	SERIES	PUBLISHER	SET (OR AUTHOR)	BAND
Sending Messages	Alphakids	Horwitz Gardner	Extending Level 23	10
Sense This	First Explorers	Kingscourt	Level 1	8
Serve Me, Stefan	Oxford Literacy Web	OUP	Stage 9: Variety	10
Seven Foolish Fishermen	PM Traditional Tales	Nelson Thornes	Gold Level	9
Shadow Dance, The	Book Project	Longman	Fiction Band 5	9
Shake, Rattle and Roll	Pathways to Literacy	Collins	Year 3: Non-fiction	10
Shampoozal	Crunchies	Orchard	Seriously Silly Stories	10
Shapes of Water, The	Skyrider	Collins	Yellow	10
Shark with no Teeth, The	Storyworld Plays	Heinemann	Stage 8	6
Sharks	Alphakids Plus	Horwitz Gardner	Transitional Level 17	7
Sharks	Oxford RT Branch Library	OUP	Oxford Reds: Pack A	9
Sharks and Rays	Explorers	Kingscourt	Set 1	10
Sheep	PM Non-fiction	Nelson Thornes	Purple Level	9
Shelley Holmes, Ace Detective	Oxford Reading Tree	OUP	TreeTops Stage 12: Pack C	11
Shelley Holmes, Animal Trainer	Oxford Reading Tree	OUP	TreeTops Stage 12+: Pack F	10
Shiny Key, The	Oxford Reading Tree	OUP	Stage 6: More Owls	6
Shipwreck	All Aboard	Ginn	Stage 8: Non-fiction	9
Shoes	Pathways to Literacy	Collins	Year 2	7
Shoo, Fly!	Storyteller	Kingscourt	Set 6	6
Shooter Shrinker, The	Alphakids	Horwitz Gardner	Extending Level 23	10
Shooting Star, The	PM Storybooks	Nelson Thornes	Gold Set C	9
Shopping List, The	Storyteller	Kingscourt	Set 6	6
Short Pants	Spotlight on Plays	Collins	Age 8+	11
Shrinking Mouse	Individual Titles	Red Fox	Hutchins, Pat	7
Shut in the Barn	Alphakids Plus	Horwitz Gardner	Transitional Level 15	6
Sidetracked Sam	Literacy Links Plus Topic	Kingscourt	Fluent B	7
Silent World, A	Literacy Links Plus Topic	Kingscourt	Fluent C	11
Silly Billy	Individual Titles	Random House	Hutchins, Pat	7
Silly Sons and Dozy Daughters	Crunchies	Orchard	Twice Upon a Time	9
Silva the Seal	Alphakids Plus	Horwitz Gardner	Transitional Level 15	6
Silver and Prince	PM Storybooks	Nelson Thornes	Silver Set C	10
Simple Rhyming Dictionary, A	Pelican Big Books	Longman	Palmer, Sue	6
Simple Solution!	Literacy Links Plus Topic	Kingscourt	Fluent A	8
Singing Princess, The	Rigby Star	Rigby	White Level	10
Sir Andrew the Brave	Alphakids	Horwitz Gardner	Extending Level 21	8
Skate Rider	Alphakids Plus	Horwitz Gardner	Transitional Level 16	7
Skateboarding	PM Non-Fiction	Nelson Thornes	Emerald	11
Skating at Rainbow Lake	PM Storybooks	Nelson Thornes	Silver Set B	10
Skeleton on the Bus, The	Literacy Links Plus	Kingscourt	Fluent B	7
Ski Lesson, The	Storyteller	Kingscourt	Set 6	6
Skunks	PM Non-fiction	Nelson Thornes	Gold Level	9
Sky Watch	Explorers	Kingscourt	Set 1	10
Sleeping Beauty	Genre Range	Longman	Emergent Trad Tales	7
Sleeping Beauty, The	PM Traditional Tales	Nelson Thornes	Silver Level	10
Sleepy Sammy	Crunchies	Orchard	Colour Crackers	8
Slinky Malinki	Individual Titles	Picture Puffin	Dodd, Lynley	8
Slugs	All Aboard	Ginn	Stage 5: Non-fiction	6
Sly Fox and Little Red Hen	PM Traditional Tales	Nelson Thornes	Purple Level	8
Smallest Tree, The	Literacy Links Plus	Kingscourt	Fluent D	7
Smudger and the Smelly Fish	Rockets	A&C Black	Ryan, Margaret	10
Smugglers of Mourne, The	Book Project	Longman	Fiction Band 6	9

TITLE	SERIES	PUBLISHER	SET (OR AUTHOR)	BAND
Snail	Stopwatch	A&C Black		9
Snails	Alphakids	Horwitz Gardner	Transitional Level 13	6
Snakes	Oxford RT Branch Library	OUP	Oxford Reds: Pack A	10
Sneaky Deals and Tricky Tricks	Crunchies	Orchard	Twice Upon a Time	8
Sneaky Snake, The	Tristars	Horwitz Gardner	Stage A	9
Snooty Prune	Oxford Reading Tree	OUP	TreeTops Stage 12: Pack C	11
Snow Goes to Town	Literacy Links Plus	Kingscourt	Fluent C	10
Snow Maze, The	Sprinters	Walker	Mark, Jan	9
Snow Queen, The	New Way	Nelson Thornes	Orange Parallel Books	10
Snow Storm, The	Oxford Reading Tree	OUP	More Jackdaws Anthologies	11
Snow White and the Seven Dwarfs	PM Traditional Tales	Nelson Thornes	Gold Level	9
Snowboarding Diary	PM Non-fiction	Nelson Thornes	Emerald	11
Snug as a Bug	Pathways to Literacy	Collins	Year 2	11
Sock Gobbler and Other Stories, The	Skyrider	Collins	Yellow	9
Solo Flyer	PM Storybooks	Nelson Thornes	Gold Set A	9
Solve This!	Storyteller	Kingscourt	Set 8	8
Something Soft for Danny Bear	Literacy Links Plus	Kingscourt	Fluent A	7
Songs, Alphabet & Playground Rhymes	Genre Range	Longman	Emergent Poetry	9
Sonic Sid	All Aboard	Ginn	Stage 7: Sam & Rosie	6
Sounds	Lighthouse	Ginn	Gold: 2	9
Sounds All Round	First Explorers	Kingscourt	Level 2	10
Soup with Obby	Literacy Land	Longmans	Story Street: Step 8	11
Sour Grapes	Alphakids	Horwitz Gardner	Extending Level 21	9
Souvenirs	Literacy Links Plus	Kingscourt	Fluent A	7
Space Adventure	Oxford Reading Tree	OUP	More Jackdaws Anthologies	10
Space Football	Rockets	A&C Black	Smith, Wendy	10
Space Travel	Alphakids	Horwitz Gardner	Transitional Level 15	7
Spanish Omelet	PM Storybooks	Nelson Thornes	Silver Set C	10
Special Cake, The	Cambridge Reading	CUP	Y2 B: Familiar Settings	10
Special Clothes	All Aboard	Ginn	Stage 4: Non-fiction	6
Special Ride, The	PM Storybooks	Nelson Thornes	Gold Set B	9
Speedy's Day Out	All Aboard	Ginn	Stage 5 Set A: Sam & Rosie	6
Spell Shell, The	Oxford RT Rhyme & Analogy	OUP	Story Rhymes: Pack A	10
Spider and Buffalo	Storyteller	Kingscourt	Set 11	11
Spider Man, The	Crunchies	Orchard	Little Horrors	8
Spiders	Oxford RT Branch Library	OUP	Oxford Reds: Pack B	9
Spiders Are Amazing	Oxford Literacy Web	OUP	Non-fiction: Animals	8
Spiders Spin Silk	National Geographic	Rigby	Turquoise Level	9
Spoilt Holiday, The	Oxford Reading Tree	OUP	Jackdaws Anthologies	10
Spooky Riddles	Beginner Books	Collins	Brown, Marc	6
Spooky!	Oxford Reading Tree	OUP	TreeTops Stage 13: Pack C	11
Spooky!	Oxford Reading Tree	OUP	TreeTops Stage 13: Playscripts	11
Sport Rules	The News	Horwitz Gardner		11
Sports for You	The News	Horwitz Gardner		11
Spy on Spiders	First Explorers	Kingscourt	Level 2	10
Squink, The	Oxford Reading Tree	OUP	TreeTops Stage 10: Pack A	8
Squirrels	Storyteller	Kingscourt	Set 9	9
Standing Tall	Storyworld Bridges	Heinemann	Stage 11	11
Star is Born, A	Rockets	A&C Black	Smith, Wendy	9
Star Striker	Storyworld Bridges	Heinemann	Stage 12	11
Star Struck	Oxford Reading Tree	OUP	TreeTops Stage 13+: Pack D	11

TITLE	SERIES	PUBLISHER	SET (OR AUTHOR)	BAND
Staying Alive	Alphakids	Horwitz Gardner	Transitional Level 17	8
Steggie's Way	Literacy World	Heinemann	Stage 1	10
Stella's Staying Put	Crunchies	Orchard	Colour Crackers	8
Stephen and the Family Nose	All Aboard	Ginn	Stage 9: Novel	10
Stick in the Mud	Pathways to Literacy	Collins	Year 3	11
Stone Soup	PM Traditional Tales	Nelson Thornes	Turquoise Level	7
Stop Thief!	Lighthouse	Ginn	Purple: 7	8
Storm at Sea	Storyworld Bridges	Heinemann	Stage 11	11
Storm Castle	Oxford Reading Tree	OUP	Stage 9: Magpies	7
Storm is Coming, A	AlphaWorld	Horwitz Gardner	Band 6: Orange	6
Story of Jeans, The	Discovery World Links	Heinemann	Stage E	9
Story of Running Water, The	Cambridge Reading	CUP	Y1 C: Range of Cultures	7
Story of Running Water, The	Cambridge Reading	CUP	Y1: Playscripts	7
Story of William Tell, The	PM Storybooks	Nelson Thornes	Silver Set C	10
Story Poems	Genre Range	Longman	Emergent Poetry	9
Storytellers	Storyteller	Kingscourt	Set 10	10
Strange Creatures	Skyrider	Collins	Yellow	10
Strange Dream, The	Oxford Literacy Web	OUP	Stage 7: Variety	7
Strange Plants	National Geographic	Rigby	Gold Level	10
Strange Shoe, The	PM Traditional Tales	Nelson Thornes	Silver Level	10
Stranger's Gift, The	Literacy Links Plus Topic	Kingscourt	Fluent D	7
Strawberry Picking	Cambridge Reading	CUP	Y2 A: Familiar Settings	8
Strength in Numbers	Infosteps	Kingscourt	Set 1	9
Stuff-it-in Specials, The	Rockets	A&C Black	Wallace, Karen	9
Stupid Trousers	Oxford Reading Tree	OUP	TreeTops Stage 10: Playscript	9
Stupid Trousers	Oxford Reading Tree	OUP	TreeTops Stage 10: Pack C	9
Submarine Adventure	Oxford Reading Tree	OUP	Stage 6 & 7: More Owls B	7
Sugar and Spice and All Things Nice	Storyteller	Kingscourt	Set 10	10
Summer Fair, The	Oxford Literacy Web	OUP	Stage 8: Duck Green	7
Sun and Moon	Pathways to Literacy	Collins	Year 3	10
Sun, Sand and Space	Rockets	A&C Black	Smith, Wendy	9
Super Sea Birds	Alphakids Plus	Horwitz Gardner	Transitional Level 17	8
SuperDad the Super Hero	Individual Titles	Macdonald	Rayner, Shoo	8
Superdog	Oxford Reading Tree	OUP	Stage 9: Magpies	7
Supersonic Engine Juice	Oxford RT Rhyme & Analogy	OUP	Story Rhymes: Pack A	7
Super-Tuned!	PM Chapter Books	Nelson Thornes	Emerald Set B	11
Surf Carnival, The	PM Storybooks	Nelson Thornes	Purple Set B	8
Surprise Dinner, The	PM Storybooks	Nelson Thornes	Gold Set B	9
Surprise Party	Tristars	Horwitz Gardner	Stage A	10
Surprise, The	Oxford Reading Tree	OUP	Stage 8: More Robins	9
Survival Adventure	Oxford Reading Tree	OUP	Stage 9: Magpies	8
Surviving the Volcano	Literacy Land	Longmans	Info Trail – Fluent	11
Survivors	Infosteps	Kingscourt	Set 1	10
Swamp Man, The	Crunchies	Orchard	Little Horrors	9
Swan Lake	New Way	Nelson Thornes	Orange Parallel Books	10
Swan Rescue	All Aboard	Ginn	Stage 6: Sam & Rosie	6
Sweetcorn	What's for Lunch?	Franklin Watts	Claire Llewellyn	9
Sweets	Book Project Non-fiction A	Longman	Food	8
T				
Tadpole and Frog	Stopwatch	A&C Black		7
Taking Good Holiday Photos	Spotlight on Fact	Collins	Y2: The Seaside	9

TITLE	SERIES	PUBLISHER	SET (OR AUTHOR)	BAND
Taking the Cat's Way Home	Sprinters	Walker	Mark, Jan	10
Tale of a Turban, The	Oxford Literacy Web	OUP	Stage 7: Variety	9
Tale of the Turnip, The	PM Traditional Tales	Nelson Thornes	Orange Level	6
Tale Twisters	Navigator	Rigby	Short Stories - Brown Level	10
Talent Quest, The	PM Storybooks	Nelson Thornes	Silver Set B	10
Tales from the Playground	Lightning	Ginn	Brown Level, Term 1	10
Tales on a Cold Dark Night	Book Project	Longman	Fiction Band 7	11
Tales, Fables and Rhymes	Tristars	Horwitz Gardner	Stage B	11
Talk Back	The News	Horwitz Gardner		11
Tall Tales	PM Chapter Books	Nelson Thornes	Emerald Set A	11
Taming Tessa	Literacy Land	Longmans	Story Street: Step 11	11
Tap into Sap	Infosteps	Kingscourt	Set 1	9
Tarquin the Wonder Horse	Sprinters	Walker	Crebbin, June	11
Tasmanian Devils	PM Non-fiction	Nelson Thornes	Gold Level	9
Tea with Grumpyboots	Literacy Land	Longmans	Story Street: Step 10	10
Teacher, Teacher	Oxford Literacy Web	OUP	Poetry Stages: 1–5	7
Teeny Tiny Teddy, A	Oxford Literacy Web	OUP	Poetry Stages: 1–5	7
Television: Making a Programme	All Aboard	Ginn	Stage 8: Non-fiction	9
Tell Me Another	Pathways to Literacy	Collins	Year 3	9
Tell-tale	Story Chest	Kingscourt	Stage 6	9
Ten Apples Up On Top	Beginner Books	Collins	Le Seig, Theo	7
Terrible Birthday Present, The	Oxford Reading Tree	OUP	TreeTops Stage 12: Pack C	11
Tessa on TV	Oxford Literacy Web	OUP	Stage 9: Variety	9
That's Not My Hobby!	Rigby Star	Rigby	Turquoise Level	7
That's Nothing!	Oxford RT Rhyme & Analogy	OUP	Story Rhymes: Pack B	9
That's the Life!	Storyteller	Kingscourt	Set 6	6
The Jam Street Puzzle	Oxford Reading Tree	OUP	TreeTops All Stars: Pack 3	11
Then and Now	Discovery World Links	Heinemann	Stage D	9
Then and Now	Pathways to Literacy	Collins	Year 2	10
There's No Place Like Home	Skyrider	Collins	Yellow	11
Things with Wings	Storyteller	Kingscourt	Set 10	10
Think About It!	Literacy Land	Longmans	Info Trail – Competent	10
This is the Mum	Oxford Literacy Web	OUP	Poetry Stages: 1–5	6
Thomas Edison	Famous People, Famous Lives	Franklin Watts	Famous Scientists & Inventors	10
Thor's Hammer	Oxford Literacy Web	OUP	Playscripts	11
Those Birds!	Storyteller	Kingscourt	Set 9	9
Those Tricky Animals	Literacy Links Plus Topic	Kingscourt	Fluent A	10
Three Billy Goats Gruff, The	Literacy Links Plus	Kingscourt	Traditional Tales	7
Three Billy Goats Gruff, The	PM Traditional Tales	Nelson Thornes	Orange Level	6
Three by the Sea	Individual Titles	Red Fox	Marshall, James	7
Three Little Pigs, The	PM Traditional Tales	Nelson Thornes	Orange Level	6
Three Magicians, The	Literacy Links Plus	Kingscourt	Fluent D	9
Three Robbers, The	Individual Titles	Roberts Rineherts	Ungerer, Toni	8
Three Sillies, The	Literacy Links Plus	Kingscourt	Fluent C	10
Three Tales	All Aboard	Ginn	Stage 10: Short Stories	11
Three Tales from Scotland	Pathways to Literacy	Collins	Year 3	10
Three Wishes, The	Alphakids Plus	Horwitz Gardner	Transitional Level 16	6
Three Wishes, The	Storyworlds	Heinemann	Stage 8: Once Upon a Time	7
Three-spined Sticklebacks & Their Young	Book Project Non-fiction A	Longman	Animals	8
Tiddalik	Story Chest	Kingscourt	Stage 7	10
Tiger and the Jackal, The	Storyworld Plays	Heinemann	Stage 8	6

TITLE	SERIES	PUBLISHER	SET (OR AUTHOR)	BAND
Tiger and the Jackal, The	Storyworlds	Heinemann	Stage 8: Once Upon a Time	7
Tiger Dreams	Cambridge Reading	CUP	Y1 C: Narrative Recount	8
Tiger Hunt	Rigby Star	Rigby	Gold Level	9
Tiger, Tiger	Pathways to Literacy	Collins	Year 3	10
Tigers	Alphakids Plus	Horwitz Gardner	Transitional Level 13	6
Tigers	Oxford Literacy Web	OUP	Non-fiction: Animals	8
Tillie McGillie's Fantastical Chair	Sprinters	Walker	French, Vivian	10
Time Travellers	Rockets	A&C Black	Smith, Wendy	10
Tina the Tiniest Girl	Crunchies	Orchard	The One And Only	8
Tiny Tim	Crunchies	Orchard	Colour Crackers	9
Titanic Survivor	Oxford Reading Tree	OUP	Stage 11: True Stories	11
To Market, To Market	Infosteps	Kingscourt	Set 1	10
Toad Crossing	All Aboard	Ginn	Stage 8: Sam & Rosie	8
Toads and Their Young	Book Project Non-fiction A	Longman	Animals	9
Toby and BJ	PM Storybooks	Nelson Thornes	Orange Set A	6
Toby and the Accident	PM Storybooks	Nelson Thornes	Turquoise Set A	7
Toby and the Big Red Van	PM Storybooks	Nelson Thornes	Orange Set B	6
Toby and the Big Tree	PM Storybooks	Nelson Thornes	Orange Set A	6
Toby at Sandy Bay	PM Storybooks	Nelson Thornes	Purple Set C	8
Today, August 17, 1929	Tristars	Horwitz Gardner	Stage B	11
Toffee and Marmalade	Oxford Reading Tree	OUP	TreeTops All Stars: Pack 3	10
Toilets	Book Project Non-fiction A	Longman	Homes	9
Toilets Through Time	Info Trail	Longman	Emergent History	9
Tom Thumb and the Football Team	Oxford Reading Tree	OUP	TreeTops More All Stars: Pack 2A	9
Tomb of Nebamun, The	Cambridge Reading	CUP	Y2: Non-fiction	10
Tommy in Trouble	Oxford Literacy Web	OUP	Stage 9: Variety	10
Tommy's Treasure	Literacy Links Plus	Kingscourt	Fluent A	6
Tom's Birthday Treat	Storyworld Bridges	Heinemann	Stage 10	10
Tom's Handplant	Literacy Links Plus	Kingscourt	Fluent B	10
Tom's Hats	Blue Bananas	Mammoth	Amstutz, Andree	9
Tongue Twisters, Limericks …	Genre Range	Longman	Emergent Poetry	9
Tongues	Info Trail	Longman	Emergent Science	8
Tongues	Literacy Links Plus	Kingscourt	Fluent A	10
Tons of Lovely Cakes	Literacy Land	Longmans	Genre Range – Competent	10
Tony and the Butterfly	Literacy Links Plus	Kingscourt	Fluent D	8
Too Many Babies	Crunchies	Orchard	Colour Crackers	8
Too Much Noise	Literacy Links Plus	Kingscourt	Early D	6
Tooth Book, The	Bright and Early Books	Collins	Le Seig, Theo	7
Top Step, The	Pathways to Literacy	Collins	Year 3	9
Town Animals	All Aboard	Ginn	Stage 7: Non-fiction	9
Town Dog	Oxford Reading Tree	OUP	TreeTops More All Stars: Pack 2A	9
Town Mouse and Country Mouse	PM Traditional Tales	Nelson Thornes	Purple Level	8
Toy Farm, The	PM Storybooks	Nelson Thornes	Orange Set A	6
Toys Around the World	Book Project Non-fiction A	Longman	Toys	9
Toys of the Past 50 Years	Spotlight on Fact	Collins	Y1: Toys and Games	6
Trail Riding	Alphakids Plus	Horwitz Gardner	Transitional Level 13	6
Training with Ali and Emma	Info Trail	Longman	Emergent Science	8
Trains Now and Fifty Years Ago	Book Project Non-fiction A	Longman	History of Transport	9
Trapped Genie, The	Tristars	Horwitz Gardner	Stage B	10
Travels with Magellan	Oxford Reading Tree	OUP	Stage 8: True Stories	7
Treasure Cave, The	Cambridge Reading	CUP	Y2 A: Fantasy Worlds	9

TITLE	SERIES	PUBLISHER	SET (OR AUTHOR)	BAND
Treasure Chest	Oxford Reading Tree	OUP	Stage 6: Owls	7
Treasure Hunt, The	Oxford Reading Tree	OUP	Stage 9: More Robins	9
Treats and Eats	Infosteps	Kingscourt	Set 1	10
Tree House, The	Literacy Land	Longmans	Story Street: Step 11	11
Trees	Go Facts	A&C Black	Plants	11
Trees	Literacy Links Plus	Kingscourt	Early D	7
Trees, Please!	Storyteller	Kingscourt	Set 9	9
Tricksters	Navigator	Rigby	Short Stories – Brown Level	11
Trojan Horse, The	Literacy Links Plus	Kingscourt	Fluent C	8
Troop of Little Dinosaurs, A	PM Storybooks	Nelson Thornes	Purple Set B	8
Tropical Journey, A	All Aboard	Ginn	Stage 8: Non-fiction	10
Trouble for Letang and Julie	Book Project	Longman	Fiction Band 6	9
Trouble in the Ark	Individual Titles	Picture Puffin	Rose, Gerald	7
Trouble with Gran, The	Individual Titles	Egmont	Cole, Babette	7
Trouble with Oatmeal, The	PM Chapter Books	Nelson Thornes	Emerald Set B	11
True Diary of Carly Ann Potter, The	Oxford Reading Tree	OUP	TreeTops Stage 13+: Pack D	11
Try Again, Emma	Lighthouse	Ginn	Orange: 1	6
T-Shirt Triplets, The	Literacy Links Plus	Kingscourt	Fluent B	7
Tug of War, The	Storyworlds	Heinemann	Stage 7: Once Upon a Time	6
Tulips for Dad	Cambridge Reading	CUP	Y2 A: Narrative Recount	9
Tunnels	National Geographic	Rigby	Purple Level	7
Turtle and the Crane, The	Book Project	Longman	Fiction Band 4: Cluster E	9
Turtle Flies South	Literacy Links Plus	Kingscourt	Fluent A	8
Turtle Talk	Storyteller	Kingscourt	Set 7	7
Turtle Who Danced with the Crane, The	Pelican Big Books	Longman	Cullimore, Stan	7
Turtles, Tortoises and Terrapins	Storyteller	Kingscourt	Set 11	11
Tusk Tusk	Individual Titles	Red Fox	McKee, David	7
Twelfth Floor Kids, The	Literacy World	Heinemann	Stage 1	9
Two Asian Tales	Literacy Land	Longmans	Genre Range – Fluent	11
Two Baby Elephants	Lighthouse	Ginn	Orange: 8	6
Two Brown Bears	Oxford Reading Tree	OUP	TreeTops All Stars: Pack 1	8
Two Can Toucan	Individual Titles	Red Fox	McKee, David	8
Two European Tales	Literacy Land	Longmans	Genre Range – Fluent	11
Two Folk Tales	Literacy Land	Longmans	Genre Range – Fluent	11
Two Foolish Cats, The	Literacy Links Plus	Kingscourt	Fluent A	7
Two Giants, The	Storyworlds	Heinemann	Stage 9: Once Upon a Time	10
Two Little Goldfish	PM Storybooks	Nelson Thornes	Orange Set C	6
Two Red Tugs	PM Storybooks	Nelson Thornes	Purple Set C	8
U				
Ugly Dogs and Slimy Frogs	Crunchies	Orchard	Twice Upon a Time	9
Ugly Duckling	Alphakids	Horwitz Gardner	Extending Level 20	8
Ugly Duckling, The	Individual Titles	Orchard	Beck, Ian	7
Ugly Duckling, The	New Way	Nelson Thornes	Violet Parallel Books	9
Ugly Duckling, The	PM Traditional Tales	Nelson Thornes	Turquoise Level	7
Ultimate Trainers, The	Oxford Reading Tree	OUP	TreeTops Stage 13: Pack B	11
Una's Spelling Test	Oxford Literacy Web	OUP	Stage 8: Variety	11
Uncle-and-Auntie Pat	Rockets	A&C Black	West, Colin	9
Under Attack	First Explorers	Kingscourt	Level 1	9
Under Sail	Alphakids	Horwitz Gardner	Extending Level 22	9
Under the Red Elephant	Individual Titles	Collins Colour Jets	Mark, Jan	11
Under the Sea	Alphakids	Horwitz Gardner	Extending Level 19	8

TITLE	SERIES	PUBLISHER	SET (OR AUTHOR)	BAND
Underground Railroad, The	Oxford Reading Tree	OUP	Stage 9: True Stories	9
Underwater	The News	Horwitz Gardner		11
Underwater Animals	Explorers	Kingscourt	Set 1	10
Up the Amazon	National Geographic	Rigby	White Level	10
Up the Dizzy Mountain	Literacy Land	Longmans	Story Street: Step 11	11
Upside Down Harry Brown	All Aboard	Ginn	Stage 5 Set A: Patt & Rhyme	6
Using Colour	AlphaWorld	Horwitz Gardner	Band 8: Purple	9
Using the River	Star Quest	Rigby	Star Plus	11
V				
Vagabond Crabs	Literacy Links Plus	Kingscourt	Early D	7
Vicky the High Jumper	Literacy Links Plus	Kingscourt	Fluent C	9
Victorian Adventure	Oxford Reading Tree	OUP	Stage 8: Magpies	8
Victorian Adventure	Oxford Reading Tree	OUP	Stage 8: Playscripts	7
Viking Adventure	Oxford Reading Tree	OUP	Stage 8: Magpies	7
Viking Adventure	Oxford Reading Tree	OUP	Stage 8: Playscripts	6
Village Show, The	Oxford Reading Tree	OUP	Stage 9: Robins	9
Volcano Woman	Cambridge Reading	CUP	Y2 B: Range of Cultures	10
Volcanoes	Alphakids	Horwitz Gardner	Extending Level 22	10
Volcanoes	National Geographic	Rigby	White Level	11
Vote for Me!	Alphakids	Horwitz Gardner	Extending Level 20	8
Voyage into Space	Storyworlds	Heinemann	Stage 9: Fantasy World	9
W				
Waiting for Goldie	Oxford Reading Tree	OUP	TreeTops Stage 13: Pack B	11
Walkathon, The	PM Storybooks	Nelson Thornes	Silver Set B	10
Walking	Literacy Links Plus Topic	Kingscourt	Fluent B	10
Walking in the Autumn	PM Non-fiction	Nelson Thornes	Green Level	6
Walking in the Spring	PM Non-fiction	Nelson Thornes	Green Level	6
Walking in the Summer	PM Non-fiction	Nelson Thornes	Green Level	6
Walking in the Winter	PM Non-fiction	Nelson Thornes	Green Level	6
Watch the Birdie!	Oxford Literacy Web	OUP	Stage 8: Duck Green	7
Water Can Change	National Geographic	Rigby	Turquoise Level	9
Water Experiments	Book Project Non-fiction B	Longman	Water	10
Water Falling	Literacy Links Plus	Kingscourt	Early A	6
Water Fun	Book Project Non-fiction B	Longman	Water	11
Water in the House	Book Project Non-fiction A	Longman	Homes	8
Water is a Solid, Liquid and Gas	Book Project Non-fiction B	Longman	Water	11
Waterbirds	Infosteps	Kingscourt	Set 1	10
Ways of Carrying Babies	Book Project Non-fiction A	Longman	Babies	8
We Need More Trees!	Alphakids	Horwitz Gardner	Transitional Level 15	6
We Want William!	Crunchies	Orchard	Colour Crackers	9
We Won the Lottery	Individual Titles	Collins Jumbo Jets	Rayner, Shoo	11
Wearing Glasses	All Aboard	Ginn	Stage 5: Non-fiction	7
Weather Drum, The	Cambridge Reading	CUP	Y2 B: Range of Cultures	10
Webster and the Treacle Toffee	Book Project	Longman	Fiction Band 5	9
Weird and Wacky Inventions	Tristars	Horwitz Gardner	Stage B	11
Welcome Home, Barney	Crunchies	Orchard	Colour Crackers	8
Welcome to Planet Earth	Navigator	Rigby	Non-fiction: Brown Level	11
Welsh Lamb, A	Cambridge Reading	CUP	Y2 B: Narrative Recount	8
We're Going on a Picnic	Cambridge Reading	CUP	Bridging Books	6
Whales	Alphakids Plus	Horwitz Gardner	Early Level 9	6
Whales	Oxford RT Branch Library	OUP	Oxford Reds: Pack B	10

TITLE	SERIES	PUBLISHER	SET (OR AUTHOR)	BAND
Whales	PM Non-fiction	Nelson Thornes	Silver Level	10
Whales on the World Wide Web	Alphakids	Horwitz Gardner	Extending Level 20	9
What a Load of Rubbish	Lighthouse	Ginn	Turquoise: 8	7
What am I Going to Be?	Storyteller	Kingscourt	Set 6	6
What Babies Used To Wear	Pelican Big Books	Longman	Witherington, Anne	8
What Babies Wore	Book Project Non-fiction A	Longman	Babies	10
What Can I Write?	Individual Titles	Red Fox	Selway, Martina	7
What Dinah Saw	Lighthouse	Ginn	Gold: 6	9
What Do You Know About Dolphins?	National Geographic	Rigby	Green Level	7
What Does it Eat?	All Aboard	Ginn	Stage 6: Non-fiction	9
What is a Bear?	My World Non-fiction	Horwitz Gardner		9
What is a Beaver?	My World Non-fiction	Horwitz Gardner		10
What is a Bee?	My World Non-fiction	Horwitz Gardner		10
What is a Beetle?	My World Non-fiction	Horwitz Gardner		10
What is a Bird of Prey?	My World Non-fiction	Horwitz Gardner		10
What is a Builder?	My World Non-fiction	Horwitz Gardner		10
What is a Butterfly?	My World Non-fiction	Horwitz Gardner		10
What is a Crocodile?	My World Non-fiction	Horwitz Gardner		10
What is a Frog?	My World Non-fiction	Horwitz Gardner		10
What is a Giraffe?	My World Non-fiction	Horwitz Gardner		9
What is a Hippopotamus?	My World Non-fiction	Horwitz Gardner		9
What is a Hooved Animal?	My World Non-fiction	Horwitz Gardner		10
What is a Horse?	My World Non-fiction	Horwitz Gardner		9
What is a Lion?	My World Non-fiction	Horwitz Gardner		9
What is a Monkey?	My World Non-fiction	Horwitz Gardner		9
What is a Penguin?	My World Non-fiction	Horwitz Gardner		9
What is a Spider?	My World Non-fiction	Horwitz Gardner		9
What is a Travelling Animal?	My World Non-fiction	Horwitz Gardner		10
What is a Turtle?	My World Non-fiction	Horwitz Gardner		9
What is a Wolf?	My World Non-fiction	Horwitz Gardner		9
What is an Animal of Australia?	My World Non-fiction	Horwitz Gardner		10
What is an Animal of the Amazon?	My World Non-fiction	Horwitz Gardner		10
What is an Ape?	My World Non-fiction	Horwitz Gardner		10
What is an Elephant?	My World Non-fiction	Horwitz Gardner		10
What is an Endangered Animal?	My World Non-fiction	Horwitz Gardner		10
What Mr Croc Forgot	Rockets	A&C Black	Rodgers, Frank	7
What Tommy Did	Literacy Links Plus	Kingscourt	Early B	7
What Was it Like?	Oxford Reading Tree	OUP	Stage 8: More Magpies	8
What's Cooking?	All Aboard	Ginn	Stage 7: Non-fiction	9
What's Cooking?	Skyrider	Collins	Yellow	11
What's Living at Your Place?	Skyrider	Collins	Yellow	10
Wheels	All Aboard	Ginn	Stage 6: Non-fiction	9
When Dad Went Fishing	Cambridge Reading	CUP	Bridging Books	6
When Sheep Cannot Sleep	Individual Titles	Red Fox	Kitamura, S	7
When the Truck Got Stuck!	Skyrider	Collins	Yellow	9
When the Volcano Erupted	PM Storybooks	Nelson Thornes	Turquoise Set A	7
Where the Wild Things Are	Individual Titles	Arrow Red Fox	Sendak, Maurice	8
Which Holiday?	Spotlight on Fact	Collins	Y2: The Seaside	11
White Horse, The	Literacy Links Plus	Kingscourt	Fluent D	8
Who Goes on the Bonfire?	Info Trail	Longman	Emergent History	9
Who Sank the Boat?	Individual Titles	Picture Puffin	Allen, Pamela	7

TITLE	SERIES	PUBLISHER	SET (OR AUTHOR)	BAND
Who Shares Your Home?	Tristars	Horwitz Gardner	Stage A	10
Who Shot the Movies?	The News	Horwitz Gardner		11
Who Stole the Fish?	Cambridge Reading	CUP	Bridging Books	7
Who Wants to Play with a Troll?	Oxford RT Rhyme & Analogy	OUP	Story Rhymes: Pack A	7
Why Do Cats Purr?	Literacy Land	Longmans	Info Trail – Competent	10
Why Elephants Have Long Noses	Literacy Links Plus	Kingscourt	Early D	6
Why Flamingoes Have Red Legs	New Way	Nelson Thornes	Violet Parallel Books	9
Why Flies Buzz	Literacy Links Plus	Kingscourt	Traditional Tales	8
Why Frog and Snake Can't Be Friends	Literacy Links Plus	Kingscourt	Traditional Tales	8
Why Rabbits Have Long Ears	Literacy Links Plus	Kingscourt	Fluent D	9
Why the Sea is Salty	Literacy Links Plus	Kingscourt	Fluent C	8
Why Things Move	First Explorers	Kingscourt	Level 2	11
Why Tortoise Has a Cracked Shell	Storyworld Bridges	Heinemann	Stage 10	10
Wild Cat Guide, The	Lighthouse	Ginn	Purple: 8	8
Wild Easts and the Wild West, The	Storyteller	Kingscourt	Set 8	8
William and the Dog	Oxford Reading Tree	OUP	Stage 7: Robins	9
William and the Ghost	Oxford Reading Tree	OUP	Jackdaws Anthologies	11
William and the Mouse	Oxford Reading Tree	OUP	Jackdaws Anthologies	11
William and the Pied Piper	Oxford Reading Tree	OUP	Stage 9: More Robins	9
William and the Spell	Oxford Reading Tree	OUP	More Jackdaws Anthologies	10
William's Mistake	Oxford Reading Tree	OUP	Stage 8: More Robins	9
Willow Pattern Plot, The	Oxford Reading Tree	OUP	Stage 6 & 7: More Owls B	7
Wind and Sun	Literacy Links Plus	Kingscourt	Early D	6
Wind Power	National Geographic	Rigby	Orange Level	6
Winnie the Witch	Individual Titles	OUP	Paul, Korky	8
Winning	Oxford Reading Tree	OUP	Citizenship Stories: Stage 9/10	9
Winter	Storyteller	Kingscourt	Set 6	6
Winter Woollies	Storyteller	Kingscourt	Set 8	8
Wise Girl, The	Oxford Literacy Web	OUP	Stage 9: Variety	11
Wish You Were Here	Individual Titles	Red Fox	Selway, Martina	10
Wizard Wagoo	Literacy Land	Longmans	Story Street: Step 10	10
Wolf Whistle, The	Oxford Literacy Web	OUP	Stage 7: Duck Green	7
Wolves	Oxford RT Branch Library	OUP	Oxford Reds: Pack B	9
Wolves	PM Non-fiction	Nelson Thornes	Silver Level	10
Wood	Find Out About	Franklin Watts		10
Woodcutter and the Bear, The	Rigby Star	Rigby	Star Plus	8
Wool and Fibre	Find Out About	Franklin Watts		8
Workshop, The	All Aboard	Ginn	Stage 3: Non-fiction	6
World Atlas	Discovery World Links	Heinemann	Stage F	11
World That Jack Built, The	Individual Titles	Red Fox	Brown, R	8
World's Largest Animals	Discovery World Links	Heinemann	Stage D	9
Worms at Work	Alphakids	Horwitz Gardner	Extending Level 21	9
Would You Be a Bee?	Info Trail	Longman	Beginner Science	7
Would you Like to Live on a Small Island?	Literacy Land	Longmans	Info Trail – Competent	9
Would You Rather?	Individual Titles	Red Fox	Burningham, John	7
Wrong Letter, The	Oxford Reading Tree	OUP	TreeTops Stage 10: Pack C	9
Wrong Words, The	Storyworld Bridges	Heinemann	Stage 11	11
Y				
Year with Mother Bear, A	Storyteller	Kingscourt	Set 6	6
Yellow Overalls	Literacy Links Plus	Kingscourt	Fluent C	8
You Are Special	First Explorers	Kingscourt	Level 1	9

TITLE	SERIES	PUBLISHER	SET (OR AUTHOR)	BAND
You Can Swim Jim	Individual Titles	Red Fox	Kumansky, K	6
You Can't Park an Elephant	Pathways to Literacy	Collins	Year 2	8
Your Amazing Body	Alphakids Plus	Horwitz Gardner	Early Level 11	6
You're It! Playground Games	Lightning	Ginn	Brown Level N/F	10
Yummy Scrummy	Oxford Reading Tree	OUP	TreeTops All Stars: Pack 2	10
Z				
Zala Runs for Her Life	PM Storybooks	Nelson Thornes	Purple Set A	8
Zoe at the Fancy Dress Ball	Literacy Links Plus	Kingscourt	Fluent B	9
Zoom in	Navigator	Rigby	Non-fiction: Brown Level	11
Zoom in!	Storyteller	Kingscourt	Set 10	10
Zoomababy & the Search for the Lost Dummy	Literacy Land	Longmans	Genre Range – Competent	8
Zoomababy and the Great Dog Chase	Literacy Land	Longmans	Genre Range – Competent	8
Zoomababy and the Locked Cage	Literacy Land	Longmans	Genre Range – Competent	9
Zoomababy and the Mission to Mars	Literacy Land	Longmans	Genre Range – Fluent	10
Zoomababy and the World Cup	Literacy Land	Longmans	Genre Range – Fluent	11
Zoomababy to the Rescue	Literacy Land	Longmans	Genre Range – Fluent	10

Acknowledgements

ACKNOWLEDGEMENTS

The authors and publisher are grateful to the following for permission to reproduce copyright material in this book.

A&C Black for *Tadpole and Frog* (Stopwatch books) by Christine Back and Barrie Watts; *Reptiles* (Go Facts) by Paul McEvoy.

Cambridge University Press for *The Little Red Hen* (Cambridge Plays) by Gerald Rose; *Marvel Paws* (Cambridge Reading) by Richard Brown and Kate Ruttle, illustrated by David Parkins.

Franklin Watts for *Paper* (Find Out About) by Henry Pluckrose; *Peanuts* (What's for Lunch?) by Claire Llewellyn.

Harcourt Education for *Grown-ups Make You Grumpy* (Ginn Lighthouse) by Carrie Weston; *Gobstoppers* (Rigby Navigator); *Animal Life Cycles* (Heinemann Discovery World Links) by Claire Llewellyn.

HarperCollins for *The Bike Lesson* (Beginner Books) by Stan and John Berenstain; *The Bad Dad List* (Skyracer) Anna Kenna; *The Brementown Musicians* (Spotlight on Plays) by Eleanor Boylan.

Horwitz Gardner for *The Lonely Troll* (Alphakids) by Shelley Jones, illustrated by Meredith Thomas; *Chocolate!* (Tristars) by Mary Ellen Ray.

Kingscourt/McGraw-Hill for *Rain or Shine* (Explorers Set 1); *Waterbirds* (Infosteps) by Avelyn Davidson; *Diary of a Honey-Bee* (Literacy Links Plus) by Bill Keir; *The Selfish Giant* (Literacy Links Plus) by Leanna Traill; *The Shopping List* (Storyteller) by Diane Foley.

Neate Publishing for *Comparing Giraffes and Polar Bears* (Literacy and Science series) by Bobbie Neate.

Nelson Thornes for *Walking in the Autumn* (PM Library) by Beverley Randell; *Jordan and the Northside Reps* (PM Library) by Stephen Harrison, illustrated by Al Fiorentino; *Yo-yos* (PM Non-fiction) by Cathy Hope.

Orchard Books for *Big Bad Raps* (Orchard Crunchies) by Tony Mitten; *Pipe Down, Prudle!* (Colour Crackers) by Rose Impey and Shoo Rayner.

Oxford University Press for *The Mungle Flap* (Oxford Reading Tree) by Roderick Hunt; *Man on the Moon* (Oxford Reading Tree True Stories) by Christine Butterworth.

Pearson Education for *Trains Now and Fifty Years Ago* (Longman Book Project) by Robin Jones; Pearson Education for *A Simple Rhyming Dictionary* (Longman) by Sue Palmer and Eugenia Low.

Walker Books for *No Tights for George* (Sprinters) text © 2002 June Crebbin, illustrations © 2002 Tony Ross; *Care of Henry* text © 1996 Anne Fine.